# Praise for
## *Cutting-Edge Marketing Analytics*

"*Cutting-Edge Marketing Analytics* presents managers with an excellent roadmap for marketing resource allocation. Based on my experience advising firms, I believe that the material presented in the book strikes the right balance of rigorous analysis and strategic relevance. Case studies presented in the book provide the necessary context for the application of statistical tools and allow managers and MBA students to learn the challenges in implementing analytics."

> —**V. Kumar**, Executive Director, Center for Excellence in Brand and Customer Management, and Director of the Ph.D. Program in Marketing, J. Mack Robinson College of Business, Georgia State University

"This is exactly the book I have been looking for to teach customer analytics! It will fill an important gap in the market as it teaches practical approaches to gain customer insights based on big data that is increasingly available to organizations."

> —**Harald J. van Heerde**, MSc, Ph.D., Research Professor of Marketing, Massey University, School of Communication, Journalism, and Marketing

"Retail's transformation is still in the early innings. The Internet and mobile have combined to create unprecedented insight into consumer behavior and customer preferences unbound by time or space. Mastery of marketing and customer analytics has become 'table stakes' for understanding and pleasing the customer—job one in retail. Practitioners looking for real world applications with a balanced overview of the underlying theory would be well served by reading this book."

> —**Matt Kaness**, Chief Strategy Officer, Urban Outfitters

"I strongly recommend *Cutting-Edge Marketing Analytics* for managers seeking to build an analytics-driven marketing function. In this book, the authors have struck the right balance of analytical sophistication and managerial relevance. The case studies provide a good opportunity for applying the analytics techniques to real problems."

> —**Nino Ninov**, Vice President, Strategic Research and Analysis, Rosetta Stone

# Cutting-Edge Marketing Analytics

## Real World Cases and Data Sets for Hands On Learning

### Rajkumar Venkatesan

Bank of America Research Professor of Business Administration,
Darden Graduate School of Business Administration,
University of Virginia

### Paul Farris

Landmark Communications Professor of Business Administration,
Darden Graduate School of Business Administration,
University of Virginia

### Ronald T. Wilcox

Ethyl Corporation Professor of Business Administration,
Darden Graduate School of Business Administration,
University of Virginia

Associate Publisher: Amy Neidlinger
Executive Editor: Jeanne Glasser Levine
Operations Specialist: Jodi Kemper
Cover Designer: Alan Clements
Managing Editor: Kristy Hart
Senior Project Editor: Betsy Gratner
Copy Editor: Karen Annett
Proofreader: Katie Matejka
Indexer: Tim Wright
Senior Compositor: Gloria Schurick
Manufacturing Buyer: Dan Uhrig

© 2015 by Rajkumar Venkatesan, Paul Farris, and Ronald T. Wilcox
Published by Pearson Education, Inc.
Upper Saddle River, New Jersey 07458

For information about buying this title in bulk quantities, or for special sales opportunities (which may include electronic versions; custom cover designs; and content particular to your business, training goals, marketing focus, or branding interests), please contact our corporate sales department at corpsales@pearsoned.com or (800) 382-3419.

For government sales inquiries, please contact governmentsales@pearsoned.com.

For questions about sales outside the U.S., please contact international@pearsoned.com.

Company and product names mentioned herein are the trademarks or registered trademarks of their respective owners.

Printed in the United States of America

ISBN-10: 0-13-355252-7
ISBN-13: 978-0-13-355252-2

Pearson Education LTD.
Pearson Education Australia PTY, Limited.
Pearson Education Singapore, Pte. Ltd.
Pearson Education Asia, Ltd.
Pearson Education Canada, Ltd.
Pearson Educación de Mexico, S.A. de C.V.
Pearson Education—Japan
Pearson Education Malaysia, Pte. Ltd.

Library of Congress Control Number: 2014937240

*We dedicate this book to our students for being*
*a constant source of inspiration.*

# Contents

# Foreword

My first boss once told me, "Data is your friend," meaning that good data could help a brand manager support his or her recommendations and help get things done.

Thirty plus years later, data is more than friendly—it's cool. *Moneyball* concepts are applied beyond baseball. Nate Silver's analyses inform everything from presidential elections to weather forecasting. And powered by ever bigger data sets and the digitization of everything, nowhere is analytics more important than in marketing. For almost all marketers, analytics has become a strategic imperative: not whether, but what and how?

It is in this data-driven environment that we should ask: What do business school students really need to know about marketing analytics? And how should they learn it?

Years removed from the MBA classroom, I have some ideas on this topic. I've worked in global marketing companies spanning everything from FMCG to financial services to advertising analytics. To put it bluntly, I've pretty much seen it all—what's useful, what's not, and all of the various methodologies and metrics that go with them.

Professors Raj Venkatesan, Paul Farris, and Ron Wilcox's gem of a new book, *Cutting-Edge Marketing Analytics*, finds just the right balance. It covers virtually all of the most important research and analytics methods but does so with just the right amount of detail and depth. They put their years of experience in teaching, research, and consulting to good use here. They hit the right analytic topics—the ones that add real value in the real world—with enough detail to move students beyond the conceptual to the practical.

Importantly, *Cutting-Edge Marketing Analytics* aims to do several things that not enough MBA texts should. First, it explains in clear and cogent terms each of the major analytical tools that are critical to the marketer. Second, the real world case studies provide realistic business situations and opportunities for students to learn by doing. Third, the book has a strong decision focus: not just "what have we learned?" but "what should we do?" Marketing analytics is shown to be exactly what it should be: a strategic and tactically important tool in the hands of the action-oriented marketing decision maker.

Students who use this book will enter the business world with a much greater appreciation for the power of marketing analytics—not just what tools to use when, but greater insight into how these insights are used to make practical real world decisions. As my old boss would say, data will be their friend, and with *Cutting-Edge Marketing Analytics*, this friendship should translate into real world insights, decisions, and, ultimately, business success.

—**Randall Beard**, Global Head of Advertiser Solutions, Nielsen

# Acknowledgments

We hope this book takes a step toward bringing advanced analytics to the marketing process. We owe thanks to several people who have made this endeavor possible.

We thank the coauthors of the case studies featured in the book: Samuel Bodily, Robert Maddox, George Michie, Phillip Pfeifer, and Gerry Yemen. We have enjoyed working with them and are thankful for their allowing us to use our joint work in this book. Kelly Ateya, Martha Gray, Timothy Harr, Gautam Kanaparthi, Dustin Moon, Dan Shively, Prateek Shrivastava, Mathew Weiss, and Ivy Zuckerman developed material for important sections using their research skills. We thank Earl Taylor and the speakers and attendants of the Marketing Science Institute Conference on Implementing Analytics for providing fodder for the chapter on implementation.

Shea Gibbs with Gibbscom worked tirelessly to develop several sections of the manuscript. His business knowledge and editing skills have influenced every aspect of this book.

Finally, we thank Disha, Kate, and Shannon, who graciously tolerated the time sacrificed from home and social lives for writing this book.

All the chapters in this book are based on technical notes and case studies written by the authors for Darden Business Publishing, http://store.darden.virginia.edu/. We thank Darden Business Publishing for allowing us to use the material in this book.

# About the Authors

**Rajkumar Venkatesan**

Bank of America Research Professor of Business Administration Rajkumar Venkatesan teaches "Marketing Strategy" and "Big Data in Marketing" in the MBA, Executive MBA, and Global Executive MBA programs at Darden. Venkatesan's research focuses on developing customer-centric marketing strategies that provide measurable financial results. Venkatesan's research has appeared in several journals, including the *Harvard Business Review*, *Journal of Marketing*, *Journal of Marketing Research*, *Marketing Science*, *Journal of Retailing*, *Decision Support Systems*, *Marketing Letters*, and *Journal of Service Research*. He serves as an Area Editor of the *Journal of Marketing*. Many of his research publications have been recognized with prestigious awards, such as the Don Lehmann Award and the MSI Alden G. Clayton Award. He has been selected as one of the top 20 rising young scholars in marketing by the Marketing Science Institute and as one of the top 40 professors of business administration under 40 by *Poets and Quants* magazine.

Professor Venkatesan has consulted and taught in executive education programs on marketing analytics for global firms in the technology, retailing, media, consumer packaged goods, and pharmaceutical industries. For his work with IBM, he was recognized as one of the three finalists worldwide for the Informs Practice Prize Competition.

Before coming to Darden, Venkatesan taught database marketing, marketing research, and quantitative marketing models to graduate students at the University of Connecticut. There, he was the recipient of the MBA Teacher of the Year Award. He received his PhD in marketing from the University of Houston and his BE in computer engineering from the University of Madras.

**Paul Farris**

Landmark Communications Professor Paul Farris taught at the Harvard Business School before his appointment at the University of Virginia Darden School of Business Administration. He has worked in marketing management for UNILEVER, Germany, and in account management for the LINTAS advertising agency.

Farris's general research focus is in the area of marketing productivity and measurement. His work has been published in 10 books and more than 70 articles, appearing in professional journals and publications such as the *Wall Street Journal, Harvard Business Review, Journal of Marketing, Marketing Science, Management Science, Decision Sciences, Journal of Interactive Marketing, Journal of Advertising Research, Journal of Retailing, Journal of the Academy of Marketing Science*, and the *Sloan Management Review*. Farris has coauthored award-winning articles on retailer power, marketing strategy, and advertising testing. He has served as an academic trustee of the Marketing Science Institute and is a current or past member of the editorial boards for the *Journal of Marketing*, the *Journal of Retailing*, the *International Journal of Advertising, Marketing—Journal of Research and Management*, and the *Journal of Advertising Research*. His current research is on channel conflict and building coherent systems of marketing metrics. His coauthored book, *Marketing Metrics: 50+ Metrics Every Executive Should Master*, was selected by *Strategy + Business* as the 2006 Marketing Book of the Year.

Farris has consulted and taught executive education programs for many international companies. He has served on the boards of retailers, manufacturers, and software companies. Currently, he is on the board of directors of Sto Corp., a building materials company. Farris has also provided expert testimony in a number of marketing-related legal cases.

### Ronald T. Wilcox

Ronald T. Wilcox, Ethyl Corporation Professor of Business Administration and Associate Dean of the MBA for Executives Program at the University of Virginia Darden School of Business Administration, teaches the required Marketing course in the MBA and Executive MBA programs as well as the elective "Pricing." He also teaches in numerous Executive Education programs.

His research, focused on the marketing of financial services and its interface with public policy, has appeared in leading marketing and finance journals such as the *Journal of Marketing Research, Management Science, Marketing Science*, and the *Journal of Business*. His research and writing have also appeared in the *Wall Street Journal, Washington Post, BusinessWeek, Fortune, Forbes*, and the *Weekly Standard*. He is a frequent contributor to *Forbes*. He is the author of the book *Whatever Happened to Thrift? Why Americans Don't Save and What to Do About It*, published by Yale University Press.

Wilcox joined the Darden faculty in 2001. He was formerly an assistant professor at the Carnegie Mellon Graduate School of Industrial Administration and an economist for the U.S. Securities and Exchange Commission.

# Introduction

Your friend has sent you on a treasure hunt. She has given you clues about how to find the treasure, but you'll be left to draw on your own treasure-hunting skills to put the clues to good use.

Who is this friend of yours? It's your boss, the owner of the company for which you are the marketing manager. What is the treasure you seek? It's a business advantage that will allow your company to allocate its marketing dollars optimally and come out ahead of the competition. Those clues? That's data your company has gathered about the past behavior of customers. And what are your treasure-hunting skills? They are the tools you will find in this book—the techniques needed to analyze past marketing performance and discover unknowns that will allow you to predict the future.

The broad view of how this is done is the discipline of marketing analytics—the process of creating models helpful in understanding consumer behaviors. It is the systematic use of empirical data about customers, companies, their competition and collaborators, and industry context to inform strategic marketing decisions. The function of marketing analytics can range from reports on regular marketing activities—such as paid search advertising click-through rates—to allocating marketing resources to maximize future performance of a company's digital presence.

You have a lot to learn, and there's no time to waste. You've got treasure to find.

## Why Marketing Analytics?

Dunia Finance LLC is a midsized financial services firm that operates in a unique financial market. Unlike similar institutions in the Western world, the Abu Dhabi–based company does not have the benefit of a reliable credit bureau to provide information on consumers' risk scores. Still, the company believes such scores are necessary to help it quantify decisions on product offerings. For example, risk scores indicate the interest rate Dunia should charge for a personal loan, as well as whether a personal loan customer is a good target for cross-selling credit cards. So instead of operating in the dark, the company has developed an internal system of tracking customer behavior and stores its data in a data warehouse. (For more information on Dunia Finance LLC, see Chapter 2, "Dunia Finance LLC.")[1]

Dunia is not the only company that places a high value on customer data these days. As technology has allowed firms to link customer behaviors more closely with the drivers behind those behaviors, an increasing number of companies are becoming comfortable using marketing analytics to gain a business advantage.

A 2013 report in *Forbes* magazine covered a survey of 211 senior marketers that showed that most large companies have had success using big data to understand customer behaviors. More than half (60%) of organizations that used big data a majority of the time reportedly exceeded their goals, whereas companies that used such data only occasionally reported significantly less success. Almost three quarters of companies that used big data a majority of the time were able to understand the effects of multichannel campaigns, and 70% of that group of companies said they were able to target their marketing efforts optimally.

Consider the effect of advertising. In the past, when television and print advertisements were the predominant form of pushing a firm's message, the relationship between the ads and customers' willingness to purchase the item advertised was not entirely clear. The firm rarely knew whether a customer bought the item because he or she had seen a television advertisement or because he or she had heard about it through some other channel. Collecting data about the success of the advertisements was indeed difficult.

With the advent of e-mail and web-based advertising, all that has changed. Firms are now able to closely connect their inputs (for example, ad placements) and outputs (for example, whether the target of the advertisement made a purchase). This produces a large amount of behavioral data. This data, in turn, allows companies to model existing customer behaviors and predict future behaviors more precisely. (It is important, however, to note that with big data comes a big problem—namely, the risk of false positives, or seeing patterns among chance events.)[2]

To avoid making mistakes with big data, business intuition is critical. Intuition allows the savvy marketing manager to select the correct inputs and outputs for a model. Analytics allows a company to take this traditional static dashboard of metrics or measurables and turn it into a predictive and dynamic entity.

Marketing analytics is not a new field. It simply allows companies to move beyond reports about what is happening in their businesses—and alerts about what needs to be done in response—to actually understand why something is happening based on regressions, experiments, testing, prediction, and optimization.[3] What is new is how skilled companies have become at using marketing analytics. The availability of granular customer data has transformed firms' marketing-spending decisions. Sophisticated econometrics combined with rich customer and marketing-mix data allow firms to bring science into a field that has traditionally relied on managers' intuition.[4]

## What Is in This Book?

This book functions as a how-to guide on practical and sensible marketing analytics. It focuses on the application of analytics for strategic decision making in marketing and presents analytics as the engine that provides a forward-looking and predictive perspective for marketing dashboards. The emphasis is on connecting marketing inputs to customer behavior and then using the predictive models (developed using historic information, experiments, or heuristics) to develop forward-looking, what-if scenarios.

After reading this book, you will be able to (1) understand the importance of marketing analytics for forward-looking and systematic allocation of marketing resources; (2) know how to use analytics to develop predictive marketing dashboards for an organization; (3) understand the biases inherent to analytics that derive from secondary data, the cost-benefit trade-offs in analytics, and the balance between analysis and intuition; and (4) learn how to conduct data analysis through linear regression, logistic regression, or cluster analysis to address strategic marketing challenges.

This text places a big emphasis on practical guidance and striking the right balance between technical sophistication and managerial relevance. This is accomplished by real-life cases and real-life data connected to the cases that allow you to take a hands-on approach to the analysis. The book emphasizes all three aspects of marketing analytics: statistical analysis, experiments, and managerial intuition. The website http://dmanalytics.org provides videos on implementing the analytics techniques discussed in this book using commonly available statistical analysis software.

This book emphasizes that (1) analytics needs to support broader strategy; (2) inferences are inherently biased by available data, information, and techniques; (3) managers constantly make cost-benefit trade-offs in analytics; and (4) not every strategic question is answered by analytics—smart managers know to balance analysis and intuition.

# Organization of the Book

This book is a reflection of the authors' experience of teaching graduate-level business students and executives, insights from academic research, and exposure to the practical aspects of marketing analytics through consulting engagements. The topics covered in this book represent the authors' impressions of the analytics techniques that are widely used in practice. This book is not intended to be an exhaustive review of marketing analytics techniques, but instead is intended to provide you exposure to how marketing analytics relates to strategic business issues.

Resource allocation provides a strategic and unifying framework for the wide-ranging purposes of marketing analytics within an organization; we therefore build marketing analytics around the resource-allocation framework. You can view analytics as the engine that provides a forward-looking perspective for marketing dashboards. The chapters in this book are organized around primary marketing functions. Section II, "Product Analytics," starts with analytics that relate to product management decisions, such as market segmentation and pricing. Section III, "Marketing-Mix Analytics," then moves to media or marketing-mix management decisions where the focus is on obtaining reliable estimates for price and advertising elasticity. Customer lifetime value is then presented as an organizing framework for customer analytics in Section IV, "Customer Analytics." Here you learn about tools to predict customer retention and profits. The emerging and popular field of analytics related to digital marketing is the focus of Section V, "Digital Analytics." It introduces design of experiments, search engine marketing, and mobile marketing. The book concludes by revisiting resource allocation and ties the different analytics tools with a case study that deals with allocating marketing resources for cross-selling products. Section VI, "Resource Allocation Revisited," then presents a forward-looking perspective on marketing analytics and provides an action plan for implementing marketing analytics in organizations and developing a learning organization that systematically includes insights gained from analytics in their strategic decisions.

# Endnotes

1. Gerry Yemen, Rajkumar Venkatesan, and Samuel E. Bodily, "Dunia Finance LLC (A)," UVA-M-0842 (Charlottesville, VA: Darden Business Publishing, 2012).

2. Wes Nichols, "Advertising Analytics 2.0," *Harvard Business Review* (March 2013).

3. Thomas Davenport, *Competing on Analytics: The New Science of Winning* (Boston, MA: Harvard Business School Press, 2007).

4. Nichols.

# Section I

## Resource Allocation

In this section, Chapter 1, "A Resource-Allocation Perspective for Marketing Analytics," presents the resource-allocation framework that ties together the various marketing analytics techniques to a firm's strategic decisions. Marketing managers are often faced with the decision of the level of investment in different marketing activities. This chapter presents a framework for making the resource-allocation process more data-driven. Chapter 2, "Dunia Finance LLC," presents the case study of Dunia Finance LLC, a midsized financial services firm in the United Arab Emirates (UAE). The case study presents Dunia's journey toward building a data-driven organization where marketing analytics is a critical contributor to its customer relationship efforts. Near the end of this book in Chapter 21, "Dunia Finance LLC Revisited," you'll revisit Dunia Finance to develop a cross-sell strategy that is informed by the analysis of customer transaction data.

# 1   ———————————————————————

# A Resource-Allocation Perspective for Marketing Analytics

## Introduction

Dunia Finance LLC, the midsize financial services firm in the United Arab Emirates (UAE), gains most of its customers through door-to-door sales. This makes the cost of obtaining new customers high. So the company needed to look at new ways of allocating its resources to improve its results. It decided to focus on cross-selling to existing customers to increase their customer lifetime value (CLV).

It was up to Dunia to apply a resource-allocation framework to pinpoint the best groups of customers for cross-selling. Any customer who had opted out of promotional offers was excluded. Customers close to reaching their credit card limit would be targeted for a loan. For those who had personal loans, Dunia could offer solutions based on loan type for problems the customers didn't even recognize they had.

Resource allocation is the endgame of analytics for any company. Using marketing analytics properly, any firm (not just financial services providers such as Dunia) should be able to determine the optimal level of spending it should make on each of its marketing channels to maximize success.

## The Resource-Allocation Framework

Resource allocation is a four-step process. The first step is to determine the objective function. What is the metric the company wants to set as its goal for optimization? This may be one of any number of methods of assessing business success, including conversion rates to sales, incremental margins and profits, CLV, near-term sales lift, new buyers, repeat sales, market share, retention rates, cross-sell rates, future growth potential, balance sheet equity, and business valuation.

The second step is to connect the marketing inputs of a firm to the objective of resource allocation. Business managers' intuition is of paramount importance in this step, as it allows the marketer to correctly decompose a metric. For example, if a company is examining gross profits, what are the attributes of the business that contribute to those profits, and are the relationships between the various components empirical or computational (such as identity relationships)? Figure 1-1 shows one way in which gross profits might be broken down. Sales is a function of price, advertising, sales force, and trade promotions. Because gross profits minus marketing yields net profits, manipulating marketing channels can improve sales, but the different channels are also cost centers.

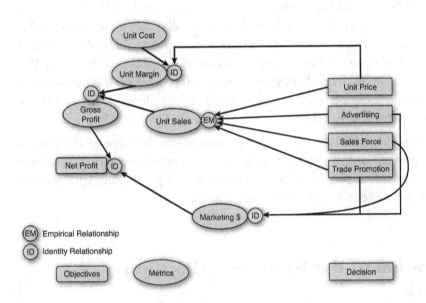

**Figure 1-1** A system-of-metrics framework for net profits

Source: Created by case writer and adapted from *Marketing Metrics.*[1]

Once the marketing inputs are mapped to the objective, as shown in Figure 1-1, the marketing manager must determine the relationships that are accounting identities versus those that are empirical. An accounting identity can be computed without any unknowns. For example, in Figure 1-1, net profit is gross profit minus marketing costs. If both gross profit and marketing costs are known, net profit can be computed easily. On the other hand, the relationship between marketing costs and unit sales is more complex and driven by numerous unknowns. You cannot directly sum the investments in marketing (for example, price, advertising, sales force, and trade promotion) to obtain sales. The relationship is termed *empirical* because the manager must analyze historical data to develop a function that transforms the marketing inputs into sales (for example, a function that describes the relationship between price and sales). The transformation function ideally develops a weight that translates a product's price into sales. These weights do not provide a perfect transformation, but rather a best guess based on historical data, wherein several factors in addition to price also affect sales. This is the main difference between an identity relationship and an empirical relationship: Empirical implies a best guess or prediction; identities are certain.

The third step in the resource-allocation process is to estimate the best weights for the empirical relationships identified in the second step. A common method for identifying these weights is to build an econometric (regression) model. Which marketing inputs of interest (for example, price, advertising, sales calls) should be considered as having an effect on the dependent variable? Once this regression model is obtained, the marketing manager can predict the precise shape of the objective function. This is the mathematical model that describes the relationship between the independent variables (for example, price, advertising, sales calls) and the dependent variable (for example, market share, profits, CLV).

In the last step of the resource-allocation process, a firm can reverse the process to identify the optimal value of the marketing inputs to maximize the objective function. This gives a detailed picture of what the company's precise marketing spend should be on each channel it uses to market its product.

# An Illustration of the Resource-Allocation Framework

Consider a pharmaceutical company in which the marketing department wants to determine the effects of sales calls on the profits it makes per customer (in this example, physicians are customers). In Figure 1-2, profits are broken down into number of new prescriptions and probability of new prescriptions. Both can be represented using a linear or logistic regression as a function of sales calls.

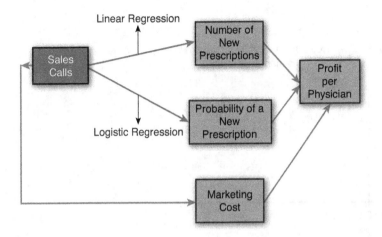

**Figure 1-2** An example of the system of metrics in the pharmaceutical industry

Source: Created by case writer.

Because sales calls also represent a marketing cost, the goal is to balance their effect on the top and bottom lines to maximize profits. The marketing manager can express the relationship between sales calls and profits mathematically and perform both linear and logistic regressions[2] as follows (Equation 1):

Profit per Physician = New Prescriptions × prob (New Prescriptions) × Gross Margin% – # of Sales Calls × Unit Cost of Sales Calls

# of New Prescriptions = $a + b1 \times ln$(# of Sales Calls)

prob (New Prescriptions) = $\exp(u) \div [1 + \exp(u)]$, where $u = c + d1 \times ln$ (# of Sales Calls)    (1)

Performing the regression analyses will determine the value of $a$, $b1$, $c$, and $d1$, giving the marketing manager a mathematical way to value sales calls with respect to their ability to increase the number of prescriptions written by physicians and the probability of a new prescription. And because sales calls are a cost center, the pharmaceutical company can maximize total profits by weighting its number of sales calls subject to optimal spending under its budget limit (see Figure 1-3).

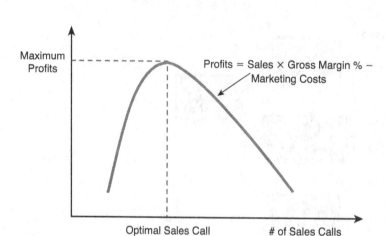

**Figure 1-3** Optimal allocation of marketing spend

Source: Created by case writer.


Table 1-1 provides hypothetical data describing the effects of sales calls on profits per physician. Say the values for $a$, $b1$, $c$, and $d1$ turn out to be 0.05, 1.5, 0.006, and 1.2 based on the regression analysis.

**Table 1-1** Numeric Example of Optimal Allocation of Marketing Spend

| $a$ | $b1$ | $c$ | $d1$ | Price | Cost of Sales Calls |
|---|---|---|---|---|---|
| 0.05 | 1.5 | 0.006 | 1.2 | 300 | 50 |

| Sales Calls | Sales | $u$ | $p$(Sales) | Profit | |
|---|---|---|---|---|---|
| 1 | 1.09 | 0.84 | 0.70 | 109.73 | |
| 2 | 1.70 | 1.32 | 0.79 | 181.65 | Current |
| 3 | 2.13 | 1.67 | 0.84 | 226.31 | |
| 4 | 2.46 | 1.94 | 0.87 | 252.30 | |
| 5 | 2.74 | 2.16 | 0.90 | 265.25 | |
| 6 | 2.97 | 2.34 | 0.91 | 268.74 | Optimal |
| 7 | 3.17 | 2.50 | 0.92 | 265.10 | |
| 8 | 3.35 | 2.64 | 0.93 | 255.94 | |
| 9 | 3.50 | 2.77 | 0.94 | 242.39 | |
| 10 | 3.65 | 2.88 | 0.95 | 225.27 | |

Source: Created by case writer.

The price of a unit (a prescription drug) is $300, and the cost of a single sales call is $50. The drug company currently calls its physicians an average of twice per month (which means that, in this example, the number of sales calls is two). Based on the estimated weights for each unknown in the described relationships, this strategy yields a profit of $181.65. If the company were to increase sales calls to six per month, the expected profits would be $268.74. Increasing sales calls beyond six per month, however, makes the cost of the sales calls higher than their incremental benefits, meaning profits start declining for sales calls of seven per month and above. In this example, six is the optimal level of sales calls because it maximizes the expected profit ($268.74) from each physician. As the example illustrates, the optimal number of sales calls that maximizes profits is critically dependent on the unknown weights of the empirical relationship.

Figure 1-4 shows a decomposition commonly used by consumer-goods companies to forecast the performance of new products. Using this model, a company can study how advertising leads to awareness and how the sales force leads to availability, among other things. Once the company understands the empirical relationships mathematically, it can calculate expected sales using simple arithmetic.

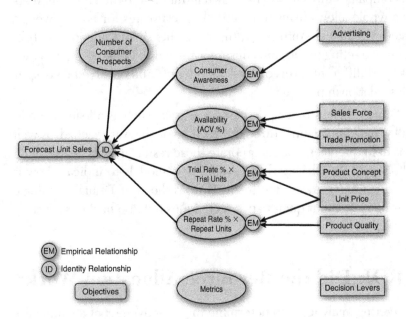

**Figure 1-4** System of metrics to forecast new product sales

Source: Created by case writer adapted from Farris, Pfeifer, Bendle, and Reibstein.

Marketing analytics relies on three pillars: econometrics, experimentation, and decision calculus (Figure 1-5).

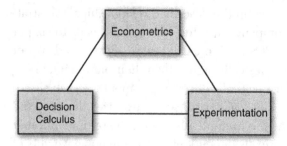

**Figure 1-5** Three pillars of marketing resource allocation

Source: Created by case writer.

Managers can use econometrics when they need to make hypotheses about their business and test them by using experiments. Where the decision calculus comes down to individual companies introducing their own intuition into the equation, marketing analytics as a whole allows firms to identify best estimates for how to weight the effects of marketing activities. Intuitively, these weights should provide the best relationship between marketing inputs and consumer response. Looking at past cases wherein a firm has tried different levels of marketing inputs and observed consumer response reveals this relationship.

In the case of Dunia, if a customer purchased a service, such as a loan or credit card, the bank would track the channel through which he or she was reached, as well as behaviors such as delinquencies, and incorporate those results into its cross-selling criteria. The results would then be used to develop new models to indicate how it should introduce future offers. According to Ali Hurbas, head of Dunia's Strategic Analytics Unit, "It is not just about quantitative techniques but also business sense."[3]

## Measuring ROI: Did the Resource Allocation Work?

The goal of marketing analytics is to determine the effectiveness of a company's various marketing strategies (such as its marketing mix). For each strategy, the company is looking to assess its return on investment (ROI).

Financial ROI is equal to profit over investment value. This is a yearly rate that is comparable to rate of return. Marketing ROI, on the other hand, is equal to profits related to marketing measures divided by the value of the marketing investment—which is actually money risked, not invested (Equation 2):

Marketing ROI = [Incremental Sales × Gross Margin –
Marketing Investment] ÷ Marketing Investment                                    (2)

Determining ROI is simple arithmetic; however, estimating and defining the effects of ROI is difficult. Imagine that Powerful Powertools spends $2 million on search engine marketing in 2012 and generates $10 million in incremental sales that year with marketing contribution margins of 50%. The company would determine its marketing ROI as follows (Equation 3):

ROI = ($10M × 0.5 – $2M) ÷ $2M = 1.5                                            (3)

A marketing manager or chief financial officer (CFO) would have therefore determined that his or her return is 150% on the marketing investment. But the manager will likely still have questions. Will the investment in 2012 also pay dividends in 2013 (for example, should some new customer acquisitions in 2013 be attributed to the investment in 2012)? How was incremental gross margin determined? What is the baseline without the search engine marketing? Will doubling the investment to $4 million double the returns to $20 million in incremental sales, or are there diminishing returns to marketing? What are the longer-term effects, and what is the CLV of the customers acquired through this campaign? The goal of analytics is to accommodate these nuances of marketing's influence on sales so that the estimate of incremental sales is an accurate reflection of reality.

One major decision regarding marketing ROI concerns the choice of average versus marginal ROI. Average ROI represents the returns for any given level of marketing investment. If an executive is interested in how total returns to marketing spending have changed over the previous two years, average ROI is the right measure. Marginal ROI, on the other hand, is the return for an additional dollar spent on marketing relative to existing investment levels. The choice between marginal and average ROI relies to a large extent on whether a marketing measure may yield diminishing returns. For linear models, average and incremental returns are the same because regardless of the current level of spending, the returns will be identical (Figure 1-6). As shown in Figure 1-7, however, the current level of investment matters when calculating incremental returns in the presence of diminishing returns.

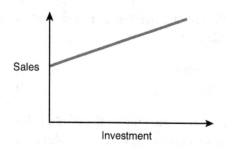

**Figure 1-6** A linear sales response curve

Source: Created by case writer.

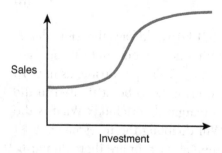

**Figure 1-7** Sales response curve with diminishing returns

Source: Created by case writer.

# Working with Econometrics: IBM and Others

To improve marketing success, companies must consistently make good decisions about which customers to select for targeting, the level of resources to be allocated to the selected customers, and nurturing the selected customers to increase future profitability. One example of a company that has successfully used CLV as an indicator of customer profitability and allocated marketing resources accordingly is IBM. In 2005, the computer and technology company used CLV as a criterion for determining the level of marketing contacts through direct mail, telesales, e-mail, and catalogs. An overview of the CLV management framework is shown in Table 1-2.

**Table 1-2** Customer Lifetime Value Management Framework

| Process | Purpose |
| --- | --- |
| Measure CLV | Obtain a measure of the potential value of IBM customers |
| Identify the drivers of CLV | Allow managers to influence CLV |
| Determine optimal level of contacts for each customer that would maximize his or her respective CLV | Guide managers about the level of investment required for each customer |
| Develop propensity models to predict which product(s) a customer is likely to purchase | Develop a product message when contacting a customer |
| Reallocate marketing contacts from low-CLV customers to high-CLV customers | Maximize marketing productivity |

Source: Created by case writer and adapted from Kumar et al (2005).[4]

In a pilot study implemented for approximately 35,000 customers, this approach led to reallocation of resources for about 14% of the customers as compared with allocation based on past spending history, the metric IBM had previously used to target customers and allocate resources (see Figure 1-8). The CLV-based resource reallocation led to a tenfold increase in revenue (amounting to about $20 million) without any changes in the level of marketing investment.

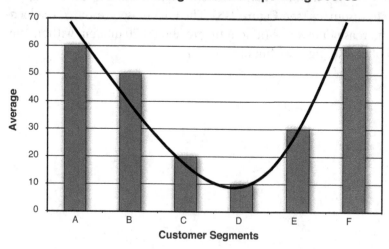

**Figure 1-8** Benefits from CLV-based resource allocation

Source: Created by case writer.

# Conclusion

Managers must understand their marketing efforts as precisely as possible to determine how much to spend on each marketing channel. If paid search advertising is the most effective way of getting a firm's message in front of the right customer, why would the company spend more on print advertising? If sales calls are profitable only up to a point, the marketing manager must know at which point the calls start costing his or her company money instead of making it.

The only way to measure the effects of marketing efforts on profitability is through the best-guess relationships revealed through marketing analytics. By using statistical analysis techniques, firms can use past customer behaviors to predict how customers will react to different marketing channels; managers can then optimize spending on each channel.

# Endnotes

1. Paul Farris, Phillip Pfeifer, Neil Bendle, and David Reibstein, *Marketing Metrics: The Definitive Guide for Measuring Marketing Performance* (Upper Saddle River, NJ: FT Press, 2010).

2. See Shea Gibbs and Rajkumar Venkatesan, "Multiple Regression in Marketing-Mix Models," UVA-M-0855 (Charlottesville, VA: Darden Business Publishing, 2013) for a discussion of linear regressions; see Shea Gibbs and Rajkumar Venkatesan, "Logistic Regression," UVA-M-0859 (Charlottesville, VA: Darden Business Publishing, 2013) for more on logistic regression analyses.

3. Gerry Yemen, Rajkumar Venkatesan, and Samuel E. Bodily, "Dunia Finance LLC (A)," UVA-M-0842 (Charlottesville, VA: Darden Business Publishing, 2012).

4. V. Kumar, Rajkumar Venkatesan, Tim Bohling, and Dennis Beckmen, "The Power of CLV: Managing Customer Lifetime Value at IBM," *Marketing Science*, 27, no. 4 (2008): 585–599.

# 2

## Dunia Finance LLC

*Analytics function has been a true franchise builder for Dunia since our launch, driving targeted cross-sell by focusing on all three Rs of consumer banking: risk, revenue, response.*

—Ali Hurbas

## Introduction

Ali Hurbas, head of the Strategic Analytics Unit (SAU) at Dunia Finance LLC (Dunia), the Abu Dhabi–based financial services company, was in an emergency meeting in Dunia's Dubai office with Rajeev Kakar and his management team in early October 2012. Kakar, executive director and founding CEO of Dunia and, concurrently, executive vice president and regional CEO for central and eastern Europe, the Middle East, and Africa for Fullerton Financial Holdings, was a veteran of the banking industry, with more than 25 years of experience in multiple markets as regional head and CEO for Citibank's Turkey, Middle East, Pakistan, and Africa consumer businesses. With investor pressure growing, Kakar told his management team, "We are facing a severe challenge. We need to quickly increase volumes and reward our good customers. And there is a need for speed to get this done!" He had put together a SWAT team, led by Hurbas, to perform this critical task of doubling business growth. (Exhibit 2-1 lists all members of the Dunia teams mentioned in the case.)

Hurbas had spent most of his career analyzing customers around the globe, so he knew there was a fine line between pitching new products to customers and alienating them. Given his experience, Hurbas appreciated Dunia's approach to marketing products: cross-selling. Executives believed their cross-selling framework had helped the organization launch into the center of the competitive Emirati financial services industry in 2008 and turn a profit by 2011—an event made even more notable for its occurrence during the global financial crisis. Just as Dunia was starting out, many others, due to involvement in debt-fueled real estate investments, were crumbling.

Working closely with his team, Hurbas had to figure out how analytics could be leveraged. Did it make sense to focus on bringing in new customers, or would ramping up cross-selling efforts to existing customers offer the volume Kakar needed to satisfy investors?

# Dunia: Into the World

As Lehman Brothers, the U.S.-based financial services company, collapsed in the fall of 2008, another financial services firm called Dunia[1] launched nearly 11,000 km (~7,000 miles) away. Dunia started as a joint venture between Singapore-based Fullerton Financial Holdings (a wholly owned subsidiary of Temasek Holdings in Singapore), Abu Dhabi's Mubadala Development Company, and Waha Capital. The new firm's business model focused on offering financial services to underserved clients in four customer segments: mass affluent market, affluent customers, mass self-employed clients, and mass salaried customers in small and midsize markets. Customer needs drove product offerings (see Table 2-1 for sub-brands and Exhibit 2-2 for market segment percentage).

**Table 2-1** Dunia Sub-Brands and United Arab Emirate (UAE) Banking Population

| Sub-Brand | Customer Segment | % of Total UAE Banking Population |
|-----------|------------------|-----------------------------------|
| Duniamoney | Salaried mass market | 40% |
| Dunia | Mass affluent | 30% |
| Duniagold | Affluent | 15% |
| Duniatrade | Self-employed mass market | 15% |

Source: Dunia. Used with permission.

Springing to life in the midst of a global financial meltdown seemed to motivate Dunia executives to create opportunity from crisis. As other financial firms reduced employee numbers, Dunia hired; as others closed branches, Dunia opened offices; as others drew back lending, Dunia sensibly grew.

At its core, Dunia did seem different. The diversity of its staff—25 nationalities and 31 languages represented, with many employees who had worked outside their respective home countries' banks for extended periods—seemed to promise that Dunia would be more mindful where other institutions had made mistakes. Indeed, Dunia promised a measured approach, with a focus on basic values and sustainable business practices. It would be customer-centric, only without the excessive risk-taking that seemed to have brought about the 2008 economic meltdown.

As the world's financial structures continued to change and geopolitical events—the tsunami and nuclear reactor crisis in Fukushima, Japan, and the Arab Spring—continued to shape its environment, Dunia became profitable within 30 months. That accomplishment, among others, had Dunia leaders convinced that their business model was working. By 2012, the company had 800 employees, 19 branches, a 24-hour call center, and a sophisticated online service (see Exhibit 2-3 for financials).

# Dunia: How Its World Worked

The UAE, a confederation of seven emirates,[2] had one of the most developed and technologically efficient banking sectors in the Middle East.[3] An increase in population (roughly 5.5 million) and high wealth levels had created much demand for financial services, so by 2012, the country was heavily banked; there were 24 local and 28 foreign banks with full operating licenses and 70 other financial institutions.[4]

The Central Bank of the United Arab Emirates (Central Bank), created in the 1980s to license companies for investment and specialized financing activities, also worked with the UAE government to set policies and act as a supervisor. Although the Central Bank did not have a federal credit bureau, there was a separate independent credit bureau called Emcredit based out of the Dubai International Financial Center (DIFC), which was founded in January 2006. The extent to which banks shared customer credit information with the central credit database (which stored an individual's negative and positive credit history) was unclear. Emcredit had another product called Embounce. The source of Embounce data was not individual banks but public prosecution in Dubai. As a criminal offense, any bounced check reported to police was recorded and submitted to Embounce. The database covered 100% of Dubai's population, but the data only included infractions, so it was not as rich as Emcredit's credit database. Moreover, check-bounce information of emirates other than Dubai (such as Abu Dhabi) was not included.

The Central Bank licensed Dunia to offer credit cards, personal and auto loans, simple insurance products linked to all of these, and corporate deposit services and financial guarantees for companies. In 2009, a new government policy offered Dunia another market opportunity: the Wage Protection System. This government regulatory system required private-sector employers to pay wages monthly through approved financial institutions. After gaining government approval, Dunia signed up companies to facilitate these transactions. "Liquidity is key to the success of any financial institution," Venu Parameshwar, Dunia CFO, said. "One of Dunia's key priorities is to ensure that our balance sheet reflects the highest degree of liquidity."

Revenue was generated through fees from originating and servicing loans, commissions, interest on credit card and loan balances, and services such as credit card protection plans and loan insurance. Dunia needed customers who carried loans but did not default, or who maintained revolving credit card balances and still made a card payment each month. In addition, the longer Dunia held a customer, the more profitable the relationship became; therefore, ensuring customer loyalty was very important. In addition, the firm needed new customers to grow and had to spend more to keep the pool a healthy size. Hurbas described a few differences between the U.S. and UAE markets:

> In a developing market like the UAE, there would be higher costs of doing business, including credit and operational cost. In the U.S., a company like ours could get 10 million names from the credit bureau and a half-percent response rate, with which you would be happy because it gives you about 30,000 or 40,000 customers. If you do that twice a month, that gives you pretty good numbers. Whereas over here, in a good month, we may still book a fraction of this kind of volume partly because UAE's population is far lower than the U.S.'s, and we don't have full-blown credit bureaus, so you can't say, "I want the customers with xyz criteria" and know exactly what type of risk you are taking. You have to rely on internal data in a developing market in order to grow prudently, which is a bigger risk challenge. Moreover, while UAE is a market full of growth opportunities, we should also be cognizant of, and factor in, several macro event risks surrounding us. The Middle East is a region going through significant changes, which bring about many risks, as well.

> Another difference between the U.S. and a developing market is the human capital required across all functions, not only in strategic analytics. A manager in a large U.S. bank typically controls a much narrower area but can afford to dig far deeper, so can be a true specialist within his/her function. On the other hand, a developing market banking associate must have broader coverage in his/her function and also needs to have a strong understanding of several other functions in order to be effective.

Another variable that increased the risk lenders faced in the UAE was its transient, expatriate work force population. When non-nationals lost their jobs, their residence visas were canceled and they had to leave the country within 30 days; by leaving the UAE for their home countries, customers could run out on loan and credit card payments, leaving banks with large credit losses. Raman Krishnan, the chief risk officer, had a tough job ensuring that the right credit policies were put in place and were dynamically assessed based on portfolio experience and market conditions. He worked closely with Hurbas to analyze the portfolio and make certain that the right metrics were in place for managing risk and reward simultaneously. Raman Krishnan explained, "Data is our most important tool in risk management. In an environment where risks are plenty, not having accurate data could lead to significant financial losses, while understanding and using data could give us a significant competitive edge."

# New Customers and a Dunia Credit Bureau of Sorts

Each new customer was assigned a Dunia customer identification number (CIN) when onboarded. In the UAE, there was no identification number comparable to a U.S. Social Security number that could be used to gather data on each person. The government had introduced an Emirates ID number, but it was still a relatively new concept in 2012. The lack of a viable credit bureau put pressure on Dunia executives to generate their own reliable statistics to help them quantify decisions on product offerings and customer value. The data to generate these statistics were kept in Dunia's data warehouse (DWH). This included static demographic data (such as age and income) captured at the time of acquisition and performance data, which was refreshed dynamically.

Each customer's CIN would be the same on all products he or she purchased, thus providing Dunia with reliable and consistent customer data. Accurate data was the key ingredient for Dunia's "customer-centric" approach. Customer centricity was at the core of Dunia. The entire organization was structured around fulfilling the needs of the customer. Processes, people, and business functions were designed with each customer segment in mind. In contrast to a product-centric approach, Dunia's customer-centric approach identified the various life stage and lifestyle needs of the customer and aimed to fulfill them using customized financial solutions. Once a customer demonstrated acceptable usage patterns and history, Dunia would consider increasing the credit granted to the customer.

All behavioral and demographic data available were captured, addressing the five Cs of credit (capacity, character, capital, collateral, and covenant) and collected within the DWH. The DWH was a multipurpose database that captured all categories of data from Dunia's several systems. These individual systems running at Dunia were chosen or designed with painstaking detail by the IT team. The DWH was completely home-grown by the Strategic Analytics Unit team and a key tool in its business. The various IT systems from front and back offices—including customer relationship manage-ment (CRM), the application processing system, the loan system, the credit card sys-tem, and the collection system—fed data into the DWH daily. As part of each system's batch update process, daily output files were produced and stored in the DWH. As a management information system (MIS), the DWH was used for list management, business analytics, statistical scoring, propensity modeling, test-versus-control design and tracking, business KPI generation, sales productivity analysis, incentive manage-ment, and limit increases.

# New Customer Acquisition

As in most consumer-lending organizations, portfolio growth was driven by a combination of "new-to-bank" customer acquisitions (direct sales–led) and deepen-ing relationships through cross-selling. The majority of new customers were gained through door-to-door sales, a model similar to the one insurance agents or financial planners used in the United States when they invited people to meet at a coffee shop or office for an information session. Several departments worked together to ensure that the right strategy was put in place for new-to-bank customer acquisitions. The team managed a very sizable group of relationship managers whose core focus was acquiring new customers.

The cost structure for booking a new loan, credit card, or insurance policy depended on the channel used to gain the business. There was a one-time booking cost for each customer. If the service was booked through a relationship officer in a Dunia branch or through a door-to-door sale by one of Dunia's 1,000 salespeople, the cost included a salesperson incentive of AED (United Arab Emirates dirhams) 400 (in U.S. dollars, USD 109); if booked through the call center, the incentive decreased by half, to AED 200 (USD 55).[5] Table 2-2 shows the effect of adding additional call center agents to the 100 already in place. The profit per agent was AED 37,000. In addition to sales incentives, there were approval costs for the various stages of appli-cation processing, such as data entry, verification, underwriting, wages/salaries, and calling costs. That figure was approximately AED 100 (USD 27) per transaction. If the booked product was a credit card, additional costs included card embossing, printing, and production, and the accompanying letter and card carrier, which totaled AED 50 (USD 14). The cost for courier delivery was another AED 50. Booking loans was less costly and had a higher probability of being collected. The UAE had a dim view of borrowers who failed to pay back loans—bouncing a check could result in a prison sentence. At Dunia, borrowers were required to provide postdated checks for each monthly installment at the time the loan was obtained.

**Table 2-2** Call Center Capacity

| Number of Call Agents Added | Number of Calls per Day | Employee Cost | Space |
| --- | --- | --- | --- |
| 1–25 | 100 each | AED 6,000 per agent | 35 sq. ft./agent |
| 26+ | 100 each | AED 3,000 per agent | 120/sq. ft./year |

Source: Dunia. Used with permission.

For a product to succeed, the deciding factor was profitability. The focus on profitability was one of the leading-edge practices adopted by the Dunia SAU team, ensuring that a holistic assessment was done on the relationship's overall value, rather than on one-dimensional metrics. The profit and loss statement incorporated all relevant revenue and expense items associated with the product. Dunia measured ROA on an annualized basis.

# The Strategic Analytics Unit and Customer Retention

Dunia was active in customer reward and progression and relationship deepening with activities such as credit card limit increases and cross-selling of other financial products. The cross-selling approach was used for existing customers and was similar to the frequently heard "Would you like fries with that?" at fast-food restaurants in the United States. Essentially, cross-selling was the strategy of selling multiple products to existing customers so that their balances (and Dunia's earnings) increased. The strategy was beneficial in two ways: The opportunity to cross-sell increased the lifetime value of the customer, and known customers were less risky because Dunia had data on their behavior. The Dunia system was set up to identify customers it could generate a profit from yet be nimble enough to take appropriate corrective actions if actual performance varied from expectations. Overall, cross-selling was less risky than acquiring new customers, required less investment to maintain, and increased probability of customer retention.

From a risk management perspective, determining which customers were eligible for cross-selling was the credit department's responsibility; once customers were cleared by that group, SAU could target them. SAU had the technical tools and historical performance, and DWH could therefore perform robust targeting.

To facilitate this approach, strong analytical capabilities were required in the form of three key elements: people, system infrastructure/technical tools, and accurate data. Dunia SAU scored high on all three counts.

Hurbas reported to Kakar (see Exhibit 2-4), ensuring independence of the critical analytics function. In most other banks and financial institutions, analytics would be a part of the credit function and called "Credit MIS," or would exist partly within marketing, finance, or IT. All analytics team members who dealt with data were gathered under one roof at Dunia, ensuring not only a single source of data—or "source of truth"—but also a broad exposure to the same team of people who handled data across all aspects of the business, as opposed to preparing reports on a one-dimensional basis within a narrow focus on a single functional area. Kakar and the rest of Dunia's senior management were the biggest supporters of analytics and promoted a culture of analytics-based decision-making throughout the organization, making analytics a part of Dunia's DNA.

To ensure that the SAU stayed sharp, Hurbas hired the team carefully. He looked for individuals who were either fresh from top schools around the world or who only had a few years' experience—always with a strong programming foundation and quantitative abilities—who also demonstrated in-depth business, financial, product, and process understanding. Because individuals bearing all of those skills were scarce, talent was incubated through senior-level, cross-functional interaction with many other departments, where training cut across various disciplines, such as finance, marketing, operations, IT, and sales.

Nesimi Monur, an industrial engineer, was Hurbas's first hire. Gauri Sawant and Ram Naveen joined the SAU team later on with IT and consumer finance backgrounds, respectively. More recently, Hurbas hired Maksym Gadomsky, who had an applied mathematics degree; Cagatay Dagistan, who had a master's in industrial engineering; and Sahil Kumar, a computer engineer with an MBA. This diverse and eclectic team helped bring added breadth, which made analytics-based decision-making more meaningful.

Parallel to Dunia's growth, the analytics function, which was one of the firm's key growth engines, was expanding. By 2012, the core SAU team was seasoned, scalable, and ready to take on more people and train them on the analytics tools and techniques, as well as on the business processes such as cross-selling.

Any customer who had previously opted out of all promotional offers was excluded from cross-sell efforts. For each product, a list of eligible customers would be extracted using behavioral criteria (for example, past delinquency incidence). Pricing and loan quantum would also be driven by SAU segmentation.

Credit card usage patterns, for example, provided a wealth of information. Every instance of a customer's credit card swipe could provide valuable insights about the customer's lifestyle and life stage and offer pointers for understanding customer needs and preferences. That way, Dunia could tailor appropriate products to meet these needs and preferences, in line with the principle of customer centricity. Dunia SAU was instrumental in taking this volume of data and extracting meaningful intelligence about the client. Dunia could offer solutions for problems customers did not know they had (for example, a new home loan may coincide with moving expenses, a hotel stay, or household furnishing purchases).

The process of contacting customers was a strategic decision, and each combination carried a different cost (Table 2-3). Efforts were made to maximize the customer response, yet Dunia was mindful not to contact a customer too frequently. Telesales calls did not exceed three per customer. SAU would give the validated list to call center agents for action.

**Table 2-3** Channel Choice Cost Sample

| Channel Choice | Cost (UAE Dirhams) | Cost (U.S. Dollars) |
|---|---|---|
| E-mail only | 0 | 0 |
| E-mail + 1 call | 0.75 | 0.20 |
| E-mail + 2 calls | 1.50 | 0.40 |
| E-mail + 3 calls | 2.25 | 0.61 |

Source: Dunia. Used with permission.

## Booking a Cross-Sell

Regardless of the cross-sell product, the front-end channel would initiate a cross-sell offer action through CRM. An offer action included electronic mailers specifying the loan or credit card amounts being sent to customers through the centralized marketing team and outbound telephone calls from the call center.

The company relied heavily on Dunia's outbound telesales team to contact eligible customers and ensure cross-sell would happen. While the outbound team ensured that call-out would happen, the marketing and product team ensured that customer communications were sent out via all channels (such as e-mail, text message, and direct mail) for the broadest reach possible. The process worked seamlessly across all units—SAU, credit, outbound calling, marketing, and operations. The analytics team played a pivotal role in ensuring well-orchestrated coordination across all involved units. This called for significant soft skills over and above the technical skills expected of analytics.

Customer responses were recorded in the CRM database, and if the customer was uninterested, the reasons for the rejection would be recorded. If the customer was interested, the new product application was created and the transaction booked. The operations team was responsible for processing applications in a cost- and time-efficient manner.

If a service such as a loan or credit card was accepted, the SAU would immediately and rigorously start tracking for delinquencies; those results would be incorporated into the criteria, and the credit and SAU departments would review results. The SAU engaged with all of Dunia's functional units and was empowered to make decisions and implement them. Cross-sell response results would be used to develop new models for predicting propensity to respond to similar future offers, and risk results were used to model and recalibrate existing behavior scores and other rule-based criteria. "It is not just about quantitative techniques, but also business sense," Hurbas said. "One must know what to analyze depending on the problem at hand versus blindly repeating analyst reports at some frequency—then it becomes MIS and not analytics, which is really actionable MIS."

## Cross-Selling and Growth Strategy

To meet this challenge, Hurbas thought he had to ensure the 10 *P*s of successful analytics:

- People—Hire top-tier *people* with specialized talent.
- Passion—The team needs to display *passion* through creativity and innovation.
- Predictability—*Predictability* of results leads to profitability.
- Profitability—*Profitability* is required for investing in good times and sustainability in stressful times.

- Proactive—Be *proactive* in identifying potential issues.

- Precision—The solution needs to be executed with *precision*.

- Power—Computing *power* has to be at the highest degree. In this case, Kakar allowed Hurbas to make maximum necessary investment into systems and hardware.

- Partnership—*Partnership* across all functional teams is a critical success factor.

- Progression—Customer *progression* has to be in line with their needs and life stage.

- Pragmatism—The solution has to be *pragmatic* for simplicity of implementation.

To form the right partnerships, Hurbas worked closely with Mariam El Samny, head of marketing and products; Barlas Balabaner, operations and technology director; Guru Balakrishna, credit policy head; Raed Shomali, contact center head; Muzaffer Hamid, operations head; Pankaj Kundra, segment distribution head; Sanjay Kao, consumer business head; Shankar Balasubramania, collections head; Venu Parameshwar, CFO; and Raman Krishnan, chief risk officer. Dunia believed that without cross-functional participation, the best solutions would fail.

There would be no sitting still in the UAE market for Dunia. In the emergency meeting, Hurbas heard loud and clear that the CEO wanted volumes increased. Hurbas was keenly aware that success relied on new ways of thinking. He believed the firm's cross-sell model offered a competitive edge, but he wondered whether Dunia should explore providing credit cards to personal loan customers. Or would increasing efforts to gain new customers be a better plan? In either event, would the company need to double the size of its call center?

# Endnotes

1. *Dunia* is Arabic for *world,* in particular the earthly world, distinct from the spiritual world or hereafter. Several other languages have retained the word and at least part of its meaning, including Bengali, Hindi, Persian, Punjabi, Turkish, and Urdu.

2. What distinguishes an emirate from other territorial units is its governance by a hereditary ruling class.

3. Economist Intelligence Unit, "United Arab Emirates: Financial Services Industry Report," June 2010, 9.

4. Banks were licensed to accept individual depositors, but financial institutions could only accept deposits from corporations.

5. All exchange rates are approximate.

# Exhibits

### Exhibit 2-1  Dunia Finance LLC: Teams

| Strategic Analytics Team | |
| --- | --- |
| Ali Hurbas | Head, Strategic Analytics |
| Nesimi Monur | Industrial engineering background and Hurbas's first hire |
| Ram Naveen | Finance background |
| Gauri Sawant | IT background |
| Maksym Gadomsky | Applied mathematics degree |
| Cagatay Dagistan | Master's in industrial engineering |
| Sahil Kumar | Computer engineering and MBA background |
| **Technology Team** | |
| Nihad Nazir | IT Solutions Head |
| Sameer Tomar | IT Systems Manager |
| **Marketing Team** | |
| Mariam El Samny | Marketing and Products Head |
| Mohan Prasannakumar | Asset Products Head |
| **Credit and Collections Team** | |
| Raman Krishnan | Chief Risk Officer |
| Guru Balakrishna | Credit Policy Head |
| Shankar Balasubramania | Collections Head |
| **New Customer Acquisition Team** | |
| Sanjay Kao | Consumer Business Head |
| Neeraj Sehgal | Sales Head, Abu Dhabi |
| Pankaj Kundra | Segment Distribution Head |
| Sunil Mathews | Segment Head, Self-Employed Mass Market |
| Rishi Tandon | Segment Head, Dunia Gold (Affluent) |
| **Operations Team** | |
| Barlas Balabaner | Operations and Technology Director |
| Muzaffer Hamid | Operations Head |
| Owais Qazi | Unit Head, Credit Operations |
| Rajat Srivastav | Unit Head, Operations |
| Vinod Thomas | Unit Head, Operations |
| Raed Shomali | Contact Center Head |

Source: Dunia. Used with permission.

**Duniamoney (Salaried Mass Market)**

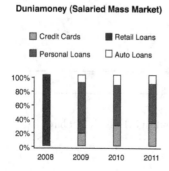

**Duniatrade (Self-Employed Mass Market)**

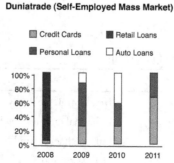

**Dunia (Salaried Mass Affluent Market)**

**Duniagold and Others (Affluent Market)**

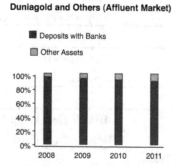

**Exhibit 2-2** Dunia Finance LLC: Monies lent by market segment in the United Arab Emirates (2008–2011)

Data source: Dunia annual reports, 2008–2012.

**Exhibit 2-3** Dunia Finance LLC: Income Statements 2008–2011 (In Thousands of UAE Dirhams)

|  | Nov. 1, 2006 to Dec. 31, 2008 | Twelve Months Ended Dec. 31, 2009 | Twelve Months Ended Dec. 31, 2010 | Twelve Months Ended Dec. 31, 2011 |
|---|---|---|---|---|
| Interest income | 5,956 | 39,131 | 86,282 | 153,397 |
| Interest expense | (54) | (1,227) | (3,386) | (12,728) |
| Net interest income | 5,902 | 37,904 | 82,896 | 140,669 |
| Commission and fee income | 62 | 7,176 | 23,152 | 64,811 |
| Other operating income | 194 | 554 | - | - |
| Operating income | 6,158 | 45,634 | 106,048 | 205,480 |
| Impairment charge, net | (336) | (25,482) | (42,174) | (54,310) |

|  | Nov. 1, 2006 to Dec. 31, 2008 | Twelve Months Ended Dec. 31, 2009 | Twelve Months Ended Dec. 31, 2010 | Twelve Months Ended Dec. 31, 2011 |
|---|---|---|---|---|
| General and administrative expenses | (115,046) | (123,040) | (140,057) | (125,655) |
| Amortization and depreciation | (5,037) | (13,594) | (11,641) | (7,398) |
| **Net Profit (Loss)** | **(114,261)** | **(116,482)** | **(87,824)** | **18,117** |

*(In Thousands of U.S. Dollars)*

|  | Nov. 1, 2006 to Dec. 31, 2008 | Twelve Months Ended Dec. 31, 2009 | Twelve Months Ended Dec. 31, 2010 | Twelve Months Ended Dec. 31, 2011 |
|---|---|---|---|---|
| Interest income | 1,621 | 10,651 | 23,486 | 41,755 |
| Interest expense | (15) | (334) | (922) | (3,465) |
| Net interest income | 1,606 | 10,317 | 22,564 | 38,290 |
| Commission and fee income | 17 | 1,953 | 6,302 | 17,642 |
| Other operating income | 53 | 151 | - | - |
| Operating income | 1,676 | 12,422 | 28,866 | 55,932 |
| Impairment charge, net | (91) | (6,936) | (11,480) | (14,783) |
| General and administrative expenses | (31,304) | (33,491) | (38,124) | (34,203) |
| Amortization and depreciation | (1,371) | (3,700) | (3,169) | (2,014) |
| **Net Profit (Loss)** | **(31,090)** | **(31,706)** | **(23,906)** | **4,931** |

**Net Income**
**(In Thousands of UAE Dirhams)**

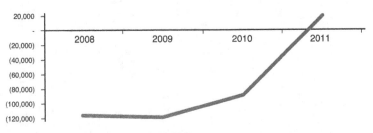

Source: Dunia directors' reports, 2008–2012.

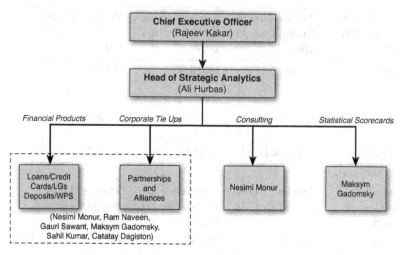

**Exhibit 2-4** Dunia Finance LLC: SAU organizational chart

Source: Dunia company documents. Used with permission.

# Assignment Questions

1. What are the differences in banking between the United States and the UAE?

2. How does analytics affect customer relationship management at Dunia?

3. How would Dunia affect customer lifetime value?

4. Is it the right time for Hurbas to focus on cross-selling or should he focus on new customer acquisition?

# Section II

## Product Analytics

This section relates to the analytics that help a manager with his or her product management decisions. In this section, you'll learn about segmentation and pricing. Chapter 3, "Cluster Analysis for Segmentation," presents k-means cluster analysis because it is flexible and can easily accommodate multiple variables for segmentation. Chapter 4, "Segmentation at Sticks Kebob Shop," details the Sticks Kebob Shop case, which presents an application of cluster analysis. You'll identify the right location for a new store for this fast-growing casual restaurant chain. The segmentation is carried out based on responses from a psychographic questionnaire. The case also allows you to take the output from segmentation to identify target segments and develop a marketing plan suitable for the target segments. Exploiting customer heterogeneity and differences across segments is a characteristic of a good resource-allocation strategy. You'll envision a firm conducting a market segmentation exercise to identify priority segments before employing the analytics techniques discussed later in this book. Analytics can then be implemented for each of the identified priority segments.

Chapter 5, "A Practical Guide to Conjoint Analysis," explores conjoint analysis and value pricing. Conjoint analysis can be connected to resource allocation by showing that stronger brands and better-quality products can charge a higher price without a discernible decrease in demand. Identification of product features that appeal to consumers can be connected to managers' product development and product line resource-allocation decisions. Chapter 6, "Portland Trail Blazers," presents the Portland Trail Blazers case, which details management's challenge of boosting regular season game attendance irrespective of the team's on-court performance. Use of conjoint analysis allows the Trail Blazers to determine the right balance between raising the stadium's seat prices and providing free concessions, such as hot dogs or team jerseys.

# 3

## Cluster Analysis for Segmentation

## Introduction

We all understand that consumers are not all alike. This provides a challenge for the development and marketing of profitable products and services. Not every offering will be right for every customer, nor will every customer be equally responsive to your marketing efforts. Segmentation is a way of organizing customers into groups with similar traits, product preferences, or expectations. Once segments are identified, marketing messages and in many cases even products can be customized for each segment. The better the segment(s) chosen for targeting by a particular organization, the more successful the organization is assumed to be in the marketplace. Since its introduction in the late 1950s, market segmentation has become a central concept of marketing practice.

Segments are constructed on the basis of customers' (1) demographic characteristics, (2) psychographics, (3) desired benefits from products/services, and (4) past-purchase and product-use behaviors. These days, most firms possess rich information about customers' actual purchase behavior, geodemographic, and psychographic characteristics. In cases where firms do not have access to detailed information about each customer, information from surveys of a representative sample of the customers can be used as the basis for segmentation.

## An Example

Consider Geico, an auto insurance company.[1] Suppose Geico plans to customize its auto insurance offerings and needs to understand what its customers view as important from their insurance provider. Geico can ask its customers to rate how

**34**

important the following two attributes are to them when considering the type of auto insurance they would use:

- Savings on premium
- Existence of a neighborhood agent

The importance of the attributes is measured using a seven-point Likert-type scale, where a rating of one represents *not important* and seven represents *very important*. Unless every respondent who is surveyed gives identical ratings, the data will contain variations that you can use to *cluster* or group respondents together, and such clusters *are* the segments. The groupings of customers are most similar to each other if they are part of the same segment and most different from each other if they are part of different segments. By inference, then, actions taken toward customers in the same segment should lead to similar responses, and actions taken toward customers in different segments should lead to different responses.

Another way of saying this is that the aspects of auto insurance that are important to any given customer in one segment will also be important to other customers in that same segment. Furthermore, those aspects that are important to that customer will be different from what is important to a customer in a different segment. Figure 3-1 shows what the analysis in this example might look like:

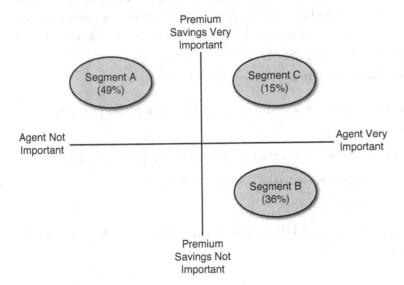

**Figure 3-1** Segmentation of Geico customers

The analysis shows three distinct segments. The majority of Geico's customers (Segment A, 49%) prefer savings on their premium, and they do not prefer having a neighborhood agent. Customers who belong to Segment B (about 36%) prefer having a neighborhood agent and premium savings is not important to them. Some customers (Segment C, 15%) prefer both the savings on their premium as well as a neighborhood agent. This analysis shows that Geico can benefit by adding an offline channel (for developing a network of neighborhood agents) to serve Segment B and also charge a higher premium to them for providing this convenience. Of course, the caveat is the increased competition with other insurance providers, such as Allstate and State Farm, who already provide this service.

# Cluster Analysis

Cluster analysis is a class of statistical techniques that can be applied to data that exhibit natural groupings. Cluster analysis makes no distinction between dependent and independent variables. The entire set of interdependent relationships is examined. Cluster analysis sorts through the raw data on customers and groups them into clusters. A *cluster* is a group of relatively homogeneous customers. Customers who belong to the same cluster are similar to each other. They are also dissimilar to customers outside the cluster, particularly customers in other clusters. The primary input for cluster analysis is a measure of similarity between customers, such as correlation coefficients, distance measures, and association coefficients.

The following are the basic steps involved in cluster analysis:

1. Formulate the problem and select the variables you want to use as the basis for clustering.

2. Compute the distance between customers along the selected variables.

3. Apply the clustering procedure to the distance measures.

4. Decide on the number of clusters.

5. Map and interpret clusters and draw conclusions—illustrative techniques like perceptual maps are useful.

### Distance Measures

The main input into any cluster analysis procedure is a measure of distance between individuals who are being clustered. The objective of a distance measure is to quantify the difference between two individuals on the variables you are using for the segmentation. A shorter (longer) distance between two individuals would imply they have similar (dissimilar) preferences on the segmentation variables. Distance between two individuals is obtained through a measure called *Euclidean distance*. If two individuals, Joe and Sam, are being clustered on the basis of $n$ variables, then the Euclidean distance between Joe and Sam is represented as:

$$\text{Euclidean Distance} = \sqrt{\left(x_{Joe,1} - x_{Sam,1}\right)^2 + \ldots + \left(x_{Joe,n} - x_{Sam,n}\right)^2}$$

where

$x_{Joe,1}$ = the value of Joe along variable 1

$x_{Sam,1}$ = the value of Sam along variable 1

A pairwise distance matrix among individuals who are being clustered can be created using the Euclidean distance measure. Extending the preceding example, consider three individuals—Joe, Sam, and Sara—who are being clustered based on their preference for premium savings and a neighborhood agent. The importance ratings on these two attributes for Joe, Sam, and Sara are shown in Table 3-1.

**Table 3-1** Sample Data for Cluster Analysis

| Individual Name | Importance Score | |
| --- | --- | --- |
| | **Premium Savings** | **Neighborhood Agent** |
| Joe | 4 | 7 |
| Sam | 3 | 4 |
| Sara | 5 | 3 |

The Euclidean distance between Joe and Sam is obtained as

$$\text{Euclidean Distance (Joe, Sam)} = \sqrt{(4-3)^2 + (7-4)^2} = 3.2$$

The first term in this Euclidean distance measure is the squared difference between Joe and Sam on the importance score for premium savings, and the second term is the squared difference between them on the importance score for neighborhood agent. The Euclidean distances are then computed for each pairwise combination of the three individuals being clustered to obtain a pairwise distance matrix. The pairwise distance matrix for Joe, Sam, and Sara is shown in Table 3-2.

**Table 3-2** Pairwise Distance Matrix

|      | Joe | Sam | Sara |
|------|-----|-----|------|
| Joe  | 0   | 3.2 | 4.1  |
| Sam  |     | 0   | 2.2  |
| Sara |     |     | 0    |

The distance between Joe and Sam is 3.2, as shown in Table 3-2. This pairwise distance matrix is then provided as an input to a clustering algorithm.

## K-Means Clustering Algorithm

K-means clustering belongs to the nonhierarchical class of clustering algorithms. It is one of the more popular algorithms used for clustering in practice because of its simplicity and speed. It is considered to be more robust to different types of variables, is more appropriate for large data sets that are common in marketing, and is less sensitive to some customers who are outliers (in other words, extremely different from others).

For K-means clustering, the user has to specify the number of clusters required before the clustering algorithm is started. The basic algorithm for K-means clustering is as follows:

1. Choose the number of clusters, $k$.

2. Generate $k$ random points as cluster centroids.

3. Assign each point to the nearest cluster centroid.

4. Recompute the new cluster centroid.

5. Repeat the two previous steps until some convergence criterion is met. Usually the convergence criterion is that the assignment of customers to clusters has not changed over multiple iterations.

A cluster centroid is simply the average of all the points in that cluster. Its coordinates are the arithmetic mean for each dimension separately over all the points in the cluster. Consider Joe, Sam, and Sara in the previous example. Let's represent them based on their importance ratings on premium savings and neighborhood agent as: Joe = {4,7}, Sam = {3,4}, Sara = {5,3}. If you assume that they belong to the same cluster, then the center for their cluster is obtained as

Cluster Centroid $Z = (z_1, z_2) = \{(4+3+5) \div 3, (7+4+3) \div 3\}$

$z_1$ is measured as the average of the ratings of Joe, Sam, and Sara on premium savings. Similarly, $z_2$ is measured as the average of their ratings on neighborhood agent. Figure 3-2 provides a visual representation of K-means clustering.

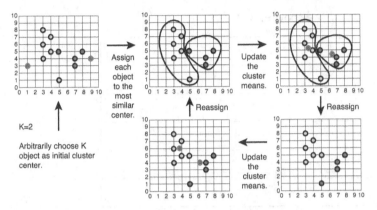

**Figure 3-2** Visual representation of K-means clustering

## Number of Clusters

One of the main issues with K-means clustering is that it does not provide an estimate of the number of clusters that exists in the data. The K-means clustering has to be repeated several times with different "Ks" (or number of clusters) to determine the number of clusters that is appropriate for the data. A commonly used method to determine the number of clusters is the *elbow criterion*.

The elbow criterion states that you should choose a number of clusters so that adding another cluster does not add sufficient information. The elbow is identified by plotting the ratio of the *within cluster variance* to *between cluster variance* against the number of clusters. The *within cluster variance* is an estimate of the average of the variance in the variables used as a basis for segmentation (importance score ratings for premium savings and neighborhood agent in the Geico example) among customers who belong to a particular cluster. The *between cluster variance* is an estimate of the variance of the segmentation basis variables between customers who belong to different segments. The objective of cluster analysis (as mentioned before) is to minimize the *within cluster variance* and maximize the *between cluster variance*. Therefore, as the number of clusters is increasing, the ratio of the *within cluster variance* to the *between cluster variance* will keep decreasing.

But at some point, the marginal gain from adding an additional cluster will drop, giving an angle in the graph (the elbow). In Figure 3-3, the elbow is indicated by the circle. The number of clusters chosen should therefore be 4.

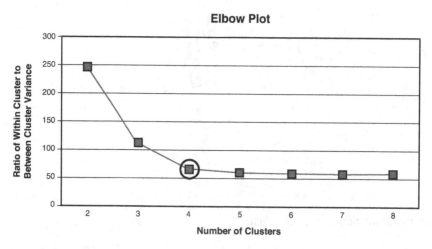

**Figure 3-3** Elbow plot for determining number of clusters

It should also be noted that the initial assignment of cluster seeds has a bearing on the final model performance. Some common methods for ensuring the stability of the results obtained from K-means clustering include:

- Running the algorithm multiple times with different starting values. When using random starting points, running the algorithm multiple times ensures a different starting point each time.

- Splitting the data randomly into two halves and running the cluster analysis separately on each half. The results are robust and stable if the number of clusters and the size of different clusters are similar in both halves.

### Profiling Clusters

Once clusters are identified, the description of the clusters in terms of the variables used for clustering—or using additional data such as demographics—helps to customize marketing strategy for each segment. This process of describing the clusters is called *profiling*. Figure 3-1 is an example of such a process. A good deal of cluster-analysis software also provides information on which cluster a customer belongs to. This information can be used to calculate the means of the profiling variables for each cluster. In the Geico example, it is useful to investigate whether the segments also differ with respect to demographic variables such as age and income. In Table 3-3, consider the distribution of age and income for Segments A, B, and C, as provided in Figure 3-1.

**Table 3-3** Age and Income Distribution for Segments

| Segment | Mean | | Range | |
|---------|------|----|-------|----|
| | **Age** | **Income ($)** | **Age** | **Income ($)** |
| A | 21 | 15,000 | 16–25 | 0–25,000 |
| B | 45 | 120,000 | 33–55 | 75,000–215,000 |
| C | 39 | 40,000 | 39–54 | 24,000–60,000 |

*Mean* represents the averages of age and income of customers belonging to a particular segment. *Range* represents the minimum and maximum values of age and income for customers in a segment. Whereas the *mean* is useful for identifying the central tendency of a segment, the *range* helps in evaluating whether the segments overlap with regard to the profile variable.

From Table 3-3, you see that Segment A customers who prefer high savings on their premium and do not prefer having a neighborhood agent tend to be younger and have low income. These could probably be college students or recent graduates who are more comfortable with transacting online. Customers who belong to Segment B, on the other hand, are older and have higher income levels. It would be interesting to evaluate if these customers also tend to be married with kids. The security of having a neighborhood agent who can help in case of an accident or emergency is very important to them, and they do not mind paying a higher price for this sense of security. These customers may also not be comfortable in transacting (or providing personal information) online.

Finally, while Segment C customers are as old as Segment B customers, they tend to have lower incomes and do not prefer to have a neighborhood agent (probably because of low disposable incomes). Identification of the segments through these demographic characteristics enables a marketer to target as well as customize communications to each segment. For example, if Geico decides to develop a network of neighborhood agents, it can first focus on neighborhoods (identified through their ZIP Codes) that match the profile of Segment B customers.

# Conclusion

Given a segmentation basis, the K-means clustering algorithm would identify clusters and the customers that belong to each cluster. Management, however, has to carefully select the variables to use for segmentation. Criteria frequently used for evaluating the effectiveness of a segmentation scheme include *identifiability*, *sustainability*, *accessibility*, and *actionability*.[2] *Identifiability* refers to the extent that managers can recognize segments in the marketplace. In the Geico example, the profiling of customers allows you to identify customer segments through their age and income information. PRIZM and ACORN are popular databases that provide geodemographic information that can be used for segmentation as well as profiling. The *sustainability* criterion is satisfied if the segments represent a large enough portion of the market to ensure profitable customization of the marketing program. The extent to which managers can reach the identified segments through their marketing campaigns is captured by the *accessibility* criterion. Finally, *actionability* refers to whether customers in the segment and the marketing mix necessary to satisfy their needs are consistent with the goals and core competencies of the firm. The success of any segmentation process therefore requires managerial intuition and careful judgment.

# Endnotes

1. Geico is used as a hypothetical example.

2. For more details, refer to Wagner Kamakura and Michel Wedel, *Market Segmentation: Conceptual and Methodological Foundations*, 2nd ed. (Norwell, MA: Kluwer Academic Publishers, 2000).

# 4

# Segmentation at Sticks Kebob Shop

## Introduction

Sticks Kebob Shop, headquartered in Charlottesville, Virginia, had a problem. But it was a good problem to have.

A restaurant chain in the fastest-growing segment of the food-service industry, Sticks expected to add about one restaurant every year or two to its portfolio starting in 2014. A sticking point was picking the right markets to enter and then deciding on (and waiting for) the right location in a market.

Since opening its first quick-service restaurant (QSR) in 2001 in Charlottesville, Sticks had added another store in town (Figure 4-1), as well as one each in Richmond and Williamsburg, Virginia. Because Richmond was a larger city, the Sticks executive team—Chris DuBois, Ty Austin, Ingmar Leliveld, and Bill Hamilton—was interested in opening a second Richmond location. Before doing so, the team wanted to gain a better sense of who Sticks's customers were, which location would attract the best customers, and how to best connect with customers.

Original location

Second location

**Figure 4-1** Sticks locations in Charlottesville

The restaurant industry veterans had a rough idea of their customer base from anecdotal evidence. An opportunity presented itself to gather survey data to confirm their hypotheses. Would the demographic and psychographic assumptions they had gathered from talking to people in stores align with the survey answers? And what would the data tell them about where to locate new stores and about which marketing channels and messages to use to promote them?

## The Sticks Story

While working at Hamiltons' at First and Main, a fine dining restaurant in Charlottesville, Virginia, Dubois and Austin realized they lacked a place to grab a good bite to eat before going into work for the night shift. When Bill Hamilton, who owned the restaurant with his wife, approached the pair about going into business together, they decided to pursue a concept that could deliver a good meal without much fuss. "We went out for some beers and decided we were going to do it," DuBois said. "We had not settled on a concept for the restaurant at the time."

The team finally settled on kebobs after kicking around ideas ranging from barbecue to curry. In 2001, the idea of the fast-casual restaurant—essentially the QSR segment minus traditional fast food—was still in its infancy. For example, Chipotle had just begun to expand outside its home state of Colorado. The idea was to offer high-quality, healthy food in a "less stuffy environment" and to deliver it quickly. As the Sticks website said, the founders wanted to "create a safe haven for fellow foodies, busy families, and health-conscious diners." It was a niche the team thought Charlottesville lacked and one they decided they could satisfy effectively.

The Sticks chain had learned a lot about its customer base over the years (for example, the executives had increased their focus on the healthy food angle). But Sticks also made sure that its cuisine remained accessible to a broader audience. Sticks didn't claim to be authentic Middle Eastern food. For example, instead of using the original term *baba ganouj* for one of its menu items, it used *roasted eggplant salad*. (See Exhibit 4-1 for a sample menu.)

## Planning for Expansion

According to DuBois, Sticks's long-term expansion plan was focused on the I-64 corridor that ran across Virginia. Richmond was the primary immediate target, since the brand had already been established there, and a second store would lend efficiencies in marketing, labor, and so on. Beyond that, the company planned to look at Newport News, Hampton Roads, Virginia Beach, Norfolk, Harrisonburg, Lynchburg, and Fredericksburg. The eventual goal was to grow from four stores to eight between 2014 and 2020, at which point the company would reassess and look at moving into Northern Virginia and the Washington, DC, area, which would require a multiple-store launch.

In addition to adding restaurants, Sticks expected to expand in two other ways. It was in the process of launching a packaged version of its signature hummus for sale in retail outlets, and it was planning to purchase a food trailer to increase its offsite vending, including at an outdoor concert series in Richmond.

The Sticks growth plan had been tempered slightly in the past several years: the Richmond location was growing more slowly than the company would have liked. The restaurant had opened right on the cusp of the 2008 recession and had improved sales by about 10% every year, but the baseline had been lower than expected. See Table 4-1 for a list of Sticks locations in 2014.

**Table 4-1** Sticks Locations, 2014

| Store Name | Address |
| --- | --- |
| Preston Avenue, Charlottesville | 917 Preston Avenue |
| | Charlottesville, VA 22903 |
| Pantops, Charlottesville | 1820 Abbey Road |
| | Charlottesville, VA 22911 |
| Willow Lawn, Richmond | 1700 Willow Lawn Dr., Willow Lawn Plaza |
| | Richmond, VA 23221 |
| Courthouse Commons, Williamsburg | 5223 Monticello Avenue |
| | Williamsburg, VA 23188 |

Source: Created by case writer.

The customer survey was an opportunity to ensure that the next store was a strong fit with its market. DuBois said its goal was to gather data that could help identify real estate options, improve the team's knowledge of customer demographics and psychographics, and provide insights as to how customers perceived Sticks in terms of value for the money and other attributes.

DuBois and Austin described typical Sticks customers—based on knowledge gained while working as managers in the two Charlottesville stores—as people "in their 30s who have a smartphone and want food that's both healthful and satisfying."

The base skewed more toward women making dining decisions for their families, but it also did well with single people ranging from their mid-20s to mid-40s and professionals on their lunch break. More recently, Sticks had identified growing interest in its Mediterranean-inspired menu from an older demographic that emphasized an active lifestyle and healthy eating.

"It may sound like a cliché, but a lot of our customers are soccer moms," DuBois said. "Soccer is a big thing in the area. We have proven to be a good fit for people who are involved in sports—either for themselves or for their kids."

The Sticks team knew that offering a quick, healthy meal option would be a big part of the restaurant's appeal when it opened in 2001, but management debated about how heavily to market that attribute; the team did not want Sticks's cuisine to be thought of as health food because most people thought of that (especially at the time) as "unsatisfying." The team also wanted to combat the idea that the restaurant was exotic and unfamiliar so it would appeal to customers who generally selected more familiar options, such as Applebee's, Arby's, or Ruby Tuesday.

DuBois and Austin said they consistently heard from customers who said that they appreciated the variety of the Sticks menu, its filling but nutritious food, its good prices, and its fast delivery. The restaurant tended to attract most customers on weekday afternoons. The volume of visits during nights and weekends were generally lower.

"The challenge is not expecting people to behave in a way you want them to, but instead letting them do more of what they already want to do themselves," Austin said. "We have to remind ourselves to work from and gradually expand people's given behaviors. We try to keep hurdles low for new customers yet offer enough options for novelty for existing customers."

# The Fast-Food Industry

Fast casual QSRs were typically restaurants that aimed to deliver food fast but looked to operate outside the traditional fast-food market, offering carefully selected ingredients and healthier options overall. For Sticks, that also meant avoiding being pigeonholed as a health food restaurant and striving to become a national brand, as opposed to being known as a college-town niche store. Sticks wanted its customers to leave the restaurant feeling full, satisfied, and as though they had made a smart dining choice.

The fast-casual industry was one of the fastest-growing segments of the restaurant business, according to *QSR* magazine, and Panera was the clear leader (Table 4-2).

According to food industry analyst Technomic, several other fast casuals were among the fastest-growing QSRs in the country (Table 4-3).

**Table 4-2** Top-10 Fast Casual Restaurants

| Fast Casual Rank | Chain | 2012 Sales (Millions) | Total Units in 2012 | Change in Units from 2011 |
|---|---|---|---|---|
| 1 | Panera | $3,861.0 | 1,652 | 111 |
| 2 | Chipotle | $2,731.2 | 1,410 | 180 |
| 3 | Jimmy John's | $1,262.8 | 1,560 | 229 |
| 4 | Zaxby's | $979.3 | 565 | 25 |
| 5 | Steak 'N Shake | $857.5 | 501 | 10 |
| 6 | Qdoba | $583.2 | 627 | 44 |
| 7 | Jason's Deli | $578.9 | 245 | 10 |
| 8 | El Pollo Loco | $563.0 | 397 | 3 |
| 9 | Boston Market | $559.0 | 469 | -12 |
| 10 | Moe's | $452.0 | 482 | 43 |

**Table 4-3** Fastest-Growing QSR Chains (More Than $200 Million in Annual Sales)

| Rank | Chain | 2011 U.S. Sales (Thousands) | 2010 U.S. Sales (Thousands) | % Change | $ Change (Thousands) |
|---|---|---|---|---|---|
| 1 | Five Guys | 950,630 | 716,105 | 32.8 | 234,525 |
| 2 | Chipotle | 2,260,548 | 1,831,922 | 23.4 | 428,626 |
| 3 | Jimmy John's | 895,000° | 735,000° | 21.8 | 160,000 |
| 4 | Firehouse Subs | 284,581 | 235,000 | 21.1 | 49,581 |
| 5 | Raising Cane's | 206,301 | 174,608 | 18.2 | 31,693 |
| 6 | Little Caesars | 1,480,000° | 1,253,000° | 18.1 | 227,000 |
| 7 | Noodles & Company | 300,000 | 261,000 | 14.9 | 39,000 |
| 8 | Wingstop | 381,660 | 332,612 | 14.7 | 49,048 |
| 9 | Chick-fil-A | 4,050,992 | 3,583,000 | 13.1 | 467,992 |
| 10 | Qdoba | 531,000° | 475,000° | 11.8 | 56,000 |

*Technomic estimate

Sticks also fell into another fast-growing segment of restaurants: ethnic food. Although the Mexican segment was the clear ethnic food leader, DuBois said Mediterranean restaurants were also growing quickly. They were part of a group (specialty fast casuals) that made up 9% of all fast-casual restaurants (Table 4-4).

**Table 4-4** Menu Composition Within Fast Casual Segment

| Rank | Category | Market Share |
|------|----------|--------------|
| 1 | Mexican | 20% |
| 2 | Bakery/Café Bagel | 18% |
| 3 | Other Sandwich | 16% |
| 4 | Hamburger | 11% |
| 5 | Chicken | 9% |
| 6 | Specialty* | 9% |
| 7 | Pizza | 7% |
| 8 | Asian | 6% |

* Barbecue, healthy, Italian, other ethnic (including Mediterranean) and soup

Sticks was somewhat unique, however, in that it marketed itself without referring to the ethnicity of its offerings. The goal of the restaurant's owners was to make the food as accessible as possible and to not intimidate customers. Sticks did not expect to attract the adventurous diner who sought out authentic ethnic food; it tried to position itself alongside Panera and Chipotle, rather than local Middle Eastern restaurants.

Still, Austin and DuBois said they watched the growth of other Mediterranean restaurants closely. For example, a larger chain from Alabama called Zoë's Kitchen had recently moved into Charlottesville and Richmond, and Taziki's (also a growing chain from the South) operated a similar concept in Richmond. In addition to those, Austin said Roti out of Chicago and Garbanzo out of Denver were other Mediterranean QSR brands worth following—both chains had high-quality management and were well funded. Despite others entering Sticks's local markets, the team didn't see competition as all bad.

"Most importantly, these larger chains help validate the concept for us," DuBois said. "They also help generate new interest in our category, which is a net benefit. But at the same time, we have to be dynamic and keep creating and emphasizing our unique points of differentiation. We are well aware of direct competition but don't want that to distract us from succeeding on our own terms."

# Sticks's Existing Marketing Initiatives

Since it launched in 2001, Sticks had made a concerted effort to better understand its customer base. Over the years, the team had changed its message in subtle ways in response to what it had learned: switching from Styrofoam containers to all reusable plates and silverware and honing its marketing message.

Sticks had used simple, brand recognition–focused advertising campaigns in the Charlottesville area to reinforce its existing reputation. In its other markets, it had focused on more extensive campaigns and making product samples available to introduce its offerings to new audiences. Its most extensive television campaign had featured animated spots. The advertisements had not shown the restaurant's food; they were more geared toward general brand recognition, DuBois said. The spots had been used extensively on Charlottesville broadcast stations, where brand recognition was most powerful for Sticks; however, the team had also used the campaign in Richmond and reported some success.

Sticks had used television to try to expand its existing customer base as well. The company had televised an announcement of a weekend discount on its popular chicken platter and saw a spike in traffic for what was otherwise a slower time of the week.

The team had used print advertisements primarily in the Richmond market, where it was looking to expand. In that city, the team determined that customers enjoyed reading the alternative newspaper *Style Weekly*, which proved to be an inexpensive way to reach the desired audience. Sticks had regularly enlisted local marketing experts to fine-tune decisions about how to reach the Richmond audience.

Sticks had found partnerships to be particularly beneficial in Charlottesville, whether in a community-service capacity or in an ongoing advertising campaign with the University of Virginia (U.Va.) sports properties. In 2013, the brand was in its second year working with U.Va. and expanded its campaign on the strength of the first year, which featured coupons in the men's basketball, baseball, and soccer team game programs. Austin and DuBois said they had counted the coupons a success, particularly the one used during the men's basketball team's ACC home games. Also in 2013, Sticks had added several U.Va. women's sports to the campaign.

The impetus behind the partnership with U.Va. was due largely to the university's own demographic and psychographic breakdown of its audience. Case writers estimated that U.Va.'s sports fans were active particularly in tennis and golf, dined in various fast-casual restaurants, enjoyed artisanal beverages, and skewed toward higher household incomes. In addition to offering it the chance to stay in view of a crowd of people similar to those Sticks believed to be its customers, the U.Va. partnership had allowed Sticks to build its brand among students.

"The gravy is to attract students as well," DuBois said. "But our main focus is the family and the long-term local resident, rather than the mostly transient students. We looked at that, and it seems to match up with who we already feel are our loyal core customers, so it lets us serve them better."

DuBois and Austin also said Sticks had considered its two alternative growth strategies—retail sales and offsite vending—to be promising marketing avenues. Finally, Sticks had offered a mobile smartphone application that enabled advance ordering and faster pickup in the store in an effort to align it with its technologically savvy base.

# Decisions

Sticks was relatively certain it had a good handle on its customer base—active people making choices for their families and working professionals looking for a quick, healthy lunch—but the team wanted to confirm that hypothesis. So management worked with an outside consultant to prepare and distribute a survey of both customers and noncustomers as follows:

1. Create a small but in-depth survey of five to ten existing customers to better inform suggestions for the questionnaires and desired outputs from the study.

2. Prepare the customer and noncustomer surveys for distribution.

3. Sample 200 existing customers, primarily from the Richmond market, using Surveymonkey.com.

4. Utilize a third-party vendor to sample 200 noncustomers online.

A quick review of the survey (Exhibit 4-2) indicated that many of the hypotheses made by the Sticks team were upheld. DuBois and Austin next wanted to identify segments among Sticks's customer base and target the unique preferences of each group. They wanted to use the segmentation information to drive their search for real estate in Richmond and determine how they should tweak their existing marketing strategy.

# Exhibits

**Exhibit 4-1** Sample Sticks menu

**Exhibit 4-2** Sticks Customer Survey Questions

1. How many times in the last week did you do the following:
   a. Make and eat lunch at home
   b. Bring your own lunch to work
   c. Buy lunch at workplace (such as a cafeteria)
   d. Buy lunch at a restaurant/food court/food truck
   e. Skip lunch and ate small snack item
   f. Other

2. Please specify the top five restaurants you have visited in the last six months in order of visit frequency.

3. Have you ever visited Sticks Kebob Shop?
   a. Yes
   b. No

4. How did you first find out about Sticks?
   a. Friend or colleague
   b. Media (print or online—FB, blog, review)
   c. Direct marketing (such as Valpak or Groupon)
   d. Driving or walking by store
   e. Catering at work (such as a menu stack)
   f. Outdoor event/food festival
   g. Other

5. Have you eaten at Sticks in the past three months?
   a. Yes
   b. No

6. In the last month, how often have you visited Sticks for the following occasions?
   a. Weekday lunch
   b. Weekday dinner
   c. Weekend lunch
   d. Weekend dinner
   e. Sticks event (catering at work, food festival)
   f. After-school snack or after sports practice
   g. Other

7. Please indicate how important the following factors are when you visit a restaurant:
   a. Convenient place to eat
   b. Variety of menu options
   c. Good value for money
   d. Healthy menu options
   e. Food taste and satisfaction
   f. Friendly staff
   g. Pleasant ambiance
   h. Consistency/reliability
   i. Part of community
   j. Other

8. Please indicate how you rate Sticks in comparison to similar restaurants that you visit regularly on the following:
    a. Convenient place to eat
    b. Variety of menu options
    c. Good value for money
    d. Healthy menu options
    e. Food taste and satisfaction
    f. Friendly staff
    g. Pleasant ambiance
    h. Consistency/reliability
    i. Part of community
    j. Other
9. What is your gender?
10. What is your age?
11. What is your approximate average annual household income?
12. How would you best describe your household type?
13. How many children, by age, currently live in your household?
14. In what ZIP Code is your home located?
15. In what ZIP Code is your work located?
16. Please indicate your best answers to the following:
    a. I tend to plan things very carefully.
    b. I sometimes have trouble controlling my spending.
    c. I think it is important to purchase products that are made locally.
    d. I carefully consider the health benefits of what I eat.
17. What is your profession?
18. If you have children living at home, in what activities do they participate?
19. In what activities or hobbies do you participate yourself?
20. In the last month, how many times have you used coupons when you visited a restaurant?
21. How do you find restaurant coupons?

# Assignment Questions

1. How do people choose the fast-food restaurant to visit?

    a. What is important: location, price, assortment, or cuisine?

2. Who do you think are Sticks's customers and what are their motivations for visiting Sticks?

3. What does the survey data tell us about differences between customers and noncustomers?

4. What survey questions would you use to identify the customer segments?

5. How many customer segments can you estimate from the survey data?

   a. What are the profiles of the customer segments?

   b. Which customer segments should Sticks target?

6. Provide a recommendation for the location of the next Sticks Kebab Shop based on the segmentation analysis and the demographic profiles of the locations in the following table.

| Location | Population | Median Age | Median Income | Consumer Spend (In Millions) | Consumer Spend per Household | Major Customer Profiles |
|---|---|---|---|---|---|---|
| A | 29,321 | 39.1 | $92,700 | $722 | $62,404 | Blue Blood Estates, Brite Lites, Li'l City, Executive Suites, Upward Bound, Winner's Circle |
| B | 34,183 | 32.5 | $31,900 | $482 | $36,720 | City Startups, Family Thrifts, Hometown Retired, New Beginnings, Sunset City Blues |
| C | 42,913 | 32.5 | $55,700 | $754 | $46,828 | Brite Lites, Li'l City, Family Thrifts, Up-and-Commers, Upward Bound, White Picket Fences |
| D | 57,509 | 34.8 | $75,500 | $1,184 | $57,880 | Brite Lites, Li'l City, Country Quires, Up-and-Commers, Upward Bound, White Picket Fences |

# 5

## A Practical Guide to Conjoint Analysis

## Introduction

*Conjoint analysis* is a marketing research technique designed to help managers determine the preferences of customers and potential customers. In particular, it seeks to determine how consumers value the different attributes that make up a product and the trade-offs they are willing to make among the different attributes or features that compose the product. As such, conjoint analysis is best suited for products that have very tangible attributes that can be easily described or quantified.

Although the history of conjoint analysis can be traced to early work in mathematical psychology,[1] its popularity has grown tremendously over the last few years as access to easy-to-use software has allowed its widespread implementation. There have been probably hundreds of applications of conjoint analysis in industrial settings.[2] Some of the more important issues for which modern conjoint analysis is used are the following:

- Predicting the market share of a proposed new product, given the current offerings of competitors
- Predicting the impact of a new competitive product on the market share of any given product in the marketplace
- Determining consumers' willingness to pay for a proposed new product
- Quantifying the trade-offs customers or potential customers are willing to make among the various attributes or features that are under consideration in the new product design

# The Anatomy of a Conjoint Analysis

Literally, conjoint analysis means an analysis of features considered jointly. The idea is that, although it is difficult for consumers to state directly how much each feature of a product is worth to them, you can infer the value of an individual feature of a product by experimentally manipulating the features of a product and observing consumers' ratings for that product or choices among competing products.

To fix your intuition here, consider the simple example of a sports car. It would be difficult for the average consumer to tell a market researcher exactly how much more valuable a car with 240 horsepower is relative to one with 220 horsepower. It is possible that a consumer might be able to come up with some dollar value, but that value may not really reflect the way that consumer would make choices if faced with a real marketplace situation. Instead, marketers have found that it is much more accurate to present individuals from the target market with a series of cars, described not only by their horsepower but by other attributes as well (for example, color, price, standard/automatic transmission) and then ask them to rate each of the cars on a numerical scale. Alternatively, the researcher presents several competing cars with different attributes and asks the consumer to choose one. By repeatedly asking the potential customers to rate the cars or choose a car from a competing set, the researcher can infer the value of each individual attribute. This is the essence of a conjoint analysis: replacing the relatively inaccurate method of asking about each attribute in isolation with a model that allows you to infer the attributes' values from a series of ratings or choices.

# The Experimental Design

A conjoint analysis begins with an experimental design. This design includes all attributes and the values of the attributes that will be tested. Conjoint analysis distinguishes between attributes and what are generally called *levels*. An attribute is self-explanatory. It could be price, color, horsepower, material used for upholstery, or presence of a sunroof, whereas a level is the specific value or realization of the attribute. For example, the attribute *color* may have the levels *red*, *blue*, and *yellow*, whereas the attribute *presence of a sunroof* will have the levels *yes* and *no*. Before a researcher begins to collect data, it is important that all the levels of each attribute to be tested are written down. Commercially available software packages require that the user provides these as input.

Continuing with the car example, an experimental design might look like the information presented in Table 5-1.

**Table 5-1** Example of Experimental Design

|  | Price | Brand | Horsepower | Upholstery | Sunroof |
|---|---|---|---|---|---|
| **Levels** | $23,000 | Toyota | 220HP | Cloth | Yes |
|  | $25,000 | Volkswagen | 250HP | Leather | No |
|  | $27,000 | Saturn | 280HP |  |  |
|  | $29,000 | Kia |  |  |  |

This is a simple design that contains a total of 15 attribute levels. Real designs often contain more attributes and levels than are presented here.

When constructing an experimental design, it is important to keep the following points in mind:

- The more tangible and understandable the levels of each attribute are to the respondents, the more valid the results of the research will be. For example, attribute levels such as *really roomy* are vague, meaning different things to different people, and should be avoided.

- The greater the number of attribute levels to be tested, the more data that will be needed to achieve the same degree of output accuracy.

- For quantitative variables (price and horsepower, in this example), the greater the distance between any two consecutive levels, the harder it will be to get a good idea of how a consumer might evaluate something in between the two (for example, $24,000).

# Data Collection

Collecting data for a conjoint analysis has been made relatively simple by the advent of dedicated off-the-shelf software. The type of conjoint analysis used dictates the exact nature of the data collected. An exhaustive discussion of the benefits and drawbacks of each of the many different types of conjoint analysis now in use is beyond the scope of this book. But those interested are encouraged to read Orme's technical paper for a good discussion of this topic.[3]

The state of the art in conjoint data collection involves using personal computers or a web-based version of the software to guide respondents through an interactive conjoint survey. The software creates the hypothetical product profiles using the experimental design provided by the researcher and estimates the attribute-level utilities from participant ratings or choices.

# Interpreting Conjoint Results

## Understanding the Basic Output

The basic results of a conjoint analysis are the estimated attribute-level utilities. Keeping with the example in Table 5-1, conjoint output might look like the output shown in Table 5-2.

**Table 5-2** Conjoint Analysis Output

| Attribute | Level | Utility (part-worth) | t-value |
| --- | --- | --- | --- |
| Price | $23,000 | 2.10 | 14.00 |
| | $25,000 | 1.15 | 7.67 |
| | $27,000 | −1.56 | 10.40 |
| | $29,000 | −1.69 | 11.27 |
| Brand | Toyota | 0.75 | 5.00 |
| | Volkswagen | 0.65 | 4.33 |
| | Saturn | −0.13 | 0.87 |
| | Kia | −1.27 | 8.47 |
| Horsepower | 220HP | −2.24 | 14.93 |
| | 250HP | 1.06 | 7.07 |
| | 280HP | 1.18 | 7.87 |
| Upholstery | Cloth | −1.60 | 10.67 |
| | Leather | 1.60 | 10.67 |
| Sunroof | Yes | 0.68 | 4.53 |
| | No | −0.68 | 4.53 |

The estimated utilities or part-worths correspond to average consumer preferences for the level of any given attribute. Within a given attribute, the estimated utilities are generally scaled in such a way that they add up to zero. So, a negative number does not mean that a given level has *negative utility*; it just means that this level is on average less preferred than a level with an estimated utility that is positive.

Conjoint analysis output is also often accompanied by t-values, a standard metric for evaluating statistical significance. Because of the way conjoint utilities are scaled, the standard interpretation of t-values can yield misleading results. For example, the level *Saturn* of the attribute *Brand* has a t-value of 0.87. In general, a t-value of this magnitude would fail a test of statistical significance; however, this t-value is generated because within the attribute *Brand,* the level *Saturn* has neither a very high nor very low relative preference. It is basically in the middle in terms of overall preference. Because of the scaling, levels that have more moderate levels of preference within a given attribute are likely to have estimated utilities close to zero, which tends to produce very low t-values (recall that the t-test is measuring the probability that the true value of a parameter is not different from zero).

A better way to think about statistical significance in this context is to examine the t-values of the levels with the highest and lowest preference within a given attribute. An applicable common practice would be if the sum of the absolute value of these two statistics is greater than three, then that given attribute is significant in the overall choice process of consumers. At a practical level, it is rare that an attribute will not be significant, and, if you find one that is, it means it probably should not have been included in the experimental design in the first place because respondents are not considering that attribute's information when they make choices.

# Conjoint Analysis Applications

As mentioned previously, there are many different possible applications of conjoint analysis. This section focuses on three very common applications: trade-off analysis, predicting market share, and determining overall attribute *importances.*

## *Trade-Off Analysis*

The utility of any given product that you might consider can be easily computed by simply summing the utilities of its attribute levels. For example, a Toyota with 280 horsepower, leather interior, no sunroof, and a price of $23,000 has a utility of 0.75 + 1.18 + 1.60 − 0.68 + 2.10 = 4.95. If the car with the same basic specifications were a Volkswagen, the overall utility would drop to 0.65 + 1.18 + 1.60 − 0.68 + 2.10 = 4.85, a drop of 0.10. This drop can be seen directly by noticing that the difference between the utility for the brand Toyota (0.75) and Volkswagen (0.65) is 0.10. In addition, because nothing else in the profile of the car has changed, this will be the exact utility difference between two cars that are the same except for this brand difference.

A natural consequence of this observation is that you use the utilities to analyze what average consumers would be willing to give up on one particular attribute to gain improvements in another. For example, how much money would they be willing to give up (price) if a sunroof was added to the vehicle? Let's look directly at this issue of the hypothetical car detailed in the previous paragraph. Adding a sunroof to the (Toyota) car would yield an overall utility of 0.75 + 1.18 + 1.60 + 0.68 + 2.10 = 6.31. This represents an increase in utility of 6.31 − 4.95 = 1.36 over the identical car without a sunroof.

This information directly implies that you can reduce the utility of price by 1.36, and average consumers would be just as happy as before the sunroof was installed. To find out how much the price can be raised, you must convert the change in utility with a change in price. You do this by first noting how much the original car costs ($23,000) and the utility associated with that figure, 2.10. You know that you can reduce the price utility by 1.36. This is equivalent to saying that you can reduce the price utility to 2.10 − 1.36 = 0.74. By referring to Table 5-2, you can immediately see that this implies a price between $25,000 and $27,000 because −1.56 < 0.74 < 1.15. In fact, if you assume a linear relationship between price and utility in the range between $25,000 and $27,000, you can solve for the exact price by performing a linear interpolation within this range.[4] Specifically, the interpolation yields:

$$\$25,000 + \frac{1.15 - 0.74}{1.15 - (-1.56)} \times \$2,000 = \$25,302.58$$

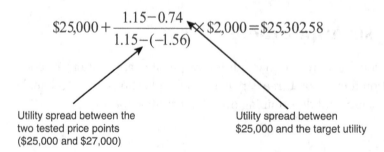

Utility spread between the two tested price points ($25,000 and $27,000)

Utility spread between $25,000 and the target utility

This implies that, if the sunroof is added, the price of the vehicle could be raised from $23,000 to about $25,300, and the average consumer's attitude would be one of indifference between the two vehicles. Qualitatively, it shows that the value of a sunroof to consumers is very substantial.

This same kind of analysis can be performed for other attributes. You could ask how much additional horsepower you would need to add if the interior was changed from leather to cloth. This particular question does present a problem, however. Because the current vehicle under consideration has 280 horsepower, and that is the maximum amount of horsepower tested by the conjoint analysis, it will be impossible to determine how much consumers will value additional horsepower. This leads to an important consideration when constructing the experimental design. That is, if the output is to be used for trade-off analysis, it is important that the range of the levels tested within each attribute span the entire range of that attribute before management would ever consider it as a realistic design alternative. If the experimental design takes this into account, you can perform trade-off analysis between any two attributes in the design.

## Market Share Forecasting

Another common application is forecasting market share. To use conjoint output for this kind of prediction, two conditions must be satisfied:

- The company must know the other products, besides its own offering, that a consumer is likely to consider when making a selection in the category.
- Each of these competitive products' important features must be included in the experimental design. In other words, you must be able to calculate the utility of not only your own product offering, but also that of the competitive products.

Market share prediction relies on the use of a multinomial logit model.[5] The basic form of the logit model is

$$Share_i = \frac{e^{U_i}}{\sum_{j=1}^{n} e^{U_j}}$$

where

$U_i$ is the estimated utility of product $i$,

$U_j$ is the estimated utility of product $j$, and

$n$ is the total number of products in the competitive set, including product $i$.

To make things clear, consider the following example. Suppose you are interested in predicting the market share of a car with the following profile: Saturn; $23,000; 220HP; cloth interior; no sunroof. You believe that when consumers consider your car, they will also consider purchasing cars that are currently on the market with the following profiles:

1. Toyota; $27,000; 250HP; cloth interior; no sunroof
2. Volkswagen; $29,000; 280HP; leather interior; no sunroof
3. Kia; $23,000; 220HP; cloth interior; no sunroof

For the Saturn and its associated product profile, the estimated utility is 2.10 − 0.13 − 2.24 − 1.60 − 0.68 = −2.55. Similarly, the utilities of the three competing products can be calculated:

1. −1.56 + 0.75 + 1.06 − 1.60 − 0.68 = −2.03
2. −1.69 + 0.65 + 1.18 + 1.60 − 0.68 = 1.06
3. 2.10 − 1.27 − 2.24 − 1.60 − 0.68 = −3.69

With these utilities in hand, you can now directly apply the logit model to forecast market share for the Saturn. This is given by the following:

$$Share_{Saturn} = \frac{e^{-2.55}}{e^{-2.55} + e^{-2.03} + e^{1.06} + e^{-3.69}} = 0.025 \text{ or } 2.5\%$$

This implies that this particular Saturn vehicle will achieve a 2.5% market share within the specified competitive set. The market share of any vehicle that can be described by the experimental design and a set of competitive vehicles, also described by the experimental design, can be found in a similar manner.

### Determining Attribute Importance

A researcher may also be interested in determining the importance of any individual attribute in the consumers' decision processes. Quantifying these attribute importances using the conjoint output is straightforward and can provide both interesting and useful insights into consumer behavior.

Intuitively, the variance of the estimated utilities within a given attribute tells you something about how important the attribute is in the choice process. Take, for example, the attributes *Sunroof* and *Upholstery*, both of which have only two levels. If you understand the material up to this point, it should be reasonably clear that *Upholstery* is a more important attribute than *Sunroof*. That is because the utility difference between having a sunroof and not having a sunroof (2 × 0.68 = 1.36) is smaller than the utility difference between having leather versus cloth interior (2 × 1.60 = 3.20).

The common metric used to measure attribute importances is

$$I_i = \frac{\bar{U}_i - \underline{U}_i}{\sum_{j=1}^{n} \bar{U}_j - \underline{U}_j}$$

where:

$I_i$ is the importance of any given attribute $i$,

$\bar{U}$ is the highest utility level within a given attribute (subscripts indicate which attribute), and

$\underline{U}$ is the lowest utility level within a given attribute.

This equation is really quite intuitive. To calculate the importance of any given attribute, you just take the difference between the highest and lowest utility level of that attribute and divide this by the sum of the differences between the highest and lowest utility level for all attributes (including the one in question). The resulting number will always lie between zero and one and is generally interpreted as the percent decision weight of an attribute in the overall choice process.

It also should be clear at this point that this estimated attribute importance depends critically on your experimental design. In particular, if you increase the distance between the most extreme levels of any given attribute, you will almost certainly increase the overall attribute importance. For example, if the tested price range was $21,000–$31,000 instead of $23,000–$29,000 (Table 5-1), this is very likely to increase the estimate attribute importance of price.

Let's now consider a concrete example using the attribute *Horsepower*. The importance of this attribute is calculated as follows:

$$I_{Horsepower} = \frac{1.18 + 2.24}{((2.10 + 1.69) + (0.75 + 1.27) + (1.18 + 2.24) + (1.60 + 1.60) + (0.68 + 0.68))} = 0.25$$

In the example, 25% of the overall decision weight is assigned to *Horsepower*. You may verify through analogous calculations that the decision weight for *Price* is about 27%; *Brand,* about 15%; *Sunroof,* about 10%; and *Upholstery,* about 23%. The numbers provide a very intuitive metric for thinking about the importance of each attribute in the decision process.

# Conclusion

Conjoint analysis has a broad array of possible applications. Many of these applications are variants of the three very common applications presented here. The increasingly widespread availability of conjoint analysis software—both PC and web-enabled—points to its continued growth as a marketing decision aid.

This chapter has presented what is generally known as *aggregate-level* conjoint analysis. That is, all of the respondents are pooled into one group, and a single set of attribute-level utilities are estimated from the ratings or choices provided by the people in this group. Recent advancements in conjoint analysis have enabled researchers to estimate different utilities for different groups of respondents and even, in some cases, for individual respondents. Although the mathematics necessary for this procedure is sometimes quite complex, it is now possible to estimate the attribute-level utilities and to compute trade-off analyses for *each individual respondent*. This has some significant advantages over aggregate-level analysis, particularly when considering marketing segmentation issues. Either way, the data collection and the basic interpretation of the output remain the same. Although there is currently no textbook that can provide answers to all the questions that might arise when applying this technique in a business setting, there is, as of this writing, a very good and surprisingly comprehensive collection of technical papers located on the site of a company that markets conjoint analysis software (http://www.sawtoothsoftware.com/techpap.shtml). These provide answers to many of the practical implementation questions a user may face.

# Endnotes

1. R. Duncan Luce and John W. Tukey, "Simultaneous Conjoint Measurement: A New Type of Fundamental Measurement," *Journal of Mathematical Psychology* 1 (February 1964): 1–27.

2. Paul E. Green, Abba M. Krieger, and Yoram Wind, "Thirty Years of Conjoint Analysis: Reflections and Prospects," *Interfaces* 31 (May–June 2001): 56–73.

3. Bryan K. Orme, "Which Conjoint Method Should I Use?," *Sawtooth Software Technical Paper* (2003). A copy of this paper is available at http://www.sawtoothsoftware.com/download/techpap/whichmth.pdf (accessed April 3, 2012).

4. This is a common way to approximate the relationship between the value of the attribute and its utility for attribute values that were not directly tested by the conjoint analysis. The closer the tested levels are to each other, the more accurate this approximation. Also notice that this interpolation can only be performed for quantitative attributes such as price. Interpolating between qualitative attributes, such as brand, is nonsensical.

5. Please refer to Chapter 13, "Logistic Regression," for the basics of the logit model. Also, most econometrics textbooks will have information on logit models.

# 6

## Portland Trail Blazers

*We have a new group sales operation in place and we're looking for dramatic results there.*

—Steve Patterson, President, Portland Trail Blazers

## Introduction

Less than a month after the 2005 NBA All-Star break, the Portland Trail Blazers were in upheaval. On the court, they had just fired their coach of the past four seasons and were 22–36, in danger of one of the worst seasons in franchise history. Off the court, the Blazers organization was facing considerable challenges as well. The team's home arena, the Rose Garden, had filed for Chapter 11 bankruptcy and was being run by the building's creditors.

The arena, a virtual lock to sell out just three seasons before, had seen attendance numbers fall more than 15% since the 2003 season (Figure 6-1). During the same time, the organization had only been successful in renewing nine of the 46 luxury-suite contracts that came due in 2005, and 42 of the 70 luxury suites sat empty during the season.[1] Television interest also declined, with a Portland-area Nielsen share of just 5% when the Blazers played the Minneapolis Timberwolves (weather coverage generally received up to 20%).[2]

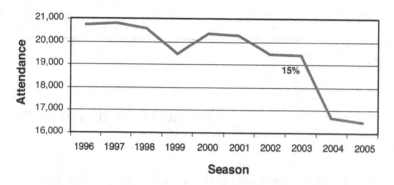

**Figure 6-1** Average home attendance, 1996–2007

Source: Portland Trail Blazers.

A similar story was occurring in the sale of the team's "club seats"—special seats for Blazers games that were sold on a multiyear contract and came with club perks. Of 1,800 club seats in 2005, 700 remained available, most of them because subscribers had dropped their contracts during the previous season.

## The Portland Sports Market

The Trail Blazers had a monopoly on the professional sports market in Portland, Oregon. Without a dominant university sports program affiliated with the city, the team competed only with minor league baseball and hockey for its share of the city's sporting dollars. With a population of just under two million people in the metro area, Portland was the fourth-smallest market in the NBA.

Each year, the Blazers tracked Portland-area residents' general perception of the team (see Figure 6-2). The historically strong relationship between the team and the city had soured over the past few seasons—the percentage of people perceiving the team negatively had increased tenfold since 2000. Fan support had dwindled due to a number of widely publicized player transgressions, including marijuana use, fighting with teammates, and an incident involving animal cruelty.[3]

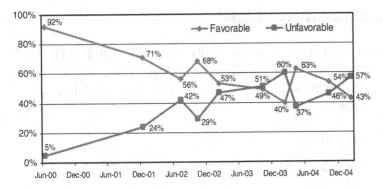

**Figure 6-2** Portland-area residents' general perception of the Portland Trail Blazers

Source: Portland Trail Blazers.

# Multigame Ticket Packages

One of the more successful Blazers promotions during the past few seasons had been multigame ticket packages. This program allowed fans to purchase tickets for a number of games at once, and usually included at least one marquee opponent, a game for which individual tickets were difficult to find. Trail Blazers' management saw this program as an effective tool to

- Increase ticket sales for less popular games (typically bundled in the package with tickets for hard-to-find games)

- Increase overall ticket sales because the multigame packages acted as an effective incentive for those who planned on attending only one or two games during the season to increase the number of games they attended

- Develop more of an ongoing relationship with fans who could potentially become future season ticket holders

Despite the program's relative success, management wanted to explore all potential packages and better understand which options were most popular with fans. The program's goal was to offer a multigame ticket package that had a high appeal to fans while still being profitable to the team and not undermining current pricing policies.

# Designing the Research Study

The Trail Blazers management team hired Acuity Market Research, a Portland-based research firm, to help design their multigame package study. Together, they determined there were six aspects of the multigame ticket packages that drove a customer's decision to purchase:

- The team the Blazers played
- The day of the week the game was played
- The number of games included in the package
- The location of the seats
- The price (per seat) of the package
- The promotional item included in the package

The project team designed a study utilizing conjoint analysis to ascertain the importance of the individual attributes, as well as the likely response of the market to specific multigame ticket packages. Some things were givens: (1) There were a high number of teams in the NBA (30 including the Blazers) and (2) the dates of the games included in the package could not be changed. Those attributes would not be included as part of the conjoint products. Instead, questions pertaining to favorite teams and days to watch a game were asked individually, after the conjoint portion of the survey.

An e-mail went out from the Blazers' director of database and Internet marketing to 960 fans who had purchased multigame ticket packages or season tickets in the past but were not current season ticket holders. The project team decided it was more important to get feedback from people who had expressed some level of commitment to purchasing Blazers tickets in the past than from general fans of the team, and the team knew it had current e-mail addresses for this group. Although new fans were always purchasing multigame or season ticket packages, Blazers management believed past purchasers were likely the best prospects for new multigame packages.

The initial e-mail explained the purpose of the study and asked fans to participate. One week later, a reminder e-mail was sent in hopes of increasing the overall response rate of the study. Both e-mails contained a link to an online conjoint-based survey, which included 20 different conjoint choice tasks (an example is included in Exhibit 6-1), Blazers-specific questions, and a battery of demographic questions. Most respondents took 10 to 15 minutes to complete the survey.

Participants were given a chance to win free tickets to Blazers games, as well as autographed Blazers items, such as jerseys, basketballs, and posters, for taking part in the survey.

# Study Findings

The e-mail solicitations received a total of 204 valid responses (a 21% response rate). Exhibit 6-1 includes summary statistics regarding demographics and past Blazers-game attendance.

Acuity began its analysis of the multigame packages by computing the attribute-level utility scores to better understand the stand-alone preference of each of the individual attribute levels. Table 6-1 shows the utility score data.

**Table 6-1**  Utility Score Data

| Utility | Number of Games |
|---------|-----------------|
| 0.03257 | Three-game create-your-own pack, including one elite team and two very good teams |
| 0.24383 | Six-game create-your-own pack, including two elite teams and four very good teams |
| –0.2764 | Ten-game create-your-own pack, including any combination of teams |

| Utility | Ticket Price |
|---------|--------------|
| 0.65646 | $15 per seat per game |
| 0.22011 | $25 per seat per game |
| 0.126 | $35 per seat per game |
| –1.00257 | $60 per seat per game |

| Utility | Ticket Location |
|---------|-----------------|
| –0.73169 | 300 level, behind the baskets |
| –0.43716 | 300 level, on the corners |
| 0.15736 | 300 level, midcourt |
| 1.01148 | 200 level, midcourt |

| Utility | Promotional Item |
|---------|------------------|
| 0.12511 | Priority for home playoff tickets |
| 0.17428 | Hot dog and soda with each ticket |
| 0.00158 | Trail Blazer apparel (hat, jersey, etc.) |
| 0.01689 | $20 gift certificate for popular local restaurant |
| –0.31786 | No promotional item |

Source: Portland Trail Blazers.

Although the conjoint study allowed all the attributes and levels to be randomly assigned, in reality the Blazers were unwilling to allow certain price and seating combinations—no matter how well received they were—due to the cost structure of the arena. They disallowed (1) 200-level seats for less than $60 and (2) 300-level, midcourt seats for less than $25.

# Cost of Multigame Packages

Although the fan preference was extremely important to Blazers management, any multigame packages the group designed had to be financially attractive and align with the organization's strategic goals. Each of the multigame ticket package attributes had costs and strategic implications associated with it.

## Number of Games

The Blazers preferred the six-game package because it offered the capability of pairing the most popular teams with games that were more difficult to sell tickets to (for example, weekday games, less competitive teams, and so on). The next preference would be a ten-game package, because it allowed the team to efficiently sell a large number of the remaining games to a single fan.

## Seat Location

Although nearly all the Blazers' stadium costs were fixed expenses, the organization still applied a cost to each of the seat locations in the stadium. This cost structure had to be met, at a minimum, for any tickets that were sold and differed based on seat location. Table 6-2 shows the minimum seat pricing.

**Table 6-2** Fixed Costs Based on Seat Location

| Seat Location | Fixed Cost |
| --- | --- |
| 300 level, behind the baskets | $10.00 |
| 300 level, on the corners | $12.00 |
| 300 level, midcourt | $18.00 |
| 200 level, midcourt | $40.00 |

Source: Portland Trail Blazers.

## Promotional Items

A direct cost was associated with each of the promotional items the Blazers might offer fans. For example, if the Blazers were to offer a hot dog and soda with each ticket, they would have to pay the Rose Garden's vendor services a negotiated price of $3.25 per package. The $20 gift certificate to a popular restaurant was purchased for a negotiated price of $10. The restaurateur deeply discounted the gift certificates in exchange for the marketing exposure.

The only promotional item without a direct cost was offering priority for home playoff tickets, given that the tickets were still sold at full retail price and multigame ticket holders just received priority in purchasing available tickets. Table 6-3 presents the unit cost of each of the potential promotional items.

**Table 6-3** Cost of Promotional Items

| Promotional Item | Cost |
|---|---|
| Priority for playoff tickets | $0.00 |
| Hot dog and soda with each ticket | $3.25 |
| Trail Blazers apparel (hat, jersey, etc.) | $12.00 |
| $20 gift certificate to a popular restaurant | $10.00 |

Source: Portland Trail Blazers.

Utilizing the conjoint information, in addition to the other data available from the survey, the Blazers management team felt prepared to design the multigame package they believed the fans would most prefer. What attributes were most important to the fans? What should the Blazers' multigame package include? Should there be more than one? How profitable would each of the packages be?

# Endnotes

1. Todd Murphy, "Have Arena, Need People," *Portland Tribune*, August 10, 2004.

2. Pete Schulberg, "Blazers Start Losing with Viewers, Too," *Portland Tribune*, January 21, 2005.

3. Andy Giegerich, "Beleaguered Blazers Play by the Numbers," *Portland Business Journal*, October 29, 2004.

# Exhibits

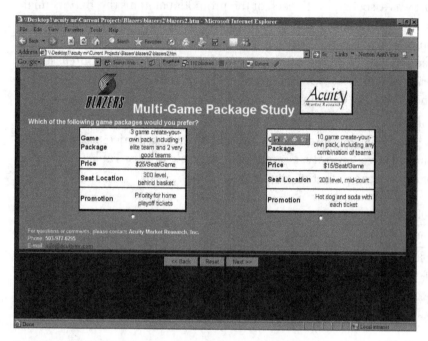

**Exhibit 6-1a**  Portland Trail Blazers example: online conjoint survey

Source: Portland Trail Blazers.

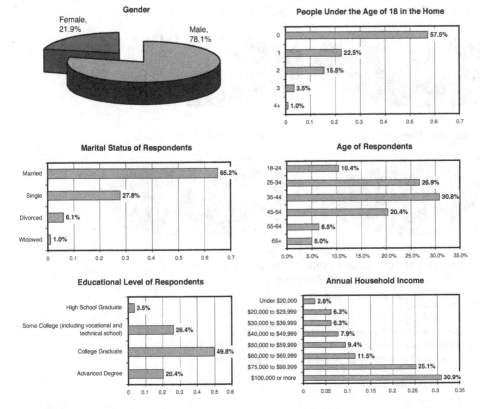

**Exhibit 6-1b** Study demographics

Source: Portland Trail Blazers.

**Have Purchased Multi-Game Tickets**

**Have Purchased Single-Game Tickets**

No, 23.2%
Yes, 76.8%

Yes, 58.1%
No, 41.9%

**Have Purchased Season Tickets**

**Have Purchased Other Tickets**

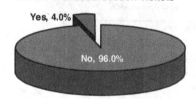

Yes, 4.0%
No, 96.0%

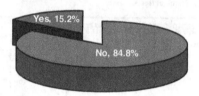

Yes, 15.2%
No, 84.8%

**Number of Trail Blazer Home Games Attended in Past Two Seasons**

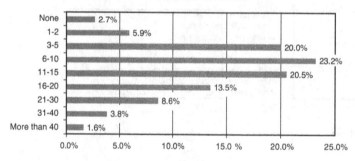

| | |
|---|---|
| None | 2.7% |
| 1-2 | 5.9% |
| 3-5 | 20.0% |
| 6-10 | 23.2% |
| 11-15 | 20.5% |
| 16-20 | 13.5% |
| 21-30 | 8.6% |
| 31-40 | 3.8% |
| More than 40 | 1.6% |

0.0%    5.0%    10.0%    15.0 %    20.0%    25.0%

**Exhibit 6-1c** Game attendance behavior

Source: Portland Trail Blazers.

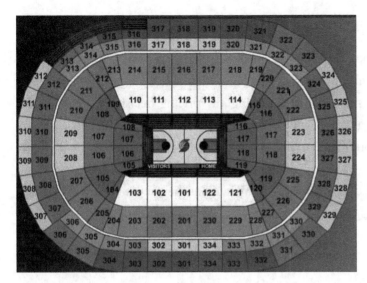

**Exhibit 6-1d** Rose Garden seating chart

Source: Portland Trail Blazers.

## Assignment Questions

1. Which attribute does the conjoint analysis indicate is most important in the overall purchase decision?

2. Are the conjoint results useful in making any pricing decisions? What useful information can be gleaned from the research?

3. What about the promotional items? Are they worth giving away (free) to season ticket holders?

4. What about the size of ticket packages? What does the conjoint analysis suggest?

5. What should the management of the Portland Trail Blazers do?

# Section III

## Marketing-Mix Analytics

This section presents multiple regression analysis. A fundamental premise of marketing-mix analytics is that the mix elements affect customer behavior simultaneously. Therefore, models that estimate elasticity should reflect this notion. It is therefore necessary to estimate the joint effect of the marketing mix on customer behavior. Chapter 7, "Multiple Regression in Marketing-Mix Models," and Chapter 8, "Design of Price and Advertising Elasticity Models," provide the definition of elasticity, present the log-log linear model framework for estimating elasticity, and list the control variables that are necessary to include in marketing-mix models to avoid biased elasticity estimates.

You can apply the process of estimating price and advertising elasticity models in the context of the vodka industry. The data provides 13 years of sales, price, and advertising data across channels for 28 vodka brands. Chapter 9, "SVEDKA Vodka," provides a case-study context to apply the estimated price and advertising elasticity to the context of a brand within the vodka industry.

When you have completed this section, you should have a good understanding of the workhorse of resource allocation: estimating marketing-mix elasticity. The chapters in this section provide ample discussion of unit roots in time series analysis, conditional effects, statistical versus economic significance, and omitted variable bias.

# 7

## Multiple Regression in Marketing-Mix Models

## Introduction

The movie *Moneyball* has a lot to teach us about optimizing a company's marketing mix. In the movie, the management of the Oakland Athletics discovers that the baseball team can get ahead by changing its perspective and looking at data differently than its competitors.

The A's know most major-league teams use batting average (hits over real opportunities) as the prevailing metric for determining the worth of a hitter. Traditional wisdom says, "You hit more, you win more." So the players who have more hits per at bat[1] are generally the most sought after and are paid the most money. But by examining the outcome of decades of baseball games, the A's find a variable they believe to be more predictive of success. It is not only hits that help a baseball team win; walks count too. Getting on base and not making outs is more closely correlated with winning games than hits alone.

The team's management takes the analysis of the data and uses it to buy undervalued players—players who don't necessarily have the highest batting averages but who do have high on-base percentages. For a small-market team such as the A's, which has less money to spend on players than other franchises, this strategy changes the game.

*Moneyball* is about baseball, but the idea also works in the context of business marketing. Although management often makes assumptions, by actually analyzing the data, a business can better understand how to succeed. And if a business can find an important variable before others begin using it, management can build its strategy around that variable to gain an advantage.

# Reviewing Single-Variable Regressions for Marketing

Single-variable regression analyses allow you to predict outcomes using one variable. Although such analyses are often oversimplifications of real-world marketing problems, it is necessary to understand them before moving on to more illustrative multivariable analyses.

Consider the following common marketing-mix example for a hypothetical company, No More Germs, which sells toothpaste. To determine the relationship between the number of promotions the company does and the number of units it sells, the company plots its known data on an x–y plane (Figure 7-1). On the x-axis, the company plots the number of promotions (such as price reductions) it could have in a month. On the y-axis, No More Germs plots the number of purchases made by customers for each level of promotions.

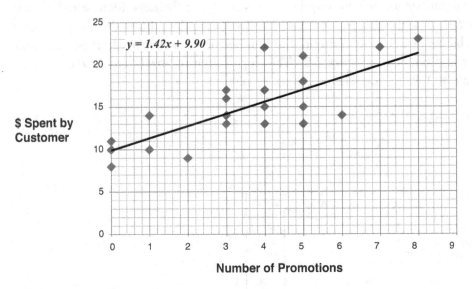

**Figure 7-1** Illustration of single-variable regression

Source: All figures created by case writer unless otherwise specified.

In this example, No More Germs has data covering a time period of 29 weeks, promotions ranging between 0 and 9, and corresponding sales from 10 to 23. A linear, single-variable regression analysis can be run on this data with the aid of computer software.[2] The results will help No More Germs examine the relationship between the number of promotions and the number of sales to customers by producing a function that describes the relationship. The objective is to draw a line that at each point represents the number of sales that are likely for any given number of promotions. In this case, the *x* variable—or independent variable—is the number of promotions. The *y* variable—or dependent variable (known as such because it depends on *x*)—is units sold.

The function produced by the regression is intended to cover as many of the known data points as possible and/or reduce the distance between the line and the points as much as possible. This allows the data analyst to accurately predict sales that are likely, given the number of promotions in other sample sets of data (in this case, if data from other weeks is used). The equation from the regression analysis for the best-fit straight line for No More Germs is $y = 1.42x + 9.9$.

The most critical outputs of the regression for the marketing manager are two coefficients: the intercept (9.9) and the slope (1.42) of the line. The intercept represents the number of sales that are likely when promotions are 0, which is equal to 9.9 in this example. This is the point where the line crosses the *y*-axis. The slope of the line describes the relationship between sales (*y*, or the dependent variable) and promotions (*x*, or the independent variable) by stating the ratio of the change in *y* to a unit change in *x*. In the example, the number of sales changes 1.42 per one-unit increase in promotions (Figure 7-2). The slope (often referred to as "rise over run") is, therefore, $1.42 \div 1$, or 1.42.

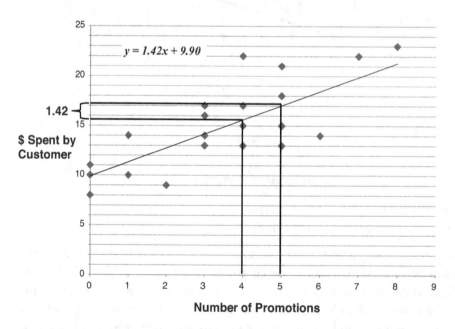

**Figure 7-2** Illustration of slope in a single-variable regression

Three things can be determined immediately by looking at the slope of the line: (1) If the number is positive, the relationship between the two variables is positive, meaning as the independent variable increases, so does the dependent variable; (2) if the slope of the line is 0, no changes are observed in the dependent variable as the independent variable changes (in other words, the variables are not correlated); and (3) if the slope of the line is negative, a change in the independent variable will produce the opposite effect in the dependent variable (in this case, No More Germs' sales would decrease if promotions increased).

Remember that although in this case the relationship between promotions and sales is obvious, in most cases a regression analysis is used to show a relationship between variables that are not as clearly related. For example, what if No More Germs wanted to know what kind of effect web advertising had on sales of its products? The company's marketing manager might not know how effective web ads are compared with print ads, for example, and the regression would assist him or her in deciding where to put the company's advertising dollars.

The output of No More Germs' sample regression (which is typical of these reports) is shown in Table 7-1. Although the analysis yields multiple statistics, the most critical for marketing analysts (in addition to the coefficients of the equation) are r squared and p-value. In this example, r squared is 60%, meaning the line described by this function is appropriate for explaining 60% of the data points. This indicates how accurate the function is within the current sample of data. (Note: A typical marketing-focused regression would have an r squared of about 20% to 30%, as there are numerous factors that affect sales—such as competition, weather, and so on—that would be unknown before running the analysis.)

**Table 7-1** Illustration of Output from Single-Variable Regression Analysis

**Regression Statistics**

| | |
|---|---|
| Multiple r | 0.775 |
| R squared | 0.601 |
| Adjusted r squared | 0.586 |
| Standard error | 2.566 |
| Observations | 29 |

**ANOVA**

| | df | SS | MS | F | Sig F |
|---|---|---|---|---|---|
| Regression | 1 | 267.28 | 267.28 | 40.60 | 0.00 |
| Residual | 27 | 177.75 | 6.58 | | |
| Total | 28 | 445.03 | | | |

|  | Coefficients | SE | t-Statistic | p-Value |
|---|---|---|---|---|
| Intercept | 9.90 | 0.85 | 11.60 | 0.00 |
| Number of promotions | 1.42 | 0.22 | 6.37 | 0.00 |

To better understand the meaning of r squared, imagine your regression output indicates an r squared of 0. The resulting plot will look like a disorderly circle of data (Figure 7-3).

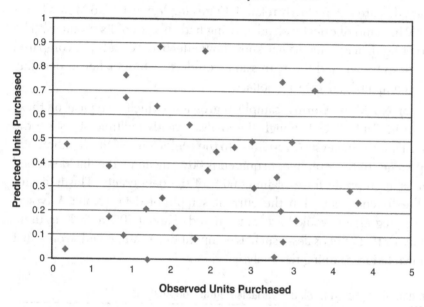

**Figure 7-3** Illustration of r squared = 0%

A line cannot be produced that will explain any of the data. Now imagine r squared is 100%. In this case, all of the data points (dots) will be on a line (Figure 7-4). The line accounts for all of the points in the data set. All regression analyses will result in lines with accuracy somewhere in between these extremes.

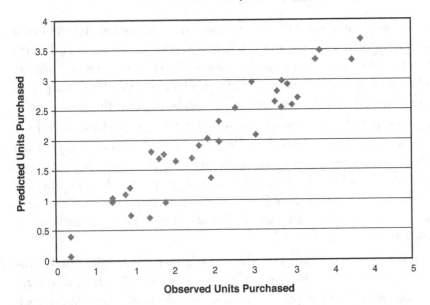

**Figure 7-4**  Illustration of r squared = 100%

P-value describes the significance of the findings given the sample size. But what does *significant* mean? In this population sample, 29 observations are made. Because this is a regression analysis of a small sample, you want to know whether you will still see the resulting coefficients if you include another 29 observations or another 29,000 observations. Will the slope of the line be 1.42, or will it be 0 or negative? Here, the p-value indicates there is a 0% chance the coefficients will change beyond the standard error given the addition of more data points or different samples. Most important, it indicates a 0% chance the slope will become negative, indicating the opposite relationship between the variables than what is indicated by the regression. In other words, regardless of how many times the data is sampled, the relationship will hold.

In addition to these critical outputs of a regression analysis, it might be beneficial to be familiar with one other value. In this example, t-stat is a reflection of p-value; however, depending on the regression or model used, the name of this value may change (for example, chi-square). P-value, on the other hand, will always be referred to in the same way. Particularly for marketing managers, who in most cases will need to be smart consumers of regression outputs but will not have to run the analyses themselves, p-value will provide adequate information about the significance of the findings.

# Adding Variables to the Regression

Now let's consider an analysis of the effects of multiple variables on the number of units purchased by hypothetical consumers. When marketing managers work through a problem, they have to gather data to find a solution. In this case, you are going to start with a solution (here, a true model) and use only data that you know is a part of that model to determine how effective a regression can be at predicting outcomes.

The data shown in Table 7-2 reflects an analysis of three variables: price paid, whether the unit was on feature (highlighted in a mailer or other promotion but not necessarily at a reduced price), and whether the unit was on a store display (on an endcap or stand-alone cardboard cutout). In this case, you know the true effect of each of these variables on the outcome because you created the model. This is evidenced by the fact that you have an r squared of 99% (with the 1% error inserted randomly in the true model you created).

Because this is a hypothetical situation, the data is known to coincide with the true model (Table 7-3), in which the intercept is 6.22, the price coefficient is –2.28 (meaning the slope is downward and, as price increases, sales decrease), the feature coefficient is 0.38, and the display coefficient is 0.22 (meaning the slope is upward and, as feature and display increase, sales increase). Also, because this is the true model, r squared is 0.99, indicating an extremely low chance of error.

But imagine you are a marketing manager, and you don't have access to the true model. (In fact, no one can know the true model in any real-world situation.) Looking only at the data, you must approximate the true model as closely as possible. Imagine now that you don't think price is important in your model, and consider only feature and display. As shown in Table 7-3, the resulting coefficients describing the effect those variables have on units purchased are higher than in the true model.

Because you would not have access to the true model in a real-world situation, what would these results influence you as a manager to do? You would expect that feature and display would be more effective than they in fact are and invest more heavily in those marketing strategies. As shown in the true model, however, price has a great effect on units purchased, and the effects of feature and display are therefore overstated in the estimated model.

To correct such a bias, intuition comes into play. First, a good marketing manager should know from experience that price has a significant effect on units purchased. A good marketing manager should also know that when items are on feature and display, they tend to come with a reduced price. In other words, price and feature/display tend to be negatively correlated.

**Table 7-2** Hypothetical Data on Sales of No More Germs Toothpaste

Units Purchased = $a + b_1 \times$ Price Paid + $b_2 \times$ Feature + $b_3 \times$ Display + Error

| Customer | Price Paid | Feature | Display | Units Purchased |
|----------|-----------|---------|---------|-----------------|
| 1 | 1.50 | 0 | 0 | 3 |
| 1 | 2.56 | 1 | 1 | 1 |
| 1 | 1.62 | 1 | 0 | 3 |
| 2 | 2.41 | 1 | 0 | 1 |
| 2 | 2.37 | 0 | 1 | 1 |
| 2 | 2.23 | 0 | 1 | 1 |
| 2 | 2.65 | 0 | 0 | 0 |
| 2 | 2.06 | 1 | 0 | 2 |
| 2 | 2.12 | 1 | 1 | 2 |
| 3 | 2.31 | 0 | 1 | 1 |
| 3 | 1.69 | 1 | 1 | 3 |
| 3 | 1.37 | 1 | 1 | 4 |
| 3 | 1.82 | 0 | 0 | 2 |
| 3 | 1.54 | 0 | 1 | 3 |
| 3 | 1.29 | 1 | 1 | 4 |
| 3 | 1.96 | 1 | 0 | 2 |
| 3 | 2.20 | 0 | 0 | 1 |
| 3 | 1.55 | 1 | 0 | 3 |
| 3 | 2.01 | 0 | 1 | 2 |
| 4 | 2.07 | 0 | 1 | 2 |
| 4 | 2.79 | 1 | 0 | 0 |
| 4 | 2.15 | 0 | 0 | 1 |
| 4 | 2.50 | 1 | 0 | 1 |

Feature and Display:

1 = Yes

0 = No

This is what is known as an *omitted-variable bias* because the estimated model has not taken into account a variable that has a significant effect on what is being measured. Although such biases may not always be as obvious as in this example, they are common in multivariable regression analyses, and this is the main point of differentiation when moving away from single-variable analyses (which are, by nature, oversimplified and, at least in terms of marketing, fail to fully explain most real-world situations).

**Table 7-3** Model Estimates Using Hypothetical Data

|  | True Model | Estimated Model |
| --- | --- | --- |
| Intercept | 6.22 | 1.14 |
| Price | –2.28 | ----- |
| Feature | .38 | .892 |
| Display | .22 | .758 |
| R squared | .99 | .305 |

To ensure a bias is not detrimental to the findings of a regression analysis, you must examine the direction of the bias. In this case, the bias is positive because feature and display have a higher coefficient in the estimated model than in the true model. But how do you know the direction of the bias if you do not know the true model? Again, some intuition and experience are necessary. You know price and sales have a negative correlation. You know price and feature and price and display also have a negative correlation. The direction of the bias when price is the omitted variable is the product of the sign of the correlation between price and units purchased and the sign of the correlation between price and feature and display. The product of a negative and a negative is a positive, so in this case, the bias is positive (Table 7-4).

**Table 7-4** Correlation Between Independent and Dependent Variables

|  | Price | Feature | Display | Units Purchased |
| --- | --- | --- | --- | --- |
| Price | 1 | (0.25) | (0.24) | (0.98) |
| Feature |  | 1 | (0.09) | 0.45 |
| Display |  |  | 1 | 0.32 |
| Units Purchased |  |  |  | 1 |

|  |  | Price | Bias |
| --- | --- | --- | --- |
| Direction of Bias in Feature = [Sign of Correlation Between Price and Units] × [Sign of Correlation Between Price and Feature] | Units | –ve (negative) |  |
|  | Feature | –ve (negative) | +ve (positive) |
|  | Display | –ve (negative) | +ve (positive) |

Another way to think about omitted variables is shown in Figure 7-5. Here, $x$ and $y$ are shown with respect to some omitted variable, $z$. By examining this relationship, the marketing manager can determine the direction of the bias created by omitting that variable.

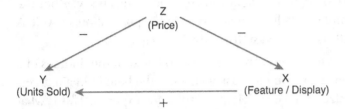

**Figure 7-5** Illustration of omitted variable bias

Note that an omitted variable is only a problem when it affects both whatever is included in the model and the dependent variable. If it is not correlated with other independent variables in the model, removing it will reduce r squared, but it will not affect the coefficient of the variables included in the model. In the current example, the variation in units is being assigned to feature and display, when in fact it should be assigned to price. If the changes in one variable did not affect another, whatever variation in the dependent variable was being captured would still reflect reality. For example, weather can have a profound effect on sales (for example, a hurricane keeping buyers in Florida from making it to stores for an extended period), but hurricanes need not necessarily affect the feature or display plans for a brand. If weather and feature and display plans are not correlated, then inclusion of weather is not necessary to obtain accurate estimates of feature or display.

In this example, you have what is known as an optimistic model, which can be a concern for marketing managers. When presenting such results to decision makers, the findings will be overstated because a significant variable (price) was omitted. Although you cannot include everything in your model, knowing whether the results are conservative or optimistic is beneficial. Typically, a conservative model (one that has a negative bias) is best. Investing in a marketing channel shown to be effective by a conservative model may still represent lost opportunity if the amount of the investment is low, but it will not represent an outright mistake in resource allocation.

When do you know if you have the true model? You never know, but examining the four Ps (product, price, place, and promotion) is a good place to start. The results of a regression analysis are only hypotheses, and they should be tested in field experiments to ensure their validity.

# Economic Significance: Acting on Regression Outputs

There are two types of significance, statistical and economic. Statistical significance is related to the p-value, or statistical significance, which indicates whether the relationship observed in a sample is likely to be observed in the population, as well. A p-value less than 0.1 is typically considered statistically significant.

But how do you know when it makes economic sense to invest in the findings of a regression? As a marketing manager, you must ask yourself if the benefit of a marketing intervention (such as the size of the coefficient) justifies the expense. This is what is known as economic significance.

Consider the single-variable-regression example in which you examined promotions versus purchases. The benefit provided from one promotion was found to be an increase in number of sales of 1.42. This was found to be a statistically significant finding. To determine economic significance, you must weigh this benefit against the cost of doing a promotion, taking into account the gross profit from the sale of a single unit.

Assume that the gross profit per unit is $5 and the cost of a promotion is $0.50. Therefore, profit = (units purchased × gross profit) – (cost of promotion × number of promotions), or:

$$\text{Profit} = 1.42 \times 5 - 0.50 \times 1 = 7.1 - 0.5 = 6.6$$

In this example, the company will make $6.60 per promotion. But if the cost of the promotion increases or the company makes less gross profit per unit, the economic significance of the promotion could quickly be lost. In other words, even if your regression findings are significant, you must first use a profit/loss function before taking action.

# Conclusion

A regression analysis is intended to help marketing managers understand the relationship between two or more variables or concepts. Typically, a company will use historic sales data or data generated through experiments to identify factors that most affect a brand's sales.

The value of a regression model is only as good as the variables selected to be in the model. Strong managerial intuition is required to identify variables (such as price, feature, and display, among others) that are most closely related to sales. For the best results, managers should also have some insight into how these variables actually relate in the real world to determine whether the results of a regression might be conservative or overly optimistic. This intuition is the artistic or creative side of analytics and is necessary to move a regression beyond a statistical exercise and turn it into something valuable for a business.

# Endnotes

1. *Webster's Third New International Dictionary, Unabridged,* defines "at bat" as "an official turn at batting charged to a baseball player except when the player walks, sacrifices, is hit by a pitched ball, or is interfered with by the catcher."

2. For more information on how to perform a regression using computer software, please visit Darden Marketing Analytics at http://dmanalytics.org/.

# 8

## Design of Price and Advertising Elasticity Models

## Introduction

The marketing mix that a manager may deploy can affect the sales of a product and can be categorized under the traditional four *P*s of marketing (product, price, promotion, and placement). But the perennial question managers face concerns the combination of these different marketing-mix variables that will give them maximized sales, highest share, lowest inventory, or maximized margins. Quite often, these questions are answered by historical data: for example, past sales or market share for different levels of expenditures on these marketing-mix variables. This chapter considers the design of models that allow managers to obtain robust price and advertising elasticity estimates.

Consider the following scenario: Belvedere vodka was introduced in the United States in 1996. This vodka traced its roots back to the Warsaw suburb of Żyrardów, Poland, and its production process went back more than 600 years. Lately, it had begun to observe a decline in its overall share of the vodka market. The company suspected the cause to be new market entrants that were capturing market share with effective advertising. To sustain the growth rate and defend its share from the competition, Belvedere was considering two options: increasing its advertising expenditure and/or reducing the pricing. Such a scenario is very common for most brands during the various stages of their brand (or product) life cycles. The first step toward solving this issue is to estimate the elasticity of a brand to its price and advertising.

## Price Elasticity of Demand

Pricing is one of the most critical variables that marketers have problems with. Based on common sense, consumers tend to buy more of a product as its price goes down, and using the same logic, they will buy less if the price goes up. Price elasticity of demand (explained in Figure 8-1) is a measure to show the responsiveness of the quantity demanded of a good (or service) to a change in its price; it gives the percentage change in quantity demanded in response to a 1% change in price (holding constant all the other variables in the marketing mix).[1] A product with a price elasticity above 1 is said to be elastic, as changes in demand are relatively large compared with changes in price. Correspondingly, a product whose elasticity goes below 1 is deemed inelastic.

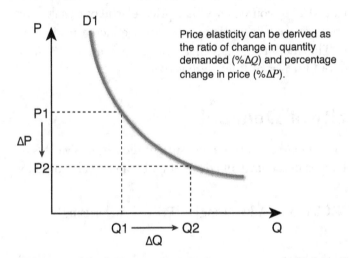

Price elasticity can be derived as the ratio of change in quantity demanded (%$\Delta Q$) and percentage change in price (%$\Delta P$).

**Figure 8-1**  Price elasticity of demand

Source: Created by case writer.

Price elasticity of demand (PED) can be calculated using Equation 1:

$$PED = [\text{Change in Sales} \div \text{Change in Price}] \times [\text{Price} \div \text{Sales}] =$$
$$(\Delta Q \div \Delta P) \times (P \div Q) \tag{1}$$

Or if you have a sample of historical sales and price data, then you can regress the sales against price, and the coefficient of this regression gives price elasticity, as shown in Equation 2:[2]

$$PED = \text{Coefficient of Price When } Ln(\text{sales}) \text{ Is Regressed on } Ln(\text{price}) \tag{2}$$

Here, you are assuming that the Ln-Ln model (that is, dependent Ln(sales) regressed on independent Ln(price)) gives you a better linear model in Equation 3:

$$Ln(\text{sales}) = \alpha_1 + \beta_1 \times Ln(\text{price}) + \varepsilon_1 \tag{3}$$

where $\beta_1$ represents the price elasticity in the preceding case and $\epsilon_1$ is the random error term drawn from a normal distribution (the standard assumption in a linear regression model).

Assuming consumers are rational and reasonably informed, the coefficient (and hence the price elasticity) should be negative. Therefore, the phrase *greater price sensitivity* means more negative price elasticity, and similarly *less price sensitivity* means less negative price elasticity.

Refer to Exhibit 8-1 for Belvedere's sales and price data and the regression results. With a regression coefficient of –1.259, you can say that price elasticity of sales for Belvedere is high (or, its customers are fairly price sensitive). Reducing price may have a positive effect on sales. This model suggests that a price decrease of 1% may result in 1.259% sales increase of 9L cases of Belvedere vodka.

# Advertising Elasticity of Demand

The advertising elasticity of demand (AED) is a measure of the responsiveness in the demand of a product to changes in the level of advertising. It can be calculated by using Equation 4:

AED = [Change in Sales ÷ Change in Advertising] × [Price ÷ Advertising]

$$= (\Delta Q \div \Delta A) \times (A \div Q) \tag{4}$$

Let us suppose that the total advertising exposure in period 1 was $100 and total sales were 200 units. Then, in period 2, the advertising was increased to $125 and the total sales were 300 units. Here, an advertising spend increase of $25 resulted in a sales increase of 100 units. So, AED = (100 ÷ $25) × (200 ÷ $100) = 8. In other words, a 1% increase in advertising results in an 8% increase in sales. Similar to the procedure for price elasticity, the basic formulation to estimate advertising elasticity is to run a regression of log of sales (or market share) on log of advertising. The coefficient of the log of advertising will be the estimate of advertising elasticity (Equation 5):

$$Ln(\text{sales}) = \alpha_2 + \beta_2 \times Ln(\text{advertising}) + \epsilon_1 \tag{5}$$

where $\beta_2$ is the advertising elasticity of demand and $\epsilon_1$ is the random error term drawn from a normal distribution.

All other factors remaining equal, an increase in advertising is expected to result in a positive shift in demand and hence a positive advertising elasticity. AED can be utilized by a firm to make sure its advertising expenses are in line, though an increase in demand may not be the only desired outcome of advertising.

Refer to Exhibit 8-2 for regression results of Belvedere's sales and advertising data. A regression coefficient of –0.013 and low t-stat value suggest that changing advertising expenses may have no effect on Belvedere's sales or that the change cannot be predicted. Elasticities (or sensitivities) can be used for short-term advertising effects[3]—values less than 0 imply negative returns to advertising and greater than 1 imply the firm is underadvertising. So the value should range from 0 to 1. The previous simple regression model took advertising expenditure as one simple independent variable by combining expenditures for all possible media. But different media (such as print, display, in-store, television) may have varied effects on the demand of a product based on its characteristics. More analysis is required to study the effect of different media, and if required, more than one variable should be incorporated in the regression model to get a better-fitting model and help the marketing manager decide on the advertising expenditure—both the total amount and its distribution across different media.

## Building a Comprehensive Model

If both PED and AED are significant, the regression model should include both price and advertising as independent variables (Equation 6):

$$Ln(\text{sales}) = \alpha + \beta_1 \times Ln(\text{price}) + \beta_2 \times Ln(\text{advertising}) + \varepsilon_1 \tag{6}$$

Bias is a commonly used term to describe the effect of omitted variables. It is used where there are systematic differences in the estimated elasticity (due to errors in estimation, not environmental differences) and the true elasticity in the market. This bias may be caused by omission of variables, which may be correlated with those included in the equation. The decision to include or omit certain variables in the model other than price and advertising will therefore depend on the correlation of a variable with the dependent variable and its correlation with other independent variables. If advertising elasticity is higher than the true value, then it is said to be a positive bias, but if it is lower than the true value, then it is called a negative bias. Conversely, if price elasticity is more negative than the true value, then it is said to be a positive bias, and if it is less negative, then it is called a negative bias (see Figure 8-2).

---

If the true model is as follows:

$$Ln(Y) = \alpha_0 + \alpha_1 \times Ln(\text{price}) + \alpha_2 \times Z + \varepsilon,$$

but you estimate the model to be

$$Ln(Y) = \beta_0 + \beta_1 \times Ln(\text{price}) + \varepsilon,$$

the true value of coefficient $\beta_1$ will be the sum of the estimated coefficient $\beta_1$ and the bias:

$$\beta_1{}^{\text{true}} = \beta_1 + \text{bias}$$

---

If $r$ is the covariance between independent variables, $Ln$(price) and Z, then the bias can be proven to be the product of the coefficient of the omitted variable $(\alpha_2)$ and some function of covariance of independent variables $[f(r)]$:

Bias = $\alpha_2 \times f(r)$

- If the dependent variable is not related to the omitted variable, then there is no bias (=0).
- If the included independent variable (here, $Ln$(price)) is not correlated to the omitted variable (covariance is zero), then there is no bias (=0).
- If $\alpha_2$ (correlation between the omitted variable and the dependent variable) and $r$ (covariance between independent variables) are of same sign, then the bias is positive.
- If $\alpha_2$ and $r$ are of different signs, then the bias is negative.

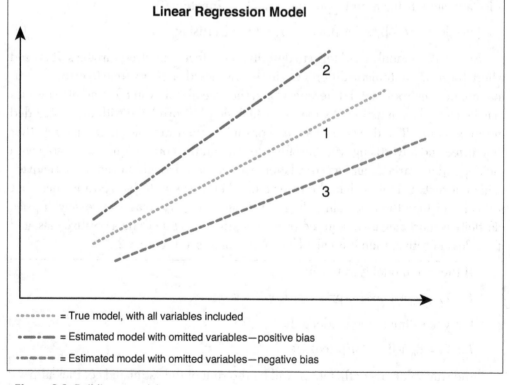

**Linear Regression Model**

⋯⋯⋯ = True model, with all variables included

▪━▪━▪ = Estimated model with omitted variables—positive bias

▪━▪━▪ = Estimated model with omitted variables—negative bias

**Figure 8-2** Building a model

Source: Created by case writer.

The following sections detail some major factors that would need to be included in a comprehensive marketing-mix model for price and advertising elasticity.

## Product Quality

If consumers are even minimally informed about the product quality, then the better-quality product would be able to command higher prices. With this assumption, the correlation coefficient for a regression model on price and quality will be positive. Therefore, if higher-quality products also sell more, the omission of quality from the model would lead to positive bias of price elasticity. This means that the estimated price elasticity in a model without product quality would be more negative than a model that includes product quality.

## Distribution

The more widely the product is available to customers, the better the sales of that product. But the relationship between distribution and price (and between distribution and sales) is not straightforward. Firms with high-priced brands typically have selective (or exclusive) distribution channels. If this strategy holds, the omission of distribution would lead to less-negative price elasticity (or a negative bias).

## Brand Life Cycle

As a brand matures, consumers' knowledge about that brand (e.g., deals, prices, comparables, availability) increases. Also, the early adopters of a brand are less price-sensitive. Therefore, price elasticity tends to increase (or become more negative) over the life cycle of a brand.

## Time Series Data Versus Cross-Sectional Data

Price elasticity for a brand will have two components: (1) a within-brand component, a measure of sensitivity to prices of a particular brand over time, and (2) a between-brands component, a measure of sensitivity to differences between brands. Because consumers mostly respond to prices at the point of purchase, using only a snapshot of data across brands without any time variation leaves out the within-brand component of elasticity. If the within-brand component is weak (less negative), then this sort of data aggregation over time would lead to a positive bias in price and advertising elasticity. Price elasticity would be more negative and advertising elasticity would be more positive if the model used data across brands for a single time period. When prices and advertising are included over time, it is better if the frequency of the time series reflects the product's purchase cycle. For example, for consumer packaged goods, the price and advertising elasticities are more accurate if the sales, pricing, and advertising decisions are sampled every week so that they are reflective of consumers' typical grocery trip frequency.

## Carry-Over Effect of Advertising

Advertising rarely has an immediate effect on sales. If you take into account the effect of advertising on sales for the current period, more often than not, those effects would be in the form of spikes and they would be relatively small (quite fragile) as compared with other marketing variables. Some research indicates that the current effect of price is 20 times larger than the current effect of advertising. The portion of advertising that retains its effect and affects consumers even beyond the period of its exposure is known as the carry-over effect. Depending on the product type, consumer segment, and firm's strategy, there could be several reasons for this carry-over effect: delayed consumer response due to their backup inventory, delayed exposure to the ad, shortage of retail inventory, and so on. Therefore, to account for the total effect of advertising one needs to include both the current and the carry-over effect.

The Koyck model provides a way to capture the carry-over effect of advertising: It enhances the basic linear marketing-mix model by including a lagged dependent variable as an additional independent variable. So, as per the enhanced model, sales of the current period depend on sales of the prior period and all the independent variables that caused prior sales, plus the current values of the same independent variables.

If the original model (before Koyck) was as shown in Equation 7:

$$Ln(Y_t) = \alpha + \beta_1 \times Ln(A_t) + \beta_1 \times B_t + \varepsilon_t \tag{7}$$

then Equation 8 is the enhanced model (by Koyck):

$$Ln(Y_t) = \alpha + \lambda \times Ln(Y_{t-1}) + \beta_1 \times Ln(A_t) + \beta_1 \times B_t + \varepsilon_t \tag{8}$$

In this model, $\beta_1$ captures the current effect of advertising, while $\beta_1 \times \lambda \div (1 - \lambda)$ can be calculated to be the carry-over effect of advertising. The higher the value of factor $\lambda$, the longer the effect of advertising will be. Similarly, the smaller the value of $\lambda$, the shorter the effects of advertising will be (in other words, sales depend more on current advertising). The total effect of advertising is the sum of current and carry-over effects; that is, $\beta_1 \div (1 \times \lambda)$.

If the advertising effects are positively correlated from one period to the next (so the last period's advertising has a positive correlation with current period's advertising), and if the past advertising has a positive correlation with the current period's sales, then the omission of the carry-over effect will result in a positive bias. In other words, managers would overestimate the current effect of advertisement in a model without the carry-over effect.

## Contextual Factors

Another factor that may come in to play is the disposable income of consumers in a region where a product is being sold. Consumers in countries (or regions) with high disposable income may be less price-sensitive. If so, then higher income would lead to lower price elasticity (less negative). At the same time, better-informed customers in a region (as well as stronger regulations and antitrust laws) may lead to increased price sensitivity.

Overall, the exogenous variables (for example, GNP and sociodemographics such as average family income, family size) generally have a positive correlation with sales, and their exclusion could have a positive bias on the model. The regional context may also have a correlation with advertising, for example, due to differences in consumer preferences, production cost structures, and geopolitical restrictions.

Table 8-1 summarizes the effect of bias due to the omission of different variables from the marketing mix.

**Table 8-1** Effect of Bias in Price and Advertising Elasticity

| Factor | Bias in Price Elasticity | Bias in Advertising Elasticity |
|---|---|---|
| Product quality | + | |
| Distribution | − | |
| Brand life cycle—early | + | |
| Absolute sales | + | |
| Time series | − | − |
| Include carry-over | | + |
| Contextual factors (income, family size, etc.) | | + |

Other factors to consider while designing the model are covered in the following sections.

## Promotion

Promotional activities can take one of two forms: (1) increasing product awareness through displays, campaigns, demonstrations, and so forth or (2) incentivizing consumers to try a company's products through coupons, rebates, and so on. Normally, firms tend to run the incentive programs along with their strategy of charging higher prices: higher prices for existing customers and rebates to acquire new customers. In such a case, prices and promotions would be positively correlated. On the other hand, the other form of promotions (increasing awareness) is generally used concurrently with lower prices. The goal is to maximize consumer awareness, and in this case, the prices and promotions would be negatively correlated. In either case, inclusion of promotion characteristics is necessary to obtain a better distinction between price and promotion effects on sales.

## Competition

Price elasticity tends to be more sensitive if the firm compares the price of its products with that of its competitors. Consumers tend to consider relative price rather than absolute price when opting for a specific brand. Therefore, an increase in price may not negatively affect sales if the competition also raises prices in the same period. Following the same logic, if a firm fails to respond to a price change from the competition, the choice may affect its sales (negative for price decline by competition and positive for price increase).

## Share Versus Volume

If sales volume is used as a dependent variable and advertising as independent, sales may be gained from a competitor (existing market) and sales may be gained from new customers (market expansion due to advertising). But if instead of sales, market share is used as a dependent variable, market expansion is eliminated as a possible reason.[4] As a result, the models using share (instead of sales) should normally have smaller elasticity.

# Conclusion

A marketing-mix model can be a strategic asset for a firm. Developing a good model requires knowledge of advanced statistics as well as a deep understanding of consumer behavior and the business context. Response models provide a good tool to aid marketing-mix decisions. They give managers a way to assess the relative importance of their different marketing-mix options. The product line may be the most effective marketing-mix option, followed by distribution, price, and promotion.[5] Managers should, however, be aware that response models assume that the market a company will face in the future would remain unchanged as compared with the past (or the time frame used to estimate the advertising and price elasticities). Price and advertising elasticities are an accurate reflection of consumer preferences, competitor reactions, the number of brands, firm strategy, and other market factors during the time of data collection. Expectations of returns from a firm's marketing-mix decisions must be informed by anticipated competitor actions and changes in the consumer preferences and competitive landscape. For this reason, it would also be a good idea to periodically update the marketing-mix models and re-estimate price and advertising elasticities.

# Endnotes

1. This is essentially never the case—as will be explored in more detail later in this chapter.

2. The coefficient and price elasticity are by definition not the same, but they are very closely related to each other, and in most of the cases, the coefficient is a close proxy for the elasticity.

3. In the case of multiplicative models, the coefficients were elasticities, whereas in the case of linear models, elasticities can be estimated by multiplying the regression coefficient by the ratio of means of the dependent variable and the advertising measure.

4. With market share as a dependent variable, the effect of advertising will appear in both numerator and denominator.

5. Berk M. Ataman, Harald J. Van Heerde, and Carl F. Mela, "The Long-Term Effect of Marketing Strategy on Brand Sales," *Journal of Marketing Research* 47, no. 5 (2010): 866–82.

# References

1. Gert Assmus, John U. Farley, and Donald R. Lehmann, "How Advertising Affects Sales: Meta-Analysis of Econometric Results," *Journal of Marketing Research* 21, no.1 (February 1984): 65–74.

2. Leonard J. Parsons, "A Rachet Model of Advertising Carryover Effects," *Journal of Marketing Research* 13, no. 1 (February 1976): 76–79.

3. Gerard J. Tellis, "The Price Elasticity of Selective Demand: A Meta-Analysis of Econometric Models of Sales," *Journal of Marketing Research* 25, no. 4 (November 1988): 331–41.

4. Gerard J. Tellis, "Modeling Marketing Mix," in *The Handbook of Marketing Research: Uses, Misuses, and Future Advances* (Thousand Oaks, CA: Sage Publications, 2006), 506–22.

# Exhibits

**Exhibit 8-1** Regression of *Ln*(sales) Versus *Ln*(price) for Belvedere Vodka

| Year | Sales (Thousands of Units) | *Ln* (Sales) (Thousands of Units) | Price (Dollars) | *Ln*(Price) (Dollars) | Advertising (Thousands of Dollars) | *Ln*(Advertising) (Thousands of Dollars) |
|---|---|---|---|---|---|---|
| 2007 | 410 | 6.016 | 215.44 | 5.373 | 20486.1 | 9.93 |
| 2006 | 381 | 5.943 | 211.45 | 5.354 | 2923.5 | 7.98 |
| 2005 | 365 | 5.900 | 207.45 | 5.335 | 4826.3 | 8.48 |
| 2004 | 369 | 5.911 | 240.87 | 5.484 | 13726.6 | 9.53 |
| 2003 | 339 | 5.826 | 241.33 | 5.486 | 10330.2 | 9.24 |
| 2002 | 306 | 5.724 | 247.55 | 5.512 | 13473.6 | 9.51 |
| 2001 | 273 | 5.609 | 240.48 | 5.483 | 9264.6 | 9.13 |

| Regression Statistics | |
|---|---|
| Multiple R | 0.67536 |
| R squared | 0.45611 |
| Adjusted R squared | 0.34733 |
| Standard error | 0.11269 |
| Observations | 7 |

|  | Coefficients | Standard Error | t Stat | P-value |
|---|---|---|---|---|
| Intercept | 12.686 | 3.340 | 3.798 | 0.013 |
| Ln (price) | −1.259 | 0.615 | −2.048 | 0.096 |

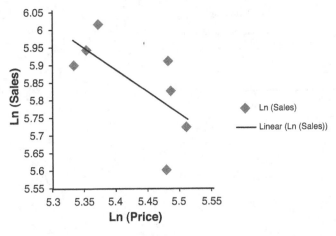

Source: Created by case writer.

**Exhibit 8-2**    Regression of *Ln*(sales) Versus *Ln*(advertising) for Belvedere Vodka

| Regression Statistics | |
|---|---|
| Multiple R | 0.06102 |
| R squared | 0.00372 |
| Adjusted R squared | −0.19553 |
| Standard error | 0.15252 |
| Observations | 7 |

|  | Coefficients | Standard Error | t-Stat | P-value |
|---|---|---|---|---|
| Intercept | 5.963 | 0.850 | 7.018 | 0.001 |
| Ln (advertising) | −0.013 | 0.093 | −0.137 | 0.897 |

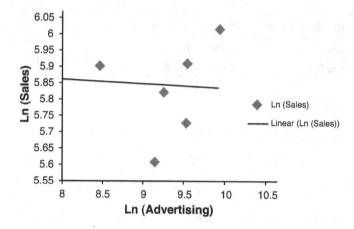

Source: Created by case writer.

# 9 ————————————————————————

## SVEDKA Vodka

## SVEDKA Vodka (A)

As he waited for his wife to meet him, Guillaume Cuvelier sat in a downtown Manhattan restaurant sipping vodka straight up. As founder and managing director of Spirits Marque One, a liquor importer, Cuvelier wondered if patrons of such an upscale bar would soon be ordering his new vodka by its name: SVEDKA. It was mid-1998, and the product was set to launch in just a few months. Scanning the bar for the competition's vodka bottles, Cuvelier ran through the marketing campaign in his head.[1]

The U.S. government defined vodka as a neutral spirit "without distinctive character, aroma, taste, or color." As one food and beverage writer explained, "Good vodka is considered to be one without the harsh, rubbing-alcohol fumes of ethanol."[2] The now-popular liquor originated in the fourteenth century in either Russia or Poland (depending on which history you believe) as a spirit distilled from rye or wheat. In the early 1800s, the introduction of filtration and dilution techniques allowed vodka to evolve into something more refined but no less potent.

As Cuvelier enjoyed his drink, the image of James Bond came to mind—described years earlier by an industry observer as "the first upscale vodka drinker."[3] Consumers were increasingly imitating Bond's discerning taste for high-priced vodka. In this climate, Cuvelier reviewed his own pricing, distribution, and positioning one last time. He hoped he was right that the vodka market was ready for a mid-priced option: Was there really an opportunity below the Bond tier and above the very low-priced products? With a small marketing budget, Cuvelier had to be correct in his efforts to position his brand as he created a new segment.

## On Trend

Trends in the marketplace inspired Cuvelier to take a closer look at opportunities in the spirits business (whiskey, gin, and vodka were among those classified as spirits). In 1991, he had received his MBA from the Darden School of Business at the conclusion of a two-year hiatus from his position with LVMH's Möet Hennessy-Louis Vuitton.

As an industry insider during the 1980s and early 1990s, Cuvelier had been inspired by Absolut vodka's success as a product, brand, and category leader. "Pre-Absolut, you could say that vodka was vodka was vodka," he said.

Cuvelier believed there was room to compete in the category by offering his own twist on the concept of name-brand vodka. With that purpose in mind, in 1998, Cuvelier founded a small entrepreneurial team of industry experts in New York City. That same year, vodka was the top-selling distilled spirit, representing 24% of total spirits consumption in the United States, up 3.6% in volume sales from 1997. The growth in premium vodka was in stark contrast to the negative long-term trend for most other spirits. (See Exhibit 9-1 for vodka sales from 1975 to 1998 and projections for the category.)

## The Market

Branded vodka dated back to the late 1860s, when Smirnoff cultivated the endorsement of the czar, engaged in comparative advertising with competitors, and paid patrons of Moscow bars to demand Smirnoff and accept no substitutes. Russia's connection with the category became prominent in the minds of many consumers. A leading imported vodka from Russia, Stolichnaya, had been introduced to the United States as recently as 1965. The brand leveraged its Russian image, evoking a strong connection to its origin and heritage. But "Stoli stumbled after the Soviet downing of Flight 007 in 1982, [which] hurt sales of many Russian products."[4] Once a Russian import, Smirnoff was eventually produced in the United States and came to dominate the domestic vodka segment, capturing almost 20% of the market share by 1998. Until the launch of Absolut, Smirnoff dominated the premium-price vodka segment with a brand name that derived authenticity from the family's Russian heritage.

The launch of Absolut in 1979 and its now-famous ad campaign helped the brand attain its pop-culture status. In 1998, Absolut spent $18 million on advertising.[5] Years later, *USA Today* reported: "Absolut had pioneered selling distilled spirits on image, persuading consumers to buy prestige in a bottle for $20. But the new prestige vodkas, at $25 to $200, have become what Absolut was 20 years ago."[6]

It took more than a decade for the Dutch Ketel One and American Skyy (then the only domestic vodka priced above $10) to enter the market. New prestige vodkas available at a high price point did indeed seem to become what Absolut once was. *The Business of Spirits* stated that the price for vodka "increased to $30 with the debut of Grey Goose, Chopin, and Belvedere in the late 1990s. Now, the debut market [was] flooded with $30 vodkas."[7]

The success of Grey Goose proved people would pay $30 for a bottle of vodka; in 1998, its sales increased 50% from the previous year.[8] Cuvelier had watched as "consumers became increasingly aware about the look, quality, and origin of vodka." (Exhibit 9-2 shows the number of new vodkas introduced from 1996 to 1998.)

Smirnoff was not alone in its high-volume sales and market share results. Brands such as Popov, Gordon's, McCormick, and Barton (each priced under $10) sold the most cases and enjoyed the largest shares.[9] A significant portion of these sales was for the larger-size plastic bottles.

Cuvelier believed that a midprice vodka could capture some volume sales from the under-$10 market. "This standard vodka category had never been expanded to include consumers who were willing to stretch their wallets a little bit," he said.

### The Product

Vodka could be manufactured inexpensively out of many different raw ingredients and didn't need to be aged. Its standard alcohol content was 40%, or 80 proof. Because the staple ingredients were relatively cheap, vodka companies invested in more complex distilling and filtering methods as well as flavor ingredients to distinguish their brands. Marketing campaigns often highlighted "more exotic backstories" to justify higher prices and profits.[10] Indeed, vodka's smoothness and thickness could vary from brand to brand. "The burn is usually associated with inexpensive vodkas," said Robert Plotkin, founder of BarMedia, a beverage consulting firm.[11]

Cuvelier was dedicated to creating a high-quality product that could be distinguished for its soft, silky drinkability. He selected Lidkoping, Sweden, as the manufacturing site. Cuvelier knew the country had recently joined the European Union, causing it to deregulate the alcohol monopoly. "My plan was to be the first to effectively develop and produce 80-proof Swedish vodka immediately after the reopening of the market," he explained. "I wanted the vodka to be from Sweden so I could take advantage of the Absolut tailwind."

SVEDKA outsourced its production to large, established industrial facilities. The glass bottles were imported from Germany, decorated in France, and shipped to the factory in Sweden to be filled with vodka. The finished product was shipped in cases to the United States.

*Wine Enthusiast* confirmed the quality of Cuvelier's product, rating SVEDKA 93 out of 100. Classifying the vodka as a "Best Buy," the review said, "We can't remember using the word 'complex' when describing a vodka before, but this one shows a tightly knit set of characteristics that deserve applause."[12]

SVEDKA would initially be available in the standard 750ml and 1.75L bottles. Larger and smaller sizes could be added once the business grew. "This gradual size rollout was common industry practice, especially for a start-up brand," Cuvelier said. While many brands were extending their selection to include flavored vodkas, SVEDKA focused on the core unflavored business for the launch.

## The Price

In addition to the option of imitating the premium prices of recent imported vodka successes, there was the under-$10-per-bottle market, which Cuvelier estimated was approximately 80% of the market volume (also known as the "standard" vodka segment, it ranged from $5 to $9 for 750ml). In fact, in 1998, 23 million cases were purchased at retail prices less than $10 per 750ml bottle (Table 9-1).[13] And then there was the third opportunity: to be a midtier player between the high and low price spectrums.

**Table 9-1** Vodka Category Price, Units Sold, Market Share, and Launch Year by Brand, 1998

| Brand | Price (750ml) | Cases (9L) (in Thousands) | Market Share (Percentage) | Launch Year |
|---|---|---|---|---|
| Grey Goose | $25.00 | 50 | 0.2 | 1997 |
| Ketel One | $18.00 | 450 | 1.3 | 1989 |
| Absolut | $16.00 | 3630 | 10.6 | 1979 |
| Stolichnaya | $16.50 | 1,100 | 3.2 | 1970 |
| Skyy | $11.50 | 702 | 2.1 | 1993 |
| Smirnoff | $10.00 | 6,720 | 19.7 | 1960 |
| Gordon's | $7.00 | 2,155 | 6.3 | 1960 |
| Popov | $6.50 | 2,230 | 6.5 | 1960 |

Note: Market share calculation is based on total case volume for imported and domestic vodka.

Data sources: Adams Business Media; Virginia Department of Alcoholic Beverage Control; case writer estimates.

Exhibit 9-3 shows the supplier case prices for vodka. In 1998, according to a Standard & Poor's survey of the alcohol industry, operating margins for U.S. alcohol beverage companies were about 20%, "well above the 12% to 14% range for packaged food companies."[14]

Cuvelier estimated that wholesaler margins for SVEDKA averaged 25%. Retailers' margins varied from 30% to 35%.

It was industry practice to offer retailers volume discounts. Cuvelier created Table 9-2 to estimate the discount levels he would be expected to offer.

**Table 9-2** Estimated Discount Levels Based on Case Quantity Discount

| Discount Level | Case Quantity Discount | Estimated Sales | Savings to Retailers |
|---|---|---|---|
| 1 | 3 | 10% | 8% |
| 2 | 5 | 15% | 13% |
| 3 | 25 | 75% | 19% |

Source: SVEDKA.

To reach a final everyday suggested retail bottle price, Cuvelier had to consider the costs along the wholesale and retail channels. The wholesaler's net laid-in costs were the sum of the free on board (FOB) price, the U.S. Federal Excise Tax (FET), state tax, and freight costs. (The FET per proof gallon was $13.50 in 1998.) SVEDKA classified the mandatory FET and individual state taxes (which varied by state) as hard production costs.

Pricing was tricky, and critics warned Cuvelier that if the price were too low, consumers might think the vodka was low-quality. But if SVEDKA were priced too high, consumers might question its value. A midrange price would risk SVEDKA's getting lost among the more premium brands. Already, higher-priced brands were encountering competition from the superpremium competitors. In *The Business of Spirits*, author Noah Rothbaum commented on the dilemma SVEDKA faced: "Many companies with high-priced spirits are concerned that their products soon will be leapfrogged by other, even more expensive brands, stealing their attention and market share."[15]

## Target Customer

Despite the risks he identified, Cuvelier was optimistic. "I believe that SVEDKA is the only brand in the vodka category to bridge the two ends of the category, appealing to both upgraders and consumers looking for the best possible value," he said. "I see SVEDKA as being at the crossroads of the market." SVEDKA wanted to capture the new vodka drinkers as the category was expanding, along with the "upgraders" who were looking for an opportunity to drink something better than the standard offerings. SVEDKA could be the vodka of choice for both price-driven groups.

In addition to considering consumer price sensitivity, Cuvelier segmented vodka drinkers into two large groups based on age and consumption behavior. Regular vodka drinkers tended to be price-conscious and loyal to a brand; consumers in this first segment were mostly older males. The second group consisted of the 21-to-35-year-old consumer, who represented 40% of the vodka market. (Exhibit 9-4 shows the breakdown of distilled spirits drinkers by category and age group.) Cuvelier thought this target group was also price-conscious, but not so brand-loyal. He was confident that SVEDKA, if positioned properly, would be able to tap into this younger crowd.

## Distribution

Off-premise (or off-trade) channels were the liquor and retail stores, while on-premise (or on-trade) channels included bars, hotels, and restaurants. Brands were usually launched simultaneously in both the on-trade locations and retail outlets. The on-premise percentage of volume was higher for premium brands because consumers often ordered drinks mixed with a specified brand-name vodka. For example, in 2003, 51% of Ketel One's volume was from on-premise. The percentages of on-premise consumption for Grey Goose, Absolut, and Stoli were 48%, 38%, and 37%, respectively.[16]

The spirits industry was a highly regulated business. Producers and importers could not sell directly to the retailers; instead, they were required to sell to licensed liquor wholesalers, who then serviced retailers. Licenses were issued by the state and therefore restricted wholesaler distributors from operating beyond any given state's jurisdiction. Cuvelier relied on a small internal sales team to manage the distributors as key clients. By leveraging relationships within the industry, "I tried to overcome the biggest hurdle of getting distributors on board," he said.

Another obstacle in distributing liquor was the issue of control states (also known as monopolies). In 18 U.S. states, accounting for about 25% of the population, state governments exercised monopoly control over the wholesaling and/or retailing of alcohol (Exhibits 9-5 and 9-6). These states, among them North Carolina, Vermont, and Washington, were scattered across the country. Michigan, Pennsylvania, Washington, and Virginia were not only control states, but also ranked among the top 15 states for retail spending on distilled spirits.[17] Most control states had higher taxes and prices than noncontrol states. For marketers, obtaining distribution meant persuading each independent state liquor commission to carry their brands.

In all cases, pricing was uniform and dictated by the state, leaving very little room for promoting brands. In most control states, retail prices were much higher than those in "open" neighbor states, but there were a few notable exceptions, such as New Hampshire and Pennsylvania. Temporary discounts and displays were allowed but highly regulated (and each state has its own set of rules) and needed to go through a lengthy approval process with the local liquor board. Shelf positioning was not negotiable. Another limitation in control states was the lack of convenience: Many had an insufficient number of stores, often with poor locations and limited operating hours.

Off-premise retailers were divided into food, drug, and liquor stores. Food stores included groceries, delis, and larger wholesale clubs. Drugstores such as Walgreens comprised the drug category. Liquor stores were further divided into the independent and control-state-owned liquor stores. Cuvelier estimated that the breakdown was 35%, 20%, and 45% for food, drug, and liquor stores, respectively. "The big chains, across all categories, were harder to penetrate, since they required high margins and heavy marketing support and established market share," he explained. "These bigger outlets relied on strong consumer pull for top brands."

For vodka, independent retailers were responsible for significant volume sales. And they could give the brand strong and sustained support because they generated higher margins on SVEDKA than high-volume established brands while offering a very competitive price. The pricing of SVEDKA, Cuvelier thought, would be attractive to them—which translated into eye-level shelf positioning, floor displays, and spontaneous retailers' recommendations. By prominently displaying SVEDKA alongside key competitors, store owners could give the brand invaluable credibility. And so SVEDKA planned to concentrate sales efforts on these midmarket retail outlets. In particular, Cuvelier intended to focus on landing the family-owned operations, considered midtier stores in terms of traffic and business, and devote very little effort to the chain stores such as large grocery and drug chains that also sold liquor in noncontrol states.

The distribution strategy for SVEDKA required a network of wholesalers and brokers. Cuvelier thought it would be difficult to gain a foothold among large wholesalers in the biggest states, so he looked for what he called "challenger" distributors where he could get more attention and support from management and sales. These operated primarily in open states. (See Exhibit 9-5 for retail sales of vodka in the top

25 states by retail sales in 1998.) Robust collateral pieces explaining the benefits of the product, brand, and company were given to all retailers as education materials.

Cuvelier believed that, given his limited budget, launching SVEDKA in the mid-market off-premise locations was the most effective strategy He instructed his sales force to secure distribution in liquor stores only. But he still harbored doubts about which particular states he should select and the order in which they would receive SVEDKA shipments.

## The Brand

The first association consumers would have with the product was its name. Cuvelier had searched for a word that evoked the vodka's Swedish heritage. During his many trips to Sweden, the word *Svensk* ("Swedish") caught his attention; it appeared everywhere. He combined it with the word "vodka" to come up with an easier-to-pronounce version: SVEDKA. Although focus groups and the packaging agency didn't confirm the wisdom of his choice, Cuvelier stayed with his intuition. (Exhibit 9-7 shows the SVEDKA bottle with its original logo, which has since been updated.)

The name was fitting for the product's positioning. Cuvelier envisioned SVEDKA as a challenger brand, with a personality like JetBlue in the airline industry or Target in fashion: an inexpensive, chic alternative. It was a fun option that challenged the status quo in a category that was taking itself too seriously. SVEDKA empowered the consumer with a different choice where there wasn't much discrepancy among the products in its category. "The category is locked in sameness," Cuvelier said. "Each brand relies on a stated marketing recipe of bottle shot plus product benefit plus cocktail recipe plus historical reference."[18]

## The Campaign

Cuvelier estimated he had about $350,000 to spend in his first year on marketing SVEDKA (not including promotions to wholesalers and retailers, which could include the discount levels, support materials, sales force incentives, and in-store promotions). He allocated this budget among media, point of sale (POS), trade shows, creative, and sampling.

Until distribution reached key markets, Cuvelier did not use traditional advertising. Generally, brands were promoted in print (with magazines as the dominant medium), outdoor, broadcast, and electronic media at an increase of 14% over the $256 million spent in 1997.[19] (Refer to Exhibit 9-8 for the total advertising expenditure in 1997 and 1998.) Cuvelier wanted SVEDKA to achieve distribution, brand awareness, and word of mouth before he launched a national campaign. He was left to reassess the best use of his dollars across the following marketing methods.

### Trade Press and PR

Cuvelier viewed trade relationships as the first step in communicating about his brand. There were a small but influential group of trade magazines and writers he needed to acquaint with SVEDKA. He bought a few full-page trade ads and entered SVEDKA in vodka contests to drum up press. He succeeded with the *Wine Enthusiast* 93 rating. Such high marks were in line with the more expensive Grey Goose (which received a 94) and Ketel One (93) and higher than the ratings for Stolichnaya (91), Skyy (90), Belvedere (89), and Absolut (90).[20] The favorable results validated the brand in the eyes of the wholesalers. Their excitement about SVEDKA would determine how quickly it was embraced by the largest, bottom portion: the core consumer. All media outreach was limited to the trade outlets. SVEDKA used its high-profile reviews to fuel favorable trade press articles. But additional public relations efforts toward larger publications were not scheduled for the launch.

### Point of Sale

Brand visibility would thus be at the store level through POS materials. Because of the emphasis on an off-premise distribution strategy, Cuvelier allocated marketing dollars toward enhancing the in-store experience (midtier liquor stores). POS and store signage (shelf, display, and window materials) helped bring the brand to life at the point of decision making and purchasing. The *Wine Enthusiast* ranking was displayed on POS pieces to provide the unknown product with credibility.

### Trade Shows

SVEDKA planned to sponsor booths at top industry trade shows. Attendees at these shows included wholesalers and retailers, as well as the media and competition. Although trade shows were costly and time-consuming, Cuvelier believed that having a presence at industry events would develop brand recognition as well as provide continuing insight into industry trends.

### Creative

The collateral materials that supported the SVEDKA booth at trade shows, in addition to the POS materials and trade press kits, fell under the creative investment line item. Cuvelier wanted all branding elements to have a cohesive look and feel for both internal and external audiences. The same images appeared as limited ads in trade magazines such as *Beverage Industry News.*

### Sampling

And finally, when the product was to be introduced in a new store, SVEDKA intended to host sampling events. SVEDKA wanted to put its own twist on the customer-engagement tactic by designing customized, branded barware test tubes. Cuvelier was certain that the ROI on these 1,000 to 1,500 sampling events per year (two to three hours per event with a small staff and collateral materials) was enormous. SVEDKA had only one shot at the launch campaign, and Cuvelier was confident in his tactics. But he did find himself reexamining his budget in the final days before his product's debut.

## Exhibits

**Exhibit 9-1a** Projections: Vodka Versus Total Distilled Spirits (In Thousands of 9L Cases)

| | Vodka | | Total Distilled Spirits | |
|---|---|---|---|---|
| Year | Cases | ACGR° | Cases | ACGR |
| 1975 | 31,898 | -.-% | 179,731 | -.-% |
| 1980 | 36,411 | 2.7 | 190,903 | 1.2 |
| 1985 | 35,681 | –0.4 | 173,508 | –1.9 |
| 1986 | 34,717 | –2.7 | 164,531 | –5.2 |
| 1987 | 33,626 | –3.1 | 162,024 | –1.5 |
| 1988 | 34,712 | 3.2 | 159,008 | –1.9 |
| 1989 | 35,054 | 1.0 | 155,865 | –2.0 |
| 1990 | 35,362 | 0.9 | 159,190 | 2.1 |
| 1991 | 33,397 | –5.6 | 147,026 | –7.6 |
| 1992 | 32,964 | –1.3 | 148,015 | 0.7 |
| 1993 | 32,441 | –1.6 | 144,162 | –2.6 |
| 1994 | 31,910 | –1.6 | 139,996 | –2.9 |
| 1995 | 32,175 | 0.8 | 137,330 | –1.9 |
| 1996 | 33,002 | 2.6 | 138,814 | 1.1 |
| 1997 | 32,912 | –0.3 | 138,740 | –0.1 |
| 1998 | 34,088 | 3.6 | 140,568 | 1.3 |

| | Vodka | | Total Distilled Spirits | |
|---|---|---|---|---|
| Year | Cases | ACGR* | Cases | ACGR |
| 1999 projected versus 1998 | 35,000 | 2.7 | 141,905 | 1.0 |
| 2003 projected versus 1998 | 35,500 | 0.8 | 143,240 | 0.4 |

*Annual compound growth rate.

Source: *Adams Liquor Handbook 1999.*

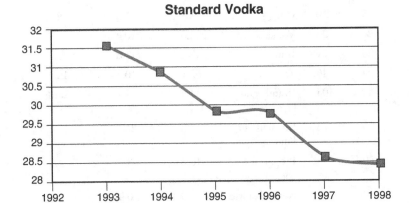

### Standard Vodka

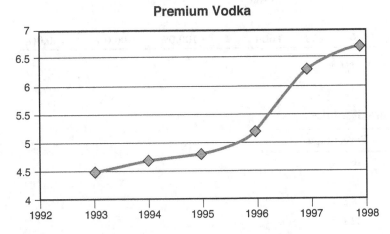

### Premium Vodka

**Exhibit 9-1b** Vodka sales, 1993 to 1998 (in millions of 9L cases)

Source: SVEDKA sales presentation, 2001.

**Exhibit 9-2** New Distilled Spirits Introductions by Category, 1996–1998

| Number of Introductions | | | | Share of Total | | | |
| --- | --- | --- | --- | --- | --- | --- | --- |
| *Category* | *1996* | *1997* | *1998* | *Category* | *1996* | *1997* | *1998* |
| U.S. whiskey | 10 | 14 | 19 | U.S. whiskey | 3.9% | 6.1% | 5.1% |
| Canadian | 7 | 1 | 5 | Canadian | 2.7 | 0.4 | 1.3 |
| Scotch | 39 | 18 | 42 | Scotch | 15.3 | 7.8 | 11.3 |
| Irish | 2 | 2 | 4 | Irish | 0.8 | 0.9 | 1.1 |
| **Total whiskey** | **58** | **35** | **70** | **Total whiskey** | **22.7%** | **15.2%** | **18.9%** |
| | | | | | | | |
| Gin | 11 | 5 | 10 | Gin | 4.3 | 2.2 | 2.7 |
| Vodka | 37 | 24 | 23 | Vodka | 14.5 | 10.4 | 6.2 |
| Rum | 31 | 26 | 27 | Rum | 12.2 | 11.3 | 7.3 |
| Tequila | 19 | 24 | 46 | Tequila | 7.5 | 10.4 | 12.4 |
| Brandy and cognac | 29 | 44 | 104 | Brandy and cognac | 11.4 | 19.1 | 28.0 |
| Cordials and liqueurs | 44 | 50 | 72 | Cordials and liqueurs | 17.3 | 21.7 | 19.4 |
| Prepared cocktails | 26 | 20 | 18 | Prepared cocktails | 10.2 | 8.7 | 4.9 |
| Neutral spirits | — | 2 | 1 | Neutral spirits | -.- | 0.9 | 0.3 |
| **Total non-whiskey** | **197** | **195** | **301** | **Total non-whiskey** | **77.3%** | **84.8%** | **81.1%** |
| | | | | | | | |
| **Total** | **255** | **230** | **371** | **Total** | **100.0%** | **100.0%** | **100.0%** |

Source: *Adams Liquor Handbook 1999*, 5.

**Exhibit 9-3** Supplier Vodka Case Prices

| Price Ranges | Percentage |
| --- | --- |
| Under $34.99 | 16.5 |
| $35.00 to $39.99 | 21.4 |
| $40.00 to $49.99 | 18.8 |
| $50.00 to $59.99 | 22.1 |
| $60.00 to $99.99 | 2.8 |
| $100.00 to $119.99 | 18.3 |
| Total | 100.0 |

Source: *Adams Liquor Handbook 1999*, 135.

**Exhibit 9-4**  Consumers of Distilled Spirits by Category and Age Group (In Percentages)

| Category | Age Groups | | | | | | Total Adults |
| | 21–24 | 25–34 | 35–44 | 45–54 | 55–64 | 65+ | |
|---|---|---|---|---|---|---|---|
| Distilled spirits | 62.7 | 60.6 | 55.2 | 53.1 | 44.4 | 35.2 | 51.7 |
| Bourbon | 15.2 | 13.6 | 12.8 | 12.3 | 12.6 | 9.5 | 12.5 |
| Blend/rye | 3.7 | 6.3 | 6.0 | 6.6 | 7.3 | 5.9 | 6.2 |
| Canadian | 6.9 | 10.0 | 11.6 | 11.3 | 13.3 | 9.1 | 10.7 |
| Scotch | 6.7 | 8.3 | 9.0 | 12.9 | 11.4 | 8.8 | 9.7 |
| Irish | 3.5 | 3.0 | 3.7 | 4.5 | 3.0 | 2.3 | 3.3 |
| Gin | 16.5 | 15.3 | 15.0 | 16.4 | 13.7 | 10.4 | 14.5 |
| Vodka | 30.4 | 29.6 | 25.5 | 24.5 | 21.8 | 15.4 | 24.3 |
| Rum | 34.4 | 28.2 | 26.0 | 23.1 | 15.8 | 7.9 | 22.1 |
| Tequila | 26.7 | 24.9 | 20.1 | 17.9 | 9.5 | 5.1 | 17.2 |
| Brandy and cognac | 4.1 | 7.3 | 8.3 | 11.0 | 8.8 | 7.7 | 8.2 |
| Cordials and liqueurs | 27.3 | 21.6 | 21.6 | 21.9 | 19.0 | 11.6 | 20.0 |
| **Adult population (in millions)** | **12.3** | **38.9** | **43.1** | **34.4** | **22.1** | **31.9** | **182.7** |

Note: Includes consumers age 21 and older only.

Sources: Simmons Market Research Bureau, Spring 1998 Study of Media and Markets; *Adams Liquor Handbook 1999*, 291.

**Exhibit 9-5**  Retail Sales for Vodka in Top 25 States, 1998 (Dollars in Millions)

| Rank | State | Sales | Control or Open | Percent Share of All Distilled Spirits |
|---|---|---|---|---|
| 1 | California | $738 | Open | 10.40 |
| 2 | Florida | $517 | Open | 6.50 |
| 3 | New York | $468 | Open | 7.40 |
| 4 | Illinois | $341 | Open | 5.00 |
| 5 | Texas | $333 | Open | 5.80 |
| 6 | New Jersey | $317 | Open | 3.90 |
| 7 | Pennsylvania | $307 | Control | 3.70 |
| 8 | Michigan | $296 | Control | 3.70 |
| 9 | Ohio | $221 | Control | 3.50 |
| 10 | Georgia | $203 | Open | 2.80 |

| Rank | State | Sales | Control or Open | Percent Share of All Distilled Spirits |
|------|-------|-------|-----------------|-----------------------------------------|
| 11 | Washington | $198 | Control | 2.50 |
| 12 | Wisconsin | $190 | Open | 2.80 |
| 13 | Connecticut | $179 | Open | 1.90 |
| 14 | Massachusetts | $177 | Open | 3.20 |
| 15 | South Carolina | $149 | Open | 1.70 |
| 16 | Arizona | $147 | Open | 1.80 |
| 17 | North Carolina | $146 | Control | 2.00 |
| 18 | Minnesota | $144 | Open | 2.10 |
| 19 | Maryland | $140 | Open | 2.00 |
| 20 | Colorado | $139 | Open | 1.90 |
| 21 | Virginia | $133 | Control | 2.00 |
| 22 | Indiana | $127 | Open | 1.90 |
| 23 | Tennessee | $117 | Open | 1.40 |
| 24 | Missouri | $113 | Open | 1.80 |
| 25 | Louisiana | $102 | Open | 1.70 |
| | **Top 25** | **$5,942** | | **84.00** |
| | **Bottom 25** | **$1,280** | | **16.50** |
| | **Total United States** | **$7,222** | | **21.20** |

| | Control | Open |
|------|---------|------|
| Top 25 | 6 | 19 |
| Total United States | 18 | 32 |
| Top 25 vodka sales, in millions | $1,301 | $4,641 |
| Top 25 percent share | 22 | 78 |

Source: *Adams Liquor Handbook 1999*, 34.

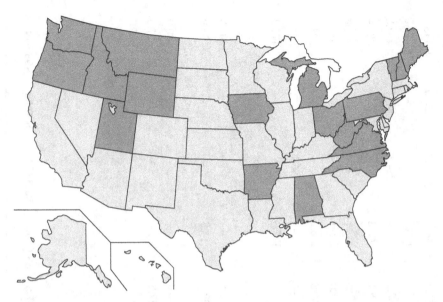

**Exhibit 9-6** Map of control (dark) and open (light) states

Source: Wikimedia Commons, http://en.wikipedia.org/wiki/File:US_States_by_alcohol_control.svg (accessed May 22, 2009).

**Exhibit 9-7** SVEDKA bottle with original logo

Source: SVEKDA.

**Exhibit 9-8** Total Advertising Expenditures for Vodka, 1997–1998 (In Thousands of Dollars)

| Brand | 1997 | | | | | 1998 | | | | |
|---|---|---|---|---|---|---|---|---|---|---|
| | Mag. | News. | Outdoor | B'cast | Total | Mag. | News. | Outdoor | B'cast | Total |
| Absolut | $27,013.9 | $201.7 | $515.7 | — | $27,731.3 | $27,617.0 | $308.2 | $1,420.4 | $161.9 | $29,507.5 |
| Smirnoff | 12,363.3 | 80.0 | 866.3 | — | 13,309.6 | 14,558.1 | 391.3 | 856.2 | 18.2 | 15,822.8 |
| Finlandia | 2,412.2 | 0.4 | 1.8 | — | 2,414.4 | 8,156.4 | 90.2 | 575.6 | 325.9 | 9,148.1 |
| Stolichnaya | 7,662.9 | 182.4 | — | — | 7,845.3 | 6,799.6 | 173.0 | — | — | 6,972.6 |
| Skyy | 3,816.8 | — | — | — | 3,816.8 | 3,259.7 | — | 224.1 | — | 3,483.8 |
| Belvedere | 116.2 | — | — | — | 116.2 | 518.1 | 863.3 | — | — | 1,381.4 |
| Grey Goose | — | — | — | — | — | — | 547.4 | — | — | 547.4 |
| Chopin | 60.3 | — | — | — | 69.3 | 274.9 | 242.1 | — | — | 517.0 |
| Argent | — | — | — | — | — | 58.2 | 236.2 | — | — | 294.4 |
| Taaka | — | — | 237.0 | — | 237.0 | — | — | 286.1 | — | 286.1 |
| Georgi | — | 156.7 | — | — | 156.7 | — | 177.3 | — | — | 177.3 |
| Fleischmann's Vodka | — | — | 137.5 | — | 137.5 | — | — | 167.4 | — | 167.4 |
| Gordon's Vodka | 2,471.8 | — | — | — | 2,471.8 | 105.8 | — | — | — | 105.8 |
| Stolichnaya Cristall | — | — | — | — | — | 82.1 | 14.8 | — | — | 96.9 |
| Rain Vodka | — | — | — | — | — | 30.0 | — | — | — | 30.0 |
| Iceberg | — | 35.6 | — | — | 35.6 | 27.3 | — | — | — | 27.3 |
| McCormick Vodka | — | — | 107.5 | — | 107.5 | — | — | 7.9 | — | 7.9 |
| Tanqueray Sterling | 2,007.8 | — | 299.1 | — | 2,306.9 | — | — | — | — | — |
| Wyborowa | — | 115.0 | — | — | 115.0 | — | — | — | — | — |
| Kremlyovskaya | 30.9 | — | — | — | 30.9 | — | — | — | — | — |
| Total Expenditure | $57,965.1 | $771.8 | $2,164.9 | — | $60,901.8 | $61,487.2 | $3,043.8 | $3,537.7 | $506.0 | $68,574.7 |

Sources: Competitive Media; *Adams Liquor Handbook 1999*, 136.

# SVEDKA Vodka (B)

SVEDKA had sold 25,000 cases by the end of 1998. Initial volume sales results, press coverage, and sales force feedback validated Guillaume Cuvelier's assessment of SVEDKA's market opportunity. Retailers and consumers responded to the product's value and appealing price. SVEDKA had identified and fulfilled a need for a high-quality imported vodka at a midlevel price point.

By 1999, SVEDKA was available in 15 of the states in its market. The number increased to 44 within three years, and, by 2003, the brand had achieved national distribution. Cuvelier told *BIN* magazine in December 2003: "As a marketer, it is most exciting for me to see the product so well displayed in store. A good product, well marketed, intrinsically translates to high volume."[21]

## The Results

In 2006, SVEDKA reached an important industry benchmark, selling one million cases. That same year, vodka was the largest growth category of any major international spirits sector.[22] According to a 2008 Information Resources, Inc., report, SVEDKA ranked fifth in the combined liquor, food, and drug categories for imported vodka (Table 9-3).[23]

**Table 9-3** Premium Imported Vodka for the 52-Week Period Ending March 23, 2008

| Rank | Brand | Sales | % Change $ versus YAG | Share of Category | 9L Case Volume | 9L Case Share |
|------|-------|-------|------------------------|-------------------|----------------|---------------|
| 1 | Absolut | $127,546,278 | 8.50% | 11.40% | 604,592 | 6.00% |
| 2 | Grey Goose | $78,157,569 | 16.70% | 7.00% | 234,779 | 2.30% |
| 3 | Ketel One | $60,311,956 | 1.60% | 5.40% | 259,929 | 2.60% |
| 4 | Stolichnaya | $54,773,915 | 7.60% | 4.90% | 302,678 | 3.00% |
| 5 | SVEDKA | $30,422,281 | 45.10% | 2.70% | 256,610 | 2.50% |
| 6 | Three Olives | $12,571,144 | 38.80% | 1.10% | 65,167 | 0.60% |
| 7 | Belvedere | $11,773,674 | 1.80% | 1.00% | 34,828 | 0.30% |
| 8 | Finlandia | $7,396,797 | −12.40% | 0.70% | 45,710 | 0.50% |

Notes: This data is useful for market shares but not for total volume or dollars sold; YAG = year ago.

Data source: Information Resources, Inc.

## The Product

Cuvelier believed that flavored vodka was a necessary step if the brand were to be viewed as a major force in the category, even if the standard vodka contributed to the majority of sales. After focus group testing, SVEDKA extended its brand, offering citron, clementine, raspberry, and vanilla flavors in 2003 and 2004. In the summer of 2009, a cherry flavor was added. These flavored versions were 37.5% alcohol, or 75 proof, whereas standard vodka was 40% alcohol, or 80 proof. All flavor varieties were priced the same as the regular vodka. Around the same time, the 200ml and 375ml sizes were introduced. And in 2008, SVEDKA tweaked the bottle design. (Exhibit 9-9 depicts the newer packaging and various flavors.)

SVEDKA continued to receive favorable product reviews, which added to the credibility it had established with the high *Wine Enthusiast* marks. For example, *F. Paul Pacult's Spirit Journal* gave SVEDKA four stars, deeming it "an outstanding value."[24] The brand won numerous awards, such as the gold medal at both the 2002 International Wine and Spirit Competition and the 2003 World Spirit Competition.

## Distribution

Cuvelier attributed much of the brand's success to his focus on distribution in the early years. "SVEDKA has essentially emerged from a core independent retail network," he said. "They have made the brand what it is today."[25] After a few years of making inroads in the off-premise channel, it became clear that SVEDKA needed a presence in the bars and restaurants as well. By 2004, Cuvelier wanted his team to focus on trendy bars where the opinion leaders decided on the next hip brand. Given SVEDKA's limited resources, this initiative targeted select accounts in key urban markets such as New York and Los Angeles, where the brand was sampled, promoted, and featured consistently.

Each year, more high-profile restaurants and clubs were added, including Starwood Hotels and Resorts Worldwide, including its trendy W luxury hotel chain, and Ruth's Chris Steak House. These were important wins for the brand. A bar's willingness to carry the product validated that SVEDKA had generated enough consumer knowledge and pull.

## The Brand

When SVEDKA hit the shelves, Cuvelier wanted to ensure that the product created an emotional connection beyond the vodka itself, a phenomenon similar to

Absolut's. During a SVEDKA corporate presentation, he said that "SVEDKA had to mean more than a product to its core audience. It was an experience, a lifestyle, and above all a fun brand."

Unlike other brands, which looked to the past for justification, Cuvelier wanted SVEDKA to suggest the future, the language of its core target. (See Exhibit 9-10 for SVEDKA's assessment of competitors' marketing campaigns from 2007–2008.) Absolut marketed its bottle silhouette in its advertisements, and other competitors such as Stoli used the heritage angle. Cuvelier believed the "tradition" message didn't make much sense for the category. Vodka, unlike other spirits such as Cognac, was not aged, so the tradition would not play an important part in the purchaser's decision.

SVEDKA's positioning as a high-quality imported vodka at an affordable price, to be enjoyed while having fun with friends, focused on the end benefits of vodka rather than telling a story about the vodka itself. SVEDKA promoted itself as both a rational and aspirational product, and Cuvelier wanted his vodka to be equated with the festive social occasions during which consumers would enjoy it.

The first step in communicating the brand was explaining it to the internal team. The sales team was trained on the product's core promises, brand attributes, and competitive positioning. Words such as *freedom, fresh thinking,* and *flirtatious* were used in presentations to describe the brand's essence. The SVEDKA consumer was described internally as a sophisticated, "casual-cool," iconoclastic, and authentic person. Above all, the brand strategy—a light-on-the-wallet yet high-quality vodka—was reinforced.[26]

### Trade Campaign (1998–2002)

In keeping with the brand's origin, the first campaign featured two young, Nordic-looking blond women, "the SVEDKA sisters," who urged consumers to "try something Swedish tonight." (See Exhibits 9-11 and 9-12 for examples of sales collateral and a tent card from this campaign.) The very first target audience was the trade, specifically the wholesalers' salespeople, most of whom were middle-age males working on commission. The goal was not only to get their attention but also to show that the brand was spending money to promote the launch in bars and stores. Given the limited budget, the campaign had to feel bigger than it really was, hence a provocative message supported with numerous point-of-sale materials. In 2000, the marketing budget of less than $350,000 covered the posters, logo roll banners, table tents, T-shirts, case cards, and shelf talkers. Each year thereafter, additional funds were allocated to support more media, public relations, and promotions.

In 2001, Cuvelier began working with a small marketing firm to execute promotions, bar nights, and sampling events. The marketing budget had more than tripled from 2000; since 1998, resources had been allocated to selling and developing the distribution network. SVEDKA models gave free Swedish massages to drum up interest in trying the product; that way, the consumer could actually experience the provocative and fun nature of SVEDKA. A limited radio buy supported the efforts in targeted local markets; however, Cuvelier spent most of the $500,000 budget to run 15 bar nights per month in three select markets.[27] The 2002 media spend was more than 100% above the previous year's. The entire SVEDKA marketing budget was up more than 30%.

### National Campaign 1: PR (2003)

As sales grew, Cuvelier faced a common marketing dilemma: how to bring his brand mainstream without alienating his initial customer base. He wanted to maintain SVEDKA's brand equity and integrity but also become known to the masses. "We think we can remain provocative and fun, but still speak to a broader group," Cuvelier told the *Wall Street Journal* in September 2005.[28] Image-conscious 21-to-30-year-old consumers remained the core audience. The answer would be to speak loud and clear in a different way. In the fall of 2003, Cuvelier was ready to take risks, invest more dollars in marketing, and introduce the brand's first national campaign. The objective was to get noticed by opinion leaders. SVEDKA relied on making noise with its ads to put itself on the map.

Marina Hahn was brought in as marketing director and applied her years of experience of building brands at Pepsi and Sony to managing SVEDKA's advertising campaign. Themed "Adult Entertainment," the ads featured such images as a nude, goose-bumped woman holding a shot glass between her breasts as someone splashes vodka into it and down her torso.[29] SVEDKA won *Impact* magazine's 2003 Hot Brand Award. SVEDKA became a brand regularly mentioned in *People, US Weekly,* and the *New York Post* as the vodka of choice among the young celebrity crowd.

### National Campaign 2: Advertising (2005)

To many, SVEDKA was known for its 2005 advertising campaign, created by the New York-based agency Amalgamated. Building on the PR campaign, marketing wanted to push things even further. SVEDKA_Grl was introduced as the futuristic and provocative mascot (Exhibit 9-13). Her sexy image appeared on the website and in advertising and buzz marketing pieces. The brand rallying cry "Voted #1 Vodka in 2033" was used in the ads to offer social commentary on hot topics of the day. SVEDKA_Grl set her own rules and delivered tongue-in-cheek messages on current events such as stem cell research and smoking bans. She appeared on billboards, bus shelters, and wallscapes in key markets such as New York, Chicago, San Francisco, and Boston.

Once again, the press responded. This time, industry associations weighed in as well. SVEDKA's ads twice drew censure from the Distilled Spirits Council (DISCUS) for using sex to sell alcohol. Although the industry's self-regulating body didn't impose a fine or require that ads be pulled, all major liquor companies that were DISCUS members voluntarily pulled or altered censured ads. SVEDKA was not a DISCUS member and did not retreat from its ad strategy. "We're not talking about Pampers here," Hahn told the *Wall Street Journal*. "We're talking about vodka."[30] SVEDKA's growth rates accelerated from 35% to 40% to 60%. Perhaps just as important as the sales results, the campaign brought life and awareness to the brand. SVEDKA had a clear personality that consumers recognized across all the marketing vehicles.

## Competition

While SVEDKA was growing, so was the number of vodkas in the market. In 2003–2004, other brands began to follow SVEDKA's strategy, updating their angles to reflect the hip, cool, and social target consumer. "This was an indicator that we had been successful," Cuvelier said. In 2005, 761 different vodka stock-keeping units (SKUs) were for sale, an increase of almost 56% from 2000, according to DISCUS.[31] The new additions reflected the trends of the times. Organic vodkas and energy vodkas entered the market in 2007.[32] Celebrity endorsements emerged as an important seal of approval: In 2007, Sean "Diddy" Combs agreed to become the spokesperson for Cîroc, which had been introduced in 2003.

The market's dynamics were changing. (Refer to Exhibit 9-14 for sales figures.) Industry data pointed to the fact that Absolut was slowing down, while Grey Goose was gaining ground.[33] Trying to protect its share of top-shelf sales, in 2004 Absolut introduced Level.[34] One thing that was increasing for the majority of brands (2005–2007) was ad spend. The top three competitors outspent SVEDKA by as much as 7 to 1 (Exhibits 9-15 and 9-16).

# Exhibits

**Exhibit 9-9** Flavor extensions and new packaging (2009)
Source: SVEDKA.

**Exhibit 9-10** Competitive Review (2007–2008)

| Brand | Positioning | Ad Strategy |
| --- | --- | --- |
| Absolut | Ideal world is Absolut world | Flavor and special-release products |
| | | Regain solidarity in category it defined |
| | | Product placements (*Sex and the City*) |
| Belvedere | Luxury | New in October 2007 |
| | | Happenstance led to product placements |
| Grey Goose | Elitist brand | Lifestyle-focused on finer things in life |
| | Best-tasting message | 35–45 audience |
| Ketel One | Club of drinkers | Clever copy |
| | | "Thank you for your support" message |
| | | Word of mouth spread the brand |
| Skyy | Ultra-hip | Lifestyle-focused |
| Smirnoff | Mixability of flavors | *New York Times* taste test |
| | Benefit oriented | Super Me |
| | Smirnoff Ice advantage | Younger male target audience |
| Stolichnaya | Authentic Russian heritage | First name in flavor |
| | Aspirational | Younger male target audience |

Sources: DISCUS, December 2007; TNS Media Intelligence, 2008.

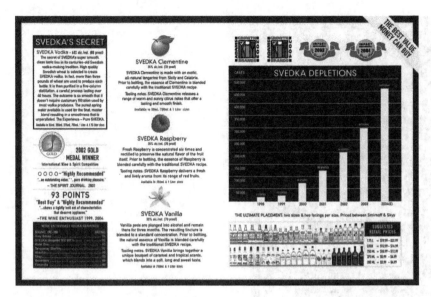

**Exhibit 9-11** Sales collateral (2004)

Source: SVEDKA.

**Exhibit 9-12** Trade campaign (2000–2002)

Source: SVEDKA.

**Exhibit 9-13** Print advertisement (2008)

Source: SVEDKA.

**Exhibit 9-14** Leading Brands of Vodka, 2002–2007 (In Thousands of 9L Cases)

| Brand | Origin | Supplier | 2002 | 2003 | 2004 | 2005 | 2006 | 2007 |
|---|---|---|---|---|---|---|---|---|
| Absolut | Sweden | Absolut Spirits Co. | 4,475 | 4,488 | 4,640 | 4,636 | 4,847 | 5,013 |
| Grey Goose | France | Bacardi USA | 1,150 | 1,400 | 1,650 | 2,075 | 2,660 | 3,325 |
| Stolichnaya | Russia | Pernod Ricard USA | 1,640 | 1,855 | 1,935 | 1,985 | 2,090 | 2,185 |
| Ketel One | Netherlands | Nolet Spirits USA | 1,054 | 1,243 | 1,438 | 1,593 | 1,753 | 1,858 |
| SVEDKA | Sweden | Constellation Spirits Marque One | 200 | 306 | 448 | 640 | 1,023 | 1,526 |
| Three Olives | United Kingdom | Proximo Spirits | 85 | 175 | 350 | 475 | 630 | 850 |

| Brand | Origin | Supplier | 2002 | 2003 | 2004 | 2005 | 2006 | 2007 |
|---|---|---|---|---|---|---|---|---|
| Belvedere Vodka | Poland | Moët Hennessy USA | 306 | 339 | 369 | 365 | 381 | 410 |
| Finlandia | Finland | Brown-Forman Beverages | 319 | 327 | 357 | 375 | 381 | 362 |

Source: *Adams Liquor Handbook 2003*, 145.

**Exhibit 9-15** Advertising Spend, 2005–2007 (Dollars in Thousands)

| Brand | 2005 Dollars | 2006 Dollars | 2007 Dollars |
|---|---|---|---|
| Absolut | $18,651.6 | $26,000.5 | $24,836.4 |
| Grey Goose | 26,931.2 | 18,878.6 | 21,809.6 |
| Ketel One | 17,892.4 | 22,608.5 | 24,171.0 |
| Imperia | 0.0 | 1,140.3 | 3,269.8 |
| Level | 9,711.0 | 8,032.6 | 4,987.4 |
| Russian Standard | 11.3 | 0.0 | 4,767.0 |
| Skyy | 12,028.9 | 11,801.0 | 14,919.0 |
| Smirnoff | 10,995.2 | 8,972.2 | 11,357.8 |
| Stolichnaya | 7,272.3 | 5,532.1 | 11,287.2 |
| SVEDKA | 730.9 | 1,614.6 | 4,209.6 |
| Three Olives | 4,668.7 | 7,106.6 | 11,385.5 |
| **Total** | **$108,893.5** | **$111,687.0** | **$137,000.3** |

Sources: SVEDKA; TNS Media Intelligence report.

**Exhibit 9-16** Media Spend (Dollars in Thousands)

| Brand | 2006 Media Spend | Depletions | Media Investment per Case Depletion | Spend Ratio versus SVEDKA |
|---|---|---|---|---|
| Absolut | $26,068 | 4,900 | $5.32 | 3 to 1 |
| Grey Goose | $19,539 | 2,660 | $7.35 | 5 to 1 |
| Ketel One | $22,609 | 1,755 | $12.88 | 8 to 1 |
| Skyy | $12,032 | 2,275 | $5.29 | 3 to 1 |
| Smirnoff | $19,630 | 8,865 | $2.21 | 2 to 1 |
| Stolichnaya | $7,354 | 2,100 | $3.50 | 2 to 1 |
| **SVEDKA** | **$1,600** | **1,037** | **$1.54** | |
| Three Olives | $7,107 | 630 | $11.28 | 7 to 1 |

Sources: SVEDKA; CMR Strategy.

# SVEDKA Vodka (C): Marketing Mix in the Vodka Industry

Associated with sophistication ever since James Bond first ordered a vodka martini "shaken, not stirred," vodka enjoyed tremendous success over the decades leading up to SVEDKA's debut. The vodka-enthusiast women of the hit HBO series *Sex and the City* provided renewed energy for vodka in early 2000, just as the more-than-40-year bump Mr. Bond had provided was losing its luster. In 2007, Smirnoff was the highest-selling spirit brand worldwide (25.7 million cases) and in the United States (9 million cases). U.S. vodka sales topped $7 billion in 2007, and two spots in the top five spirit brands worldwide belonged to vodka brands Smirnoff and Absolut.[35]

## Product

Between 2000 and 2007, the number of vodka brands increased from 14 to 26. Flavors and packaging were the more popular product variations introduced. Absolut was the first to introduce flavored vodka in 1986, using three types of peppers. The company called it Absolut Peppar (peh-PAR) and proclaimed it to be perfect for a Bloody Mary. Smirnoff and Absolut introduced the most flavors, and by 2007, Smirnoff's product line included 20 different flavors while Absolut had more than 10. Innovative packaging evolved, starting with Absolut's recognizable shape, inspired by a vintage Swedish apothecary bottle. By 2011, brands such as Vox and Cîroc were bottled in elegant frosted glass.

## Price

In 1997, Grey Goose invented the superpremium category, marketing a 750ml bottle of vodka priced above $30. Vodka retail prices varied across states because of taxes and the regulation of distributors. The wholesale price of a 9L cases of vodka was above $200 for the superpremium brands such as Chopin, Belvedere, Grey Goose, and Level, whereas the prices of some value brands such as Aristocrat, McCormick, Barton, and Crystal Palace were below $35 per 9L case.[36]

## Advertising

By 2007, the industry had spent more than $200 million on advertising through various channels, including outdoor, magazine, newspaper, and television.

TV advertising of alcoholic drinks had been controversial; indeed, for 48 years liquor producers had chosen not to air commercials. In 1996, Seagram broke that trend with network spots promoting Crown Royal and Lime Twisted Gin. In spite of the public outcry that arose, other liquor brands slowly started testing cable TV spots. Eventually, cable television came to be seen as the most suitable venue for liquor advertising.

The print ads for vodka were very sophisticated. In 1980, Absolut began featuring its bottle's distinct silhouette, a practice it continued for more than two decades. Its innovative campaign prompted an account rep at TBWA, Absolut's ad agency, to write a book in 1996 about its print campaign.

Grey Goose won the Beverage Tasting Institute award for "best-tasting vodka" in 1998 and used the title in a series of successful print campaigns in the *Wall Street Journal* and other high-end publications. In the same year, *Sex and the City* characters started asking for a "Grey Goose cosmopolitan," which extended the brand's recognition and superpremium image.

### Distribution

In 1919, a constitutional amendment banned the manufacture, sale, and transporting of alcohol in the United States. With the repeal of Prohibition in 1933, U.S. alcohol distribution was highly regulated via a three-tier system that restricted producers from direct distribution of alcohol. Producers were required to supply distributors, who then supplied retailers; consumers could purchase alcohol only from the retailers. Some states, called control states, had a monopoly over the wholesaling and/or retailing of some or all categories of alcohol. In those states, consumers could obtain alcohol only from state-run Alcohol Beverage Control stores. By 2011, there were 19 control states.

The marketing-mix model for vodka was therefore focused on balancing product line, price, and advertising decisions. Temporary price reductions were generally not allowed by the U.S. government. Further, distribution was not under alcohol producers' control.

## Conclusion: Marketing-Mix Model

SVEDKA founder Guillaume Cuvelier considered looking into historic U.S. vodka sales to evaluate the effect of new flavors, segment membership, and advertising. Consumer reactions to vodka advertising and pricing probably differed among the superpremium, premium, and value segments. New brand entries also may have had different price and advertising elasticities compared with the established brands. Finally, new flavors could have had a direct effect on vodka sales. Cuvelier wondered if he could quantify the financial value of his product's *Wine Enthusiast* certification and 2002 and 2003 gold medals. Understanding the value generated by each of the three campaigns from 1998 through 2005 would provide a good basis for the design of future campaigns. And identifying brands that directly competed with SVEDKA would allow Cuvelier to effectively allocate marketing resources. Cuvelier wanted to use historic vodka brand sales to inform his product's price and advertising budget.

# Endnotes

1. Case writer interview with Guillaume Cuvelier, October 13, 2008; unless otherwise indicated, all subsequent attributions derive from this interview.

2. Corby Kummer, "Flavorless No More," *Atlantic Monthly*, December 2004.

3. William Grimes, "Summer Places: The Super Vodkas," *New York Times*, June 2, 1991.

4. Kummer.

5. *Adams Liquor Handbook 1999* (New York: Adams Business Media), 122.

6. Theresa Howard, "Absolut Puts a New Premium on Vodka," *USA Today*, March 30, 2004.

7. Noah Rothbaum, *The Business of Spirits: How Savvy Marketers, Innovative Distillers, and Entrepreneurs Changed How We Drink* (New York: Kaplan Publishing, 2007), 46.

8. Adams Business Media. Note: Grey Goose received a 96 on the Beverage Testing Institute's well-regarded 100-point scale from the Beverage Testing Institute.

9. *Adams Liquor Handbook 1999*, 132.

10. Rothbaum, 45.

11. Jim Rendon, "Want to Profit From Vodka?" *New York Times*, October 31, 2004.

12. "Best Buy," *Wine Enthusiast*, 1999.

13. M. Shanken Communications, "Distilled Spirits Study," *Impact*, 2000.

14. *Industry Surveys: Alcoholic Beverages & Tobacco*, Standard & Poor's 166, no. 10 (March 5, 1998): 8.

15. Rothbaum, 163.

16. SVEDKA corporate presentation.

17. *Adams Liquor Handbook 1999*, 135.

18. SVEDKA corporate presentation.

19. *Adams Liquor Handbook 1999*, 227.

20. *Wine Enthusiast* ratings, 1999, 2004, and 2007.

21. "High Spirits: The Rise of SVEDKA," *BIN*, December 2003.

22. "Vodka Meets with Growing Global Appeal," *International Wine and Spirit Record*, September 2007, 6.

23. Information Resources, Inc., "52-Week Report Ending March 23, 2008, for U.S. Food, Drug, & Liquor, Vodka." Drugstores came last because it was much harder to gain distribution in that category. Even at this stage, SVEDKA was still pushing to get full distribution in this channel; that was why SVEDKA's ranking was not so high.

24. F. Paul Pacult, "SVEDKA Vodka," *F. Paul Pacult's Spirit Journal*, March 2000.

25. Case writer interview with Guillaume Cuvelier, October 13, 2008.

26. SVEDKA corporate presentation, April 9, 2001.

27. SVEDKA corporate presentation.

28. Deborah Ball, "SVEDKA Hopes to Broaden Its Edgy Appeal," *Wall Street Journal*, September 7, 2005.

29. Ken Magill, "SVEDKA Pours It On," *New York Sun*, January 5, 2004.

30. Ball.

31. Noah Rothbaum, *The Business of Spirits: How Savvy Marketers, Innovative Distillers, and Entrepreneurs Changed How We Drink* (New York: Kaplan Publishing, 2007), 43.

32. Eric Felten, "Make Mine a 020001," *Wall Street Journal*, September 1, 2007.

33. "Growth in Vodka," *Impact*, 2006.

34. Theresa Howard, "Absolut Puts a New Premium on Vodka," *USA Today*, March 30, 2004.

35. *Drinks International*, "Millionaires Club Supplement," July 2009.

36. *Adams Liquor Handbook*, 2007.

# Assignment Questions

1. What gave Cuvelier the idea that there was a market for $10.00 vodka?

2. Are there brands you can point to that have used strategies similar to those employed by SVEDKA?

3. What is the brand positioning statement that might guide integrated marketing communications? How has the positioning evolved over time? Where is it headed?

4. What advice would you give Cuvelier for SVEDKA's rollout strategy?

5. Which elements of his total marketing strategy is he relying on for success in this market?

Use the vodka industry data set to evaluate the effect of price and advertising on sales by answering the following:

6. Run a regression of the natural logarithm of change in sales on the natural logarithm of previous period's prices, and the natural log of marketing expenditures on print, outdoor, and broadcasting.

7. To understand the influence of vodka quality, run a regression by adding the tier 1 and tier 2 dummy variables (that indicate whether a vodka brand belongs to first- or second-quality tiers) to the set of independent variables in question 6.

8. To understand the influence of competition and brand power, run a regression by adding the sum of sales of all the competing brands in the previous year ("lagtotalminussales") to the independent variables in question 7.

9. To measure the sales growth of new brands compared with the existent ones, include the variable "firstintro" to the independent variable set in question 8. "Firstintro" is equal to one in the first three years after a brand is introduced and is zero elsewhere.

10. Why does the coefficient of price and advertising change in the above regressions?

11. Based on your analysis of the Vodka data, what recommendations do you have for Cuvelier regarding the marketing mix for SVEDKA?

# Section IV

## Customer Analytics

In this section, customer lifetime value (CLV) is presented as the integrating metric for customer management. Chapter 10, "Customer Lifetime Value," discusses customer profitability, and Chapter 11, "Netflix: The Customer Strikes Back," defines CLV for a subscription business and connects it to business models and market capitalization. Chapter 12, "Retail Relay," connects CLV to investments in customer acquisition activities. In contrast to Netflix, Retail Relay allows you to calculate CLV in a noncontractual setting. It provides you the opportunity to evaluate multiple customer acquisition activities based on results from pilot studies.

Chapter 13, "Logistic Regression," exposes you to logistic regression to predict customer churn and Chapter 14, "Retail Relay Revisited," allows you to implement logistic regression for predicting churn in Retail Relay.

# 10

## Customer Lifetime Value

## Introduction

As Don Peppers and Martha Rogers are fond of saying, "Some customers are more equal than others."[1] One way to examine these differences is through *customer profit (CP)*, the difference between the revenues and the costs associated with the customer relationship during a specified period. The central difference between CP and customer lifetime value (CLV) is that CP measures the past and CLV looks forward. As such, CLV can be more useful in shaping managers' decisions but is much more difficult to quantify. Quantifying CP is a matter of carefully reporting and summarizing the results of past activity, whereas quantifying CLV involves forecasting future activity.

## Customer Lifetime Value: The Present Value of the Future Cash Flows Attributed to the Customer Relationship

The concept of CLV is nothing more than the concept of present value applied to the cash flows of the customer relationship. The present value of any stream of future cash flows is designed to measure the single lump-sum value, today, of those future cash flows. CLV represents the single lump-sum value, today, of the customer relationship. Even more simply, CLV is the dollar value of the customer relationship to the firm. It is an upper bound on what the firm would be willing to pay to acquire the customer relationship as well as an upper bound on the amount the firm would be willing to pay to avoid losing the customer relationship. If you view a customer relationship as an asset of the firm, CLV would represent the dollar value of that asset.

## Cohort and Incubate

One way to project the value of future customer cash flows is to make the heroic assumption that the customers acquired several periods ago are no better or worse (in terms of their CLV) than the ones currently acquired. You then go back and collect data on a cohort of customers, all acquired at about the same time, and carefully reconstruct their cash flows over some finite number of periods. The next steps are to discount the cash flow for each customer back to the time of acquisition, to calculate the sample customers' CLVs, and then to average all sample CLVs together to produce an estimate of the CLV of each newly acquired customer. This method is referred to as the "cohort-and-incubate" approach. Equivalently, you can calculate the present value of the *total* cash flow from the cohort and divide by the number of customers to get the average CLV for the cohort. If the value of customer relationships is stable across time, the average CLV of the cohort sample is an appropriate estimator of the CLV of newly acquired customers.

As an example of this cohort-and-incubate approach, Berger, Weinberg, and Hanna (2003) followed all the customers acquired by a cruise-ship line in 1993. The 6,094 customers in the cohort of 1993 were tracked (incubated) for five years. The total net present value of the cash flows from these customers was $27,916,614. These flows included revenue from the cruises taken (the 6,094 customers took 8,660 cruises over the five-year horizon), variable cost of the cruises, and promotional costs. The total five-year net present value of the cohort expressed on a per-customer basis came out to be $27,916,614 ÷ 6,094, or $4,581 per customer. This is the average five-year CLV for the cohort. Berger, Weinberg and Hanna (2003) state in their study that

> "Prior to this analysis, [cruise-line] management would never spend more than $3,314 to acquire a passenger...Now, aware of CLV (both the concept and the actual numerical results), an advertisement that [resulted in a cost per acquisition of $3,000 to $4,000] was welcomed—especially since the CLV numbers are conservative (again, as noted, the CLV does not include any residual business after five years)."[2]

The cohort-and-incubate approach works well when customer relationships are stationary—changing slowly over time. When the value of relationships changes slowly, a company can use the value of incubated past relationships as predictive of the value of new relationships.

In situations where the value of customer relationships changes more rapidly, firms often use a simple model to forecast the value of those relationships. A model just means some assumptions about how the customer relationship will unfold.

Next, this chapter explains what is perhaps the simplest model for future customer cash flows and the equation for the present value of those expected cash flows. Although not the only model of future customer cash flows, this one is used the most.

## Customer Lifetime Value Model

The CLV formula[3] multiplies the per-period cash margin, $M$, by a long-term multiplier that represents the present value of the customer relationship's expected length:

$$CLV = \$M \left[ \frac{r}{1+d-r} \right]$$

where $r$ is the per-period retention rate and $d$ is the per-period discount rate.

So, in the model, CLV is a multiple of $M$, the per-period dollar margin (net of retention spending). The multiplicative factor represents the present value of the expected length (number of periods) of the customer relationship. When $r = 0$, the customer will never be retained and the multiplicative factor is zero. When $r = 1$, the customer is always retained and the firm receives $M$ in perpetuity. The present value of the $M$ in perpetuity turns out to be $M \div d$. For retention values in between, the CLV formula tells us the appropriate multiplier.

*Example:* An Internet service provider charges $19.95 per month. Variable costs are about $1.50 per account per month. With marketing spending of $6 per year, the company's attrition is only 0.5% per month. At a monthly discount rate of 1%, what is the CLV of a customer?

$M = (\$19.95 - \$1.50 - [\$6 \div 12])$

$= \$17.95$

$r = 0.995$

$d = 0.01$

$CLV = \$M \times (r \div [1 + d - r])$

$CLV = \$17.95 \times (0.995 \div [1 + 0.01 - 0.995])$

$CLV = (\$17.95) \times (66.33)$

$CLV = \$1,191$

## Limitations of the CLV Model

The model for customer cash flows treats the firm's customer relationships as something of a leaky bucket. In each period, a fraction (one less the retention rate) of the firm's customers leaves and is lost for good.

The CLV model has only three parameters: (1) constant margin (contribution after deducting variable costs including retention spending) per period, (2) constant retention probability per period, and (3) discount rate. Furthermore, the model assumes that in the event the customer is not retained, he or she is lost for good. Finally, the model assumes the first margin will be received (with probability equal to the retention rate) at the *end* of the first period.

One other assumption of the model is that the firm uses an infinite horizon when it calculates the present value of future cash flows. Although no firm actually has an infinite horizon, the consequences of assuming one are discussed in the following section.

The retention rate—and by extension the attrition rate—are drivers of CLV. Very small changes can make a major difference to the lifetime value calculated. Accuracy in this parameter is vital to meaningful results.

The retention rate is assumed to be constant across the life of the customer relationship. For products and services that go through a trial, conversion, and loyalty progression, retention rates will increase over the lifetime of the relationship. In those situations, the model given here might be too simple. If the firm wants to utilize a sequence of retention rates, a spreadsheet model can be used to calculate CLV.

The contribution is assumed to be constant across time. If the margin is expected to increase or decrease with the duration of the customer relationship, the simple model will not apply.

Take care not to use this CLV formula for relationships in which customer inactivity does not signal the end of the relationship. In catalogs, for example, a small percentage of the firm's customers purchase from any given catalog. Don't confuse the percentage of customers active in a given period (relevant for the cataloger) with the retention rates in this model. If customers often return to do business with the firm after a period of inactivity, the previous CLV formula does not apply.

Also take care to match the period of the model to the period of the retention events. If retention happens monthly, for example, then use a monthly model. If retention happens every six months (as for auto insurance), then use a biannual model. If cash flows are spread out within the retention period, then use their present value in the CLV formula.

## The Infinite Horizon Assumption

In some industries and companies, it is typical to calculate four- or five-year customer values instead of using the infinite time horizon inherent in the previous formula. Of course, over shorter periods, customer retention rates are less likely to be affected by major shifts in technology or competitive strategies and are more likely to be captured by historical retention rates. For managers, the question is, "Does it make a difference whether I use the infinite time horizon or, for example, the five-year customer value?" The answer to this question is, "Yes, sometimes it can make a difference because the value over five years can be less than 70% of the value over an infinite horizon."

Table 10-1 calculates the percentages of (infinite-horizon) CLV accruing in the first five years. If retention rates are higher than 80% and discount rates are lower than 20%, differences in the two approaches will be substantial. Depending on the strategic risks that companies perceive, the additional complexities of using a finite horizon may be informative.

**Table 10-1** Five-Year CLV as a Percentage of Infinite-Horizon CLV

| | Year | | | | | |
|---|---|---|---|---|---|---|
| | 1 | 2 | 3 | 4 | 5 | 6 |
| | Retention Rate | | | | | |
| | 40% | 50% | 60% | 70% | 80% | 90% |
| Discount Rate | Percent of CLV Accruing | | | | | |
| 2% | 99% | 97% | 93% | 85% | 70% | 47% |
| 4% | 99% | 97% | 94% | 86% | 73% | 51% |
| 6% | 99% | 98% | 94% | 87% | 76% | 56% |
| 8% | 99% | 98% | 95% | 89% | 78% | 60% |
| 10% | 99% | 98% | 95% | 90% | 80% | 63% |
| 12% | 99% | 98% | 96% | 90% | 81% | 66% |
| 14% | 99% | 98% | 96% | 91% | 83% | 69% |
| 16% | 100% | 99% | 96% | 92% | 84% | 72% |
| 18% | 100% | 99% | 97% | 93% | 86% | 74% |
| 20% | 100% | 99% | 97% | 93% | 87% | 76% |

## CLV with Initial Margin

If you consult other sources on CLV, you may encounter a slightly different formula for CLV:

$$CLV_{alternative} = \$M\left[\frac{1+d}{1+d-r}\right]$$

This alternative formula applies to a situation in which the initial cash flow is a certain $\$M$ received at the *beginning* of the first period. Because of this, this alternative formula always comes out to be $\$M$ higher than the original formula. It represents the value of the customer if and when acquired.

## Prospect Lifetime Value

One of the major uses of CLV is to inform prospecting decisions. A prospect is someone the firm will spend money on in an attempt to acquire him or her as a customer. The acquisition spending must be compared not just with the contribution from the immediate sales it generates, but also with the future cash flows expected from the newly acquired customer relationship (the CLV). Only with a full accounting of the value of the newly acquired customer relationship will the firm be able to make informed, economic-prospecting decisions.

The expected prospect lifetime value (PLV) will be the value expected from each prospect minus the cost of prospecting. The value expected from each prospect will be $a$—the expected fraction of prospects who will make a purchase and become customers—times ($\$M_0$ + CLV), where $\$M_0$ is the average margin the firm makes on the initial purchases net of any marketing spending used to attempt to retain the customer at the end of the first period. The cost will be $\$A$, the amount of acquisition spending per prospect. The formula for expected *PLV* is as follows:

$$PLV = a(\$M_0 + CLV) - \$A$$

If *PLV* is positive, the acquisition spending is a wise investment. If *PLV* is negative, the acquisition spending should not be made.

The *PLV* number will usually be very small. While *CLV* is sometimes in the hundreds of dollars, *PLV* can come out to be only a few pennies. Just remember that *PLV* applies to prospects, not customers. A large number of small- but positive-value prospects can add to a considerable amount of value for a firm.

*Example:* A service company plans to spend $60,000 on an advertisement reaching 75,000 readers. If the service company expects the advertisement to convince 1.2% of the readers to take advantage of a special introductory offer (priced so low that the firm makes a $10 margin on this initial purchase) and the CLV of the acquired customers is $100, is the advertisement economically attractive?

Here, $A is $0.80, a is 0.012, and $M_0$ is $10. The *PLV* of each of the 75,000 prospects is

$$PLV = a(\$M_0 + CLV) - \$A$$

$$= 0.012 \times (\$10 + \$100) - \$0.80$$

$$= \$0.52$$

The expected lifetime value of a prospect is $0.52. The total expected value of the prospecting effort will be 75,000 × $0.52 = $39,000. The proposed acquisition spending *is* economically attractive.

If you are uncertain about the 0.012 acquisition rate, you might ask what the response rate from the prospecting campaign must be in order for it to be economically successful. You can get that number using Excel's Goal Seek function to find the *a* value that sets *PLV* to zero. Or you can use a little algebra and substitute $0 in for *PLV* and solve for *a*:

$$a_{be} = \frac{\$A}{\$M_0 + CLV}$$

$$= \$0.80 \div (\$10 + \$100)$$

$$= 0.007273$$

The acquisition rate must exceed 0.7273% for the campaign to break even on an NPV basis.

## Issues with PLV

Perhaps the biggest challenge in calculating PLV is estimating the CLV. The other terms (acquisition spending, expected acquisition rates, and initial margin) all refer to flows or outcomes in the near future, whereas CLV requires longer-term projections.

Another caution worth mentioning is the decision to spend money on customer acquisition whenever PLV is positive. This rests on an assumption that the customers acquired would not have been acquired had the firm not spent the money. In other words, this approach gives the acquisition spending "full credit" for the subsequent customers acquired. If the firm has several simultaneous acquisition efforts, for example, dropping one of them might lead to increased acquisition rates for the others. Situations such as these (where one solicitation cannibalizes another) require a more complicated analysis.

The firm must be careful to search for the most economical way of acquiring new customers. If there are alternative prospecting approaches, the firm must be careful not to simply go with the first one that gives a positive projected PLV. Given a limited number of prospects, the approach that gives the highest expected PLV should be used.

Finally, you should be warned that there are other ways to perform the calculations necessary to judge the economic viability of a given prospecting effort. Although these other approaches are equivalent to the one presented here, they differ with respect to what is included in CLV.

Some approaches include the initial margin as part of CLV. For the service company example, this approach would say that the CLV is $110.

Another common approach includes both the initial margin and the expected acquisition cost per acquired customer as part of the CLV. For the service company example, this CLV equals $110 - ($60,000 \div 900) = $43.33$. Here, 900 is the expected number of new customers and $60,000 \div 900$ is the expected cost per new customer. The $43.33 is the expected value of the prospecting effort expressed on a per-customer-acquired basis. If this CLV is positive, the prospecting effort is economically attractive.

Notice that $43.33 times the 900 expected new customers equals $39,000, the same total net value from the campaign calculated in the original example. The two ways to do the calculations are equivalent.

# Retention and Customer Lifetime Value

Reichheld and Sasser (1990)[4] helped popularize the idea that customer retention is an important driver of firm financial success. They reported that "reducing defections by 5% boosts profits 25% to 85%."[5] Rather than rely on the Reichheld and Sasser percentages, you can use three approaches for quantifying the economic benefits of increased retention for a given firm.[6]

In the first approach, the firm might build an electronic spreadsheet model to forecast future company profits and cash flows as a function of a retention rate or schedule of retention rates. You could then change the retention rate or schedule of retention rates and observe what happens to profits and cash flows. These "what-if" analyses conducted using a spreadsheet model are one way to quantify the benefits of increased retention. If the firm thought, for example, that increased retention would reduce the need for future acquisition spending, that linkage could be built in to the model and captured in the what-if analyses.

The second and third approaches ask how increased retention affects the lifetime value of the customer. Whereas the preceding firm-level spreadsheet approach projects the future stream of company profits and cash flows, CLV accounts for the dollar value of the future cash flows attributed to the customer—either a single customer or (more than likely) an average customer.

In the second approach, the firm might build an electronic spreadsheet model of future cash flows associated with the customer relationship. That model might allow for margins and retention rates to increase with customer tenure. The present value of the projected future cash flows would be the estimated CLV. To quantify the economic benefits of increased retention, once again the firm could conduct what-if sensitivities using the model of customer cash flows. For example, you might multiply the schedule of retention rates by 1.01 and recalculate the CLV. The resulting number would represent the CLV if all retention rates increased by 1%.

In the third approach, the firm might assume constant margins and retention rates and perform what-if analyses directly on the formula for CLV presented earlier in this chapter.

*Example:* Consider again the customer relationship where $M = \$17.95$, $d = 0.01$, and $r = 0.995$. The calculated *CLV* was $1,191. Now suppose the firm expected $r$ to increase to 0.996 as a result of several recent customer-relationship-management initiatives.

To quantify the benefits of the expected increased retention, you calculate CLV for $r = 0.996$ and get $CLV = \$1,277$ (an increase of about 7.2%).

When using the CLV formula, remember the timing assumptions inherent in this formula. The formula applies to current customers whose next cash flow occurs in one period in the event they are retained. This timing assumption is conservative because, in actuality, the firm's current customers will be spread throughout the renewal cycle. For some customers, the renewal event will be imminent, not a full period away.

The change in CLV for a change in retention rate is a measure of the increase in dollar value of the firm's current customer base. This dollar value does not translate directly to an equivalent increase in yearly profits because there are many other factors affecting firm profits. If the firm wants to measure the impact of increased retention rate on yearly profits, a firm-level model described in the first approach is required.

The firm should also remember that increases in retention rate not only affect the value of the firm's current customers, but also the value of the firm's current prospects whenever the increases in retention rate are expected to also apply to customers the firm will acquire in the future. The economic benefits of increased retention must be compared with the costs required to achieve the increased retention rates in order to make a sound investment decision.

# Conclusion

CLV provides firms with a forward-looking metric that combines customers' retention rate, marketing spend, and cash flows. The metric is a good tool to assess the effects of increasing retention rates on future customer value and the amount a firm should spend on customer acquisition. When marketing spend is connected to retention rates and future cash flows, the metric provides a mechanism for firms to optimize marketing spending.

# Endnotes

1. Don Peppers and Martha Rogers, *Enterprise One to One: Tools for Competing in the Interactive Age* (New York: Currency Doubleday, 1997), 31.

2. Paul D. Berger, Bruce Weinberg, and Richard C. Hanna, "Customer Lifetime Value Determination and Strategic Implications for a Cruise-Ship Company," *Journal of Database Marketing and Customer Strategy Management* 11, no. 1 (2003): 49.

3. Sunil Gupta and Donald R. Lehmann "Customers as Assets," *Journal of Interactive Marketing* 17, no. 1 (2003): 9–24.

4. Frederick F. Reichheld and W. Earl Sasser Jr., "Zero Defections: Quality Comes to Services," *Harvard Business Review* (September–October 1990): 105–11.

5. Reichheld and Sasser Jr.

6. Phillip E. Pfeifer and Paul W. Farris, "The Elasticity of Customer Value to Retention: The Duration of a Customer Relationship," *Journal of Interactive Marketing* 18, no. 2 (Spring 2004): 20–31.

# 11

## Netflix: The Customer Strikes Back

## Introduction

Three years after earning his MBA, Hunter Keay was starting to make a name for himself at a leading investment bank when, in February 2012, some of his clients grew increasingly anxious about the value of their holdings in Netflix, Inc. (Netflix), the subscription-based media distribution company. Six months earlier, Netflix had announced a plan to split its on-demand video streaming and DVD mail delivery into two businesses and to increase the price of its most popular service. But in the face of near-universal criticism, Netflix had abandoned the plan within a month, only to lose 800,000 subscribers and half its stock value (Figure 11-1). Keay's clients who held Netflix wanted to know what remained of their investment.

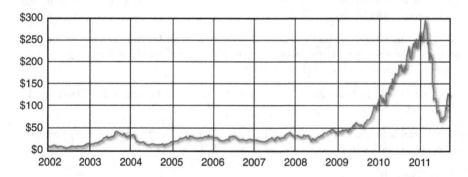

**Figure 11-1** Netflix stock price and volume, March 2002 to February 2012

Source: Yahoo! Finance.

To determine a more accurate value of Netflix stock, rather than apply one of the standard methods favored by his firm, Keay was considering the use of *customer lifetime value* (CLV). He was not certain that the metric applied in this instance, whether the firm even considered it valid, or how CLV related to the more accepted methods. He was certain about one thing, though: New technologies were transforming the industry and the ways customers received video content. The question was whether "Netflix 2: The Sequel" would ever be as popular as the original.

# An Industry Driven by Technology

The video rental industry has been substantially altered by technological developments outside the industry. Major milestones included the DVD by mail that could be ordered via the Internet, video streaming, and lately kiosks.

## The Traditional Retail Rental Store

The advent of videotape, acceptance of the VHS cassette standard, and subsequent affordability of home videocassette players in the 1980s brought with them the proliferation of the movie rental business. By the 1990s, the majority of market share had consolidated to a few participants with similar business models competing on selection, price, and especially location. National chains, such as Blockbuster and Hollywood Video, grew by staking claims at strategic locations with adequate population density. By 1990, Blockbuster professed to have a store within a ten-minute drive of 70% of the U.S. population. Mom-and-pop video stores survived by finding locations the chains did not seek.

Movie rental required that a customer leave his or her home with the intention of renting, then make a spontaneous decision based on what was available. The cost of a video rental ranged from $3.00 per week for older movies to $6.00 per three days for new releases (allowing for weekend viewing when rented on Friday, the most popular day). Small mom-and-pop stores typically had a collection of a few hundred videos for rental; a Blockbuster store had about 2,500 titles. A store's video paid for itself after 13 rentals, so films with mass appeal were the norm; nearly 70% of all films rented at Blockbuster were new releases. Limited selection and stock-outs were a common concern, as was the relative convenience of store hours.

Late returns were a thorny problem: A movie could not be rented until it was back on the shelf, and a scarcity of titles might deter a customer from returning. So video stores charged late fees, which monetized the delay and encouraged the customer to return movies promptly. In reality, as one commentator noted, late fees called attention to customer failure, in the manner of "a disapproving librarian tallying up 35 cents in overdue fines while floating the unspoken accusation you were irresponsible on top of everything else."[1] When Blockbuster eventually dropped many forms of late fees, the move resulted in a charge to revenue of $400 million. The bricks-and-mortar value proposition was eroding.

## DVD by Mail

DVD mail service started to gain popularity in the early 2000s. The subscribing customer selected a movie on a website, and a DVD would arrive at his or her home in about one business day. The customer could keep the DVD as long as he or she liked, then mail it back to the provider in the envelope provided. By selecting multiple movies and arranging them in order of priority in an online *queue*, the customer could ensure prompt delivery of subsequent selections and always have something on hand to watch as opportunities arose. Subscription tiers were based on how many movies a customer could receive simultaneously and priced accordingly, starting at $7.99 per month for one movie at a time. (See Exhibit 11-1 for a complete pricing comparison.)

## Video on Demand

Video on demand (VOD) was content distribution via an Internet-connected television, computer, or mobile device. The customer selected a movie from an online menu and, within seconds, the movie began streaming to his or her device. The customer could view the content as it was downloaded, rather than waiting for the complete file, which otherwise could take almost as long as the running time of the film. No exchange of a data-storage medium was required, so stock-outs and late fees were avoided, and a significantly larger and more eclectic catalog could be offered.

## Kiosk Rentals

Movie rental kiosks were freestanding dispensers of DVDs located in high-traffic areas with extended—sometimes 24-hour—access, such as convenience stores, grocery stores, and fast-food restaurants. Redbox, the dominant player, founded in 2003, was originally funded by McDonald's. As of 2012, Redbox claimed to have rented 1.5 billion movies from 30,000 kiosks nationwide and to operate a kiosk within a five-minute drive of two thirds of the U.S. population. Its only significant competitor, albeit a much smaller player, was Blockbuster's "Blockbuster Express" kiosks.

Kiosks revolutionized the rental price point (about $1.00 per night per movie) and changed consumer renting behavior by eliminating the planning ahead required by DVD-by-mail services and the need to go to another location required by rental stores. Plus, 24-hour access freed customers from time constraints. Selection, however, was limited by two major shortfalls: the physical space inside the kiosk and delayed releases to kiosks by movie studios wary of cannibalizing DVD sales.

# A New Range of Business Models

As content delivery methods increased, an industry participant could employ different pricing heuristics across different channels and different end-user content licenses. As such, revenue model, delivery method, and content licensing were dimensions by which each participant might be assessed (see Table 11-1).

In terms of revenue, a business was either pay-per-view or monthly subscription. Depending on the delivery method, the one-time fee of the pay-per-view model would entitle the customer to rent one DVD by mail or online streaming access for a finite time period. In the case of purchase, a one-time fee entitled the buyer to indefinite ownership of streaming content or of an actual DVD.

**Table 11-1** Perceptual Market Map for the VHS and Digital Eras

| | Revenue Model | | Delivery Method | | Content Licensing | |
|---|---|---|---|---|---|---|
| **Before 2000 (VHS)** | **À la carte** | **Subscription** | **Streaming** | **VHS** | **Rent** | **Buy** |
| Blockbuster | • | | | • | • | |
| Hollywood Video | • | | | • | • | |
| Video Update | • | | | • | • | |
| Local video store | • | | | • | • | |
| **After 2000 (Digital)** | | | | **DVD** | | |
| Amazon Prime | | • | • | | • | |
| Amazon Instant Video | • | | • | | • | • |
| Blockbuster | • | • | • | • | • | • |
| Cinema Now | • | | • | | • | • |
| DVD Café | • | • | | • | • | • |
| Greencine | | • | | • | • | |
| Hulu | Free | Free | • | | • | |
| Hulu Plus | | • | • | | • | |

| | Revenue Model | | Delivery Method | | Content Licensing | |
|---|---|---|---|---|---|---|
| **After 2000 (Digital)** | **À la carte** | **Subscription** | **Streaming** | **DVD** | **Rent** | **Buy** |
| iTunes | • | | • | | • | • |
| Netflix | | • | • | • | • | |
| Redbox | • | | | • | • | |
| Vudu | • | | • | | • | |

Source: Company websites.

Content was either delivered by physical DVD or streamed over the Internet from the service's website to the user's computer or ancillary television device, sometimes called a *streaming player*. Physical discs were still the dominant medium, but increased digital access was expected to continue (Figure 11-2). The downward pressure on physical discs was somewhat mitigated by the increasing popularity of kiosk rental systems such as Redbox. A user's right to content varied by service provider and plan, but generally fell into one of three categories: rental for a finite time period, outright purchase for unlimited personal use, or access to an entire online library from which content could be streamed.

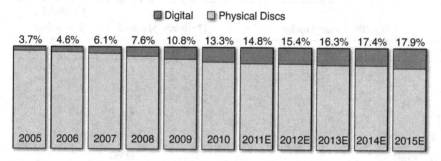

**Figure 11-2** Digital streaming as percentage of content delivery, 2005 to 2015 (projected)
Source: Mintel/Digital Entertainment Group, May 2011.

# Netflix: "Delivering Goosebumps"

Reed Hastings founded Netflix in 1997 in Los Gatos, California, after paying $40 in late fees to the local video store for *Apollo 13*, and later asking, "How come movie rentals don't work like a health club, where, whether you use it a lot or a little, you get the same charge?"[2] The key was to let people watch movies whenever they wanted.

The Netflix model was simple: Movies that consumers ordered from Netflix's website were shipped to their houses. Once consumers watched the movies, they returned them to Netflix in envelopes that were shipped along with the DVDs. Netflix claimed that it could ship videos to most customers in less than 24 hours.

Netflix's first innovation, in December 1999, was to eliminate late fees. Customers paid a fixed monthly fee of about $16, rented as many as four movies in a single order, and kept films as long as they wanted. Technically, the longer customers kept films, the lower Netflix's shipping cost per rental. Customer retention under this system, however, depended on customers renting more movies per month: the more rentals per month, the more value customers placed on the service. As Hastings stated, "If they [the customers] rent just two movies a month, they may decide it is not worth it."[3] This made Netflix's movie recommendation system extremely important: Good recommendations increased queue length, which increased retention, which increased customer lifetime value.

To expand its customer base and reduce its reliance on the most popular films, Netflix invested significantly in data mining technology. Netflix developed a simple but effective movie recommendation algorithm that compared each user's purchase to those of customers with similar tastes and then suggested films that were highly rated and unseen. These reviews, together with a catalog of close to 85,000 titles, held new releases to only 30% of rentals, and 95% of Netflix's titles were rented every quarter. Netflix was picking up revenue from a far broader distribution of preferences than a retail store could ever offer.

As the Netflix catalog grew, the recommendation system became simpler and more robust. In January 2000, Netflix introduced a new simple and accurate recommendation system called CineMatch. Each customer was prompted to rate certain movie genres and specific movies on a one- to five-star scale. The program found others in its database with similar preferences and then offered a predicted star value for each movie. As the customer rated more films, the accuracy of the data improved substantially. As Hastings stated, "Over 50% of our traffic comes via the recommendation system. It requires a lot of database work done in real time."[4] By 2007, Netflix had close to one billion movie reviews, with customers reviewing an average of 200 movies each.

CLV depended on the extent to which Netflix could leverage its large catalog by encouraging customers to rent more. Its target for per-customer monthly orders was five, the corporate average. Special promotions encouraged current customers to refer the service to friends and family; efforts resulted in an upward trend in customer retention (Figure 11-3).

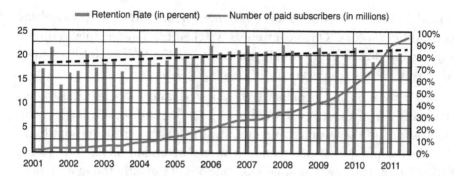

**Figure 11-3** Paid subscribers and retention rate, March 2001 to December 2011

Source: Netflix Q1 earnings report, 2012.

# Conclusion

Keay asked his analyst to compile the financial data required to calculate CLV at Netflix, but a considerable amount of work lay ahead. Was CLV an appropriate approximation of firm value in this setting? Does CLV track with market capitalization, discounted cash flows, or other traditional firm valuation techniques? How sensitive was CLV to various operational and strategic changes? And what role might be played by changes in technology? With such a public call on a volatile stock at this point in his young career, Keay could not afford to miss.

# Endnotes

1. Tara Lemmey, "Push the Positive for Customers," *BusinessWeek*, September 13, 2005.

2. Chris Taylor, "The Movie Is in the Mail," *Time*, March 18, 2002, 67.

3. Alan Cohen, "Netflix: DVDs at Your Door," *PC*, February 19, 2003.

4. Cohen.

# Exhibits

**Exhibit 11-1** Pricing Comparison (Per Month Unless Otherwise Indicated)

|  | Netflix | Amazon Prime[1] | Blockbuster | iTunes[2] | Redbox[3] |
|---|---|---|---|---|---|
| **Rental Subscription** |  |  |  |  |  |
| 2 DVDs/month, 1 out at a time | $4.99 |  |  |  |  |
| Unlimited DVDs |  |  |  |  |  |
| 1 out at a time | $7.99 |  | $9.99 |  |  |
| 2 out at a time | $11.99 |  | $14.99 |  |  |
| 3 out at a time |  |  | $19.99 |  |  |
| À la carte (VOD only) |  |  | $3.99 | $3.99 |  |
| Unlimited VOD | $7.99 | $6.58 |  |  |  |
| Unlimited VOD + DVDs |  |  |  |  |  |
| VOD + 1 DVD out at a time | $15.98 |  |  |  | $1.00 |
| VOD + 2 DVDs out at a time | $19.98 |  |  |  |  |
| VOD + 3 DVDs out at a time | $23.98 |  |  |  |  |
| VOD + 4 DVDs out at a time | $29.98 |  |  |  |  |
| **Purchase (à la carte only)** |  |  |  |  |  |
| VOD |  |  | $15.99 | $14.99 |  |
| DVD |  |  | $14.99 |  |  |

Source: Company websites.

1. Includes digital books and free shipping on items purchased from Amazon.com.

2. Per movie.

3. Per movie per night.

# Assignment Questions

1. Using the case data and the customer lifetime value formulation provided in Chapter 10, "Customer Lifetime Value," estimate the lifetime value of a Netflix customer for each quarter.

    a. Use the $CLV_{alternative}$ formula in Chapter 10's "CLV with Initial Margin" section and assume a 10% annual discount rate.

    b. In the customer lifetime value formula, you will need to compute retention rate. In the data, you have information on the total number of customers (or subscribers) per quarter and the number of new subscribers (out of the total number of subscribers) per quarter. For example, in June 2001, Netflix had 306 subscribers, and out of these 306, 88 were new subscribers. This information can be used to compute retention rate. The retention rate per quarter is the percentage of subscribers in the quarter who were also subscribers in the previous quarter. For example, the retention rate in June 2001 is equal to the percentage of customers in June 2001 who were also subscribers in March 2001.

    c. You will have to make a decision on what constitutes revenue and variable costs for Netflix to compute the margin (M).

2. How do you expect industry changes and technology advances to affect Netflix? Are these expectations validated by the trend in Netflix's customer acquisition, customer retention, customer revenue, and CLV?

3. Are Netflix's customer metrics a good indicator of its market valuation? Do CLV metrics move with more standardized valuation techniques?

4. How should Netflix react to these technology changes and new entrants? Which company is a bigger threat to Netflix: Redbox, Amazon, iTunes, or VUDU? Why?

5. Should Netflix consider selling DVDs? Why? How would it affect CLV?

# 12

## Retail Relay

*The last-mile delivery cost kills most home-delivery businesses. I knew we could find a better way.*

—Zach Buckner, CEO, Retail Relay

## Introduction

During the summer of 2007, Zach Buckner, the 31-year-old founder and CEO of Retail Relay, was again confronted with an ongoing frustration of daily suburban life. After his third trip to a local hardware store to get supplies for the same home improvement project, Buckner realized that a one-day project had now effectively become an all-weekend affair. He had spent more time shopping than installing new wiring in his 1930s-era house. Buckner had studied electrical and systems engineering and completed many consulting assignments for companies looking to improve their business operations. He drew on that knowledge and experience to come up with the concept of Retail Relay (Figure 12-1). And a new paradigm for online shopping was born.

**Figure 12-1** Retail Relay's delivery trucks, which also served as moving billboards
Source: Case writer photograph.

Although online retailing was certainly not a new concept, Buckner's approach was unique. His overall objective was to provide a solution to a problem faced by all Americans: time wasted, inefficiencies, and costs caused by the daily need to run errands. His initial concept was to provide an online means for consumers to order and purchase goods from a variety of local retailers (such as grocers, hardware stores, and clothiers), minimizing the burden of making trips to individual stores. Although the obvious solution was to provide convenient delivery service to customers' homes, Buckner soon realized there was no way to make this economically feasible.

Many online businesses that had entered the home-delivery market had failed. Perhaps the most spectacular of these early failures was Webvan, a grocery home-delivery service that at its height operated in ten metropolitan areas in the United States. Webvan built a billion-dollar order-processing, warehousing, and delivery infrastructure. Its revenues and profits never came close to covering its capital outlay, however, and in 2001, it filed for bankruptcy protection.

But not all these home-delivery businesses had failed. Bolstered by substantial growth in both online retailing and the market for fresh, organically produced food items, Long Island food purveyor Fresh Direct had enjoyed considerable success.[1] Founded in 1999, this online grocery business was built on offering custom-prepared groceries and meals for its customers. By sourcing food items directly from local farms, dairies, and fisheries and preparing meats, breads, and so on in an onsite warehouse facility, Fresh Direct was able to reduce transit time and improve the quality and freshness of its products, while also reducing costs by eliminating the need for a middleman. In that sense, Fresh Direct acted in many ways like a traditional grocery retailer, buying direct and carrying inventory. Though its delivery area was still limited mainly to Manhattan, Brooklyn, and Queens, there were plans to expand.

Buckner was determined not to repeat the mistakes of others. To make Retail Relay successful, it would be imperative to cut out "last-mile delivery costs" and to minimize up-front working capital requirements. Last-mile delivery costs greatly reduced operating margins. Getting a truckload of products to a single neighborhood or workplace location was not nearly as costly as paying for drivers and trucks to bring products to individual homes. Likewise, a simple initial distribution system would not require the kind of "Willy Wonka operation" that had strained the financial viability of so many other businesses.[2] Fresh Direct had been able to make its more expensive warehouse and home-delivery system work, but it operated in a densely populated area of New York City. Buckner wanted to find several locations that were convenient for many customers, both in location and in ease of order pickup. These pickup locations would be the "relay" point for the grocery items on their journey from farm or store to the customer's home. If these cost-reduction measures were successful, they would allow Retail Relay to provide this service to customers without charge, which effectively meant customers would pay the same price for these items as if had they had shopped at the retailers' stores themselves.

Although the original plan was to sell much more than grocery-type items, initial sales feedback confirmed that local, natural, organic, and healthy foods and household items were by far the best-selling categories. The custom leather belts did not sell. Neither did electrical wiring. Retail Relay soon narrowed its business concept, becoming a grocery- and farm-product retailer.

Even though the company abandoned the idea of selling a vast selection of non-grocery items early on, it was still important to offer customers a wide selection of grocery items. A narrow selection would not achieve the goal of reducing the amount of time customers spent grocery shopping because they might still have to stop at a store to pick up items Retail Relay did not offer. Customers wanted to buy free-range chicken and freshly picked English peas, but they also wanted to buy paper towels and laundry detergent—and, if possible, they wanted to avoid a supermarket trip entirely. Although signing up large grocery retailers as suppliers had the advantage of quickly producing a large available assortment, these large retailers had little to gain and potentially much to lose by acting as Relay's suppliers. Sales through Relay might cannibalize their own in-store sales. For this reason, the initial push for suppliers focused on smaller, boutique-type retailers, restaurants, and local farms. For smaller retailers and farms, Relay offered a promising new vehicle through which to reach a previously untapped consumer market with its goods, and their risk of cannibalization was small.

When putting forth proposals to local businesses, Retail Relay experienced overwhelming acceptance, with a 100% positive response rate from the retailers it approached with this collaborative opportunity. Retail Relay enlisted more than 40 unique suppliers, covering a wide assortment of grocery items. Large supermarkets such as Whole Foods, however, were not used as suppliers.

# Retail Relay Operations

Retail Relay set up initial operations in Charlottesville, Virginia, a city that had a population of 50,000 and that was home to the University of Virginia as well as several other large private and government employers. Although pockets of poverty existed in Charlottesville, significantly more than the average number of residents could be described as having a high level of income and/or a high level of education.[3] It also had an unusually high proportion of residents who were interested in local and organic food. Retail Relay's management team believed that Charlottesville was an ideal location in which to test its concept.

The typical customer order and product pickup process followed six discrete steps:[4]

1. Customers submitted orders and paid for them online at RetailRelay.com, selecting from what evolved into an assortment of mostly grocery and home products. Customers wanting to pick up their orders the next day had to place them by midnight the night before.

2. Orders were downloaded by Retail Relay immediately after midnight and were then broken down and transmitted to participating retailers.

3. Retailers used these orders to pack and sort bags by customer number.

4. Orders were picked up by a Retail Relay driver the following morning and returned to the warehouse, where they were manually re-sorted.

5. Orders from multiple retailers were re-sorted by customer and repacked onto the truck in the appropriate temperature zone (shelf-stable, refrigerated, frozen) (Figure 12-2). Any one customer might have bags from several retailers and multiple bags from a given retailer.

6. Finally, orders were transported to the customer pickup location in a Retail Relay truck.

**Figure 12-2** Retail Relay driver loading the truck and waiting at a pickup location

Source: Case writer photographs.

Although not as cost prohibitive as home delivery, collecting, sorting, and delivering products to the pickup location cost money. Because individual suppliers removed ordered products from their own shelves and had them ready for the Retail Relay driver near the front of the store, it took drivers very little time to collect merchandise from individual suppliers. It took very little time for the driver to move from one supplier to the next during the collection process because the community was relatively small. Overall, the costs associated with collecting merchandise from suppliers were negligible.

Sorting products by customer and distributing them to customers was costly. Because this sorting process was very labor-intensive, an individual worker could sort only about $400 of product per hour. The cost of labor, both for workers who sorted and for truck drivers, was about $15 per hour. Unlike product collection, distribution was not a quick process. Drivers had to drive to the pickup location and wait for three to four hours while customers came by to pick up their orders. On average, a driver would spend about five hours transporting product from the warehouse to the pickup location, setting up at the location, waiting for customers to pick up their orders, and then returning to the warehouse. A fully loaded truck could carry about $3,200 of merchandise and made deliveries about 200 days per year. The trucks themselves were utilitarian, lacking the comforts of longer-haul vehicles. They were also inexpensive to operate. Retail Relay estimated that the total cost of a truck, including maintenance and fuel, was about $3,000 per year.

## Prices and Promotions

The basic contract with suppliers stipulated that suppliers had to sell products to Retail Relay at 15% less than their in-store shelf price. The retail price to customers was set to the current shelf price at the supplier's brick-and-mortar establishment. Suppliers were required to enter their own product prices—using in-house-developed iPhone, BlackBerry, and Android applications—into Retail Relay's ordering system. Although it was possible for Retail Relay to audit its system to make sure its prices were indeed the same as an individual supplier's regular shelf prices, it was more difficult to know whether every deal price offered at a supplier's store was passed through to Retail Relay customers. As a practical matter, management believed that some suppliers were more diligent than others in making sure their Retail Relay price matched their true shelf price.

Retail Relay engaged in a limited amount of price promotional activity. New customers generally received a coupon for 10% off their next purchase, printed on the receipt of their first purchase. On the second purchase, they received a 5% discount coupon for a third purchase. The redemption rate of these coupons on qualified purchases was high, around 80%. The rationale behind these first- and second-purchase coupons flowed from two studies that Retail Relay did involving purchase data from customers. The first, a small pilot study, tracked the purchase activity of 81 randomly chosen customers who had made their first purchase with Retail Relay before June 2009. In constructing the pilot study, management wanted to be sure it could track these individuals over a period long enough to observe many purchase occasions. The company was growing very quickly, and many of their customers were new and, as such, had made only a small number of purchases. Given that the average inter-purchase interval for individuals in this sample was approximately three weeks, and that the end of the time frame for analysis was February 2010, it seemed reasonable to restrict the pilot group to those who had made their first purchase at least nine months earlier. Descriptive statistics for this pilot study are provided in Exhibit 12-1.

Two things stood out in the results of this pilot study. First, many people seemed to be purchasing from Retail Relay once and not returning to make another purchase. Of the 81 customers who tried Retail Relay, 32% never returned to make a second purchase. Second, the average size of the basket of goods purchased increased once an individual became experienced in dealing with Retail Relay. The average size of an individual's first purchase was $49.51, whereas someone who had ordered from Retail Relay frequently made an average purchase of $92.91 on their 20th purchase occasion. Both of these findings suggested to management that offering promotions for the second and third purchase occasion to get new customers "over the hump" might be an effective way to retain those customers.

Once the results of the pilot study were known, Retail Relay conducted a more extensive study using 587 randomly selected customers and choosing them regardless of when they had made their first purchase. The managers hoped this new, much larger sample size would provide more reliable results than those of the pilot study. Descriptive statistics for this study can be found in Exhibit 12-2. Indeed, the more extensive study showed an even larger attrition rate between the occasion of the first and second purchase—45%—a worrisome number for management. The results of the more extensive study were not convincing to everyone on the management team. In particular, some were concerned that using a sample containing many individuals who had only recently become customers would bias the analysis because management would not be able to observe anything other than their first few purchase occasions. Whether the pilot study or the larger study provided a more accurate depiction of customers' purchase patterns was an open question.

Retail Relay tested the value of home-delivered flyers as well, distributing 2,000 of them to homes in a Charlottesville subdivision. The flyers contained a coupon for 10% off the total price of a Retail Relay order. The cost of this door-to-door program, including printing, transportation, and labor, was approximately $1,200 and produced a total of seven uses, all of which were new customers.

Retail Relay also tested coupons inserted in Valpak "blue envelopes"—mailers that contained coupons and promotional offers from many companies, most of them local. Retail Relay's coupon offered $5 off any purchase of $25 or more and $15 off a purchase of $100 or more. An example of the Valpak insert can be found in Exhibit 12-3. Purchasing insert coverage across three separate mailings at a cost of $1,100, Retail Relay was able to reach approximately 60,000 homes in the greater Charlottesville area. Based on coupon redemptions, which required customers to input a promotional code when they submitted their online order, and previous purchase data, management determined these Valpak inserts were redeemed by 58 new customers and ten existing customers.

Management wanted to determine the profitability of these promotions. An important part of this analysis would be the determination of customer lifetime value (CLV), a metric that assigned a dollar value to a potential new customer. A CLV analysis of its customer-level data would allow Retail Relay to answer the question, "If I acquire a new customer, on average how much money is that customer really worth?" Appendix 12-1 provides a description of how to apply CLV analysis to the data contained in the supplemental Excel spreadsheet (UVA-M-0784X), available on the companion website, http://dmanalytics.org.

# New Customer Acquisition and Retention

Aside from its limited foray into direct-to-consumer price promotions, Retail Relay employed several tactics to recruit new customers and retain existing ones. It set up informational booths at various community functions around Charlottesville (e.g., Discovery Museum Fair, Vegetarian Festival, and Virginia Festival of the Book), and management was available for local talk radio programs that catered to Retail Relay's target audience. But by far its largest promotional investment, in terms of both time and money, was its e-mail and social media campaigns. Beginning each Sunday, promotional Retail Relay e-mails were distributed to thousands of existing customers as well as to others whose e-mail addresses had been obtained during other promotional activities. E-mail delivery was staggered to ensure that existing customers would receive messages one day prior to their regular order day to serve as a reminder as well as to offer special information in a timely manner.[5] A sample promotional e-mail can be found in Exhibit 12-4. To further promote awareness through this medium, Retail Relay established partnerships with large local employers who sent e-mail blasts out to its employee base, offering exposure to an expanded group of potential customers. Individuals could also become fans of Retail Relay on Facebook, and its Facebook page was regularly updated with new information on suppliers, recipe suggestions, and comments on what produce was starting to come in season.

Through all this activity, Zach Buckner and his recently hired new president, Arnon Katz, a 2009 graduate of the Darden School of Business, wondered if the customer acquisition and retention activities were really worth what they cost the business in time, money, and aggravation. As the customer base grew, perhaps they should simply allow word-of-mouth advertising from existing customers to filter through the rest of their target audience. Retail Relay's growth rate was robust, averaging 25% per month over the previous six months, and ramping up the home-delivered flyers or Valpak mailers did not seem to be a great use of time and money, particularly in the small market of Charlottesville.

# The Richmond Expansion

In its Charlottesville birthplace, Retail Relay was enjoying robust and profitable growth, but Buckner and Katz had already made plans to expand to other locations. On the immediate horizon was a planned expansion in summer 2010 into the Richmond, Virginia, market. Katz was put in charge of making plans for the expansion, and there was much to consider. The city of Richmond anchored a metropolitan area of approximately 1.2 million people; the population of the city proper was slightly more than 200,000. The city and surrounding metropolitan area were more economically diverse than Charlottesville.

In summer 2010, Retail Relay (renamed Relay Foods; see Figure 12-3) expanded into Richmond, Virginia. It operated profitably for the year that followed and expected to continue to do so. During fiscal year 2011, the company more than doubled in size. In 2011, the venture capital firm Battery Ventures invested about $3 million to help Relay Foods further expand its operations. The company planned to expand into other cities.

**Figure 12-3** Relay Foods' new logo
Source: Relay Foods.

Infusion of new cash presented its own set of challenges. New pickup locations would have to be selected, a new sorting facility established, and—because Richmond was 70 miles from Charlottesville—a new supplier base developed. As Katz assessed the situation, he considered whether to expand in the Richmond market with an aggressive customer acquisition effort, spending the profits the Charlottesville market had generated on promotions designed to gain rapid market penetration. He asked himself how much money a new customer was really worth and what the most effective promotional ideas for reaching new customers were.

On the flip side, Retail Relay could not add new pickup locations in Richmond and let the business grow through the same word-of-mouth advertising that had previously been successful. Katz looked over the sizable amount of purchase and promotional data he already had and thought about how he could use this information to better market the company's products in Richmond. If Retail Relay had worked well in Charlottesville, then perhaps it would work well anywhere.

# Endnotes

1. U.S. sales of organic foods stood at about $6.2 billion in 2009, after several years of growth rates exceeding 20% per year.

2. Zach Buckner used the phrase "a Willy Wonka operation" in reference to the movie *Willy Wonka and the Chocolate Factory* as a way of implying a highly elaborate and automated system.

3. "Demographics," City of Charlottesville, http://www.charlottesville.org/Index.aspx?page=576 (accessed July 21, 2011).

4. Retail Relay did offer a fee-based home-delivery option, but this constituted a small part of its business.

5. Customers often developed a regular pattern in their orders whereby it was possible to predict the most likely day of the week for their purchases.

# Exhibits

**Exhibit 12-1** Descriptive Statistics of Customer Purchases Conditioned on How Many Times an Individual Has Ordered from Retail Relay (Pilot Study)

| Order Number | Total Number of Observations in the Data | Conditional Probability of Observing Purchase Occasion $t + 1$ in the Data if Occasion $t$ is Observed° | Average Dollar Amount of Purchase |
|---|---|---|---|
| 1 | 81 | NA | $49.51 |
| 2 | 55 | 55 ÷ 81 = 68% | $62.28 |
| 3 | 44 | 44 ÷ 55 = 80% | $57.01 |
| 4 | 34 | 77% | $62.03 |
| 5 | 31 | 91% | $63.06 |
| 6 | 28 | 90% | $72.90 |
| 7 | 23 | 82% | $60.30 |
| 8 | 21 | 91% | $63.68 |
| 9 | 20 | 95% | $72.04 |
| 10 | 19 | 95% | $67.89 |
| 11 | 17 | 89% | $70.07 |
| 12 | 17 | 100% | $82.48 |
| 13 | 16 | 94% | $82.17 |
| 14 | 15 | 94% | $61.12 |
| 15 | 14 | 93% | $65.79 |
| 16 | 13 | 93% | $82.29 |

| Order Number | Total Number of Observations in the Data | Conditional Probability of Observing Purchase Occasion $t + 1$ in the Data if Occasion $t$ is Observed* | Average Dollar Amount of Purchase |
|---|---|---|---|
| 17 | 13 | 100% | $65.32 |
| 18 | 13 | 100% | $99.20 |
| 19 | 13 | 100% | $73.74 |
| 20 | 12 | 92% | $92.91 |
| 21 | 10 | 83% | $59.57 |
| 22 | 10 | 100% | $75.69 |
| 23 | 9 | 90% | $60.33 |
| 24 | 9 | 100% | $84.83 |
| 25 | 8 | 89% | $87.55 |
| 26 | 7 | 88% | $60.99 |
| 27 | 7 | 100% | $87.95 |
| 28 | 7 | 100% | $99.33 |
| 29 | 6 | 86% | $77.30 |
| 30 | 6 | 100% | $99.70 |

* For example, in the pilot study, if a customer makes two purchases, the probability that we would observe a third purchase is 80%.

Source: Retail Relay.

**Exhibit 12-2** Descriptive Statistics of Customer Purchases Conditioned on How Many Times an Individual Has Ordered from Retail Relay (Full Study)

| Order Number | Total Number of Observations in the Data | Conditional Probability of Observing Purchase Occasion $t + 1$ in the Data if Occasion $t$ is Observed | Average Dollar Amount of Purchase |
|---|---|---|---|
| 1 | 587 | NA | $46.71 |
| 2 | 322 | $322 \div 587 = 55\%$ | $56.71 |
| 3 | 240 | $240 \div 322 = 75\%$ | $57.93 |
| 4 | 188 | 78% | $56.87 |
| 5 | 156 | 83% | $58.26 |
| 6 | 127 | 81% | $66.90 |
| 7 | 103 | 81% | $63.62 |
| 8 | 89 | 86% | $70.27 |
| 9 | 73 | 82% | $63.03 |
| 10 | 62 | 85% | $62.60 |

| Order Number | Total Number of Observations in the Data | Conditional Probability of Observing Purchase Occasion $t + 1$ in the Data if Occasion $t$ is Observed | Average Dollar Amount of Purchase |
|---|---|---|---|
| 11 | 56 | 90% | $71.81 |
| 12 | 52 | 93% | $76.76 |
| 13 | 44 | 85% | $78.14 |
| 14 | 39 | 89% | $65.65 |
| 15 | 33 | 85% | $74.84 |
| 16 | 30 | 91% | $81.11 |
| 17 | 29 | 97% | $72.08 |
| 18 | 28 | 97% | $87.30 |
| 19 | 27 | 96% | $71.94 |
| 20 | 23 | 85% | $75.44 |
| 21 | 19 | 83% | $70.35 |
| 22 | 17 | 89% | $72.86 |
| 23 | 14 | 82% | $66.68 |
| 24 | 11 | 79% | $79.90 |
| 25 | 9 | 82% | $93.91 |
| 26 | 8 | 89% | $61.08 |
| 27 | 7 | 88% | $94.16 |
| 28 | 6 | 86% | $100.40 |
| 29 | 4 | 67% | $77.89 |
| 30 | 3 | 75% | $99.70 |

Source: Retail Relay.

**Exhibit 12-3**  Valpak insert

Source: Retail Relay. Used with permission.

Relay Reminder

## *The Eyes of a Farmer*

As Relay gears up for a great season of local food vendors, this week we roll out two new farms, each with a story to tell. The folks at Babes in the Wood refer to their pigs as **forest-fed**—which helps to explain the incredible taste of their pork products.

Likewise, **John Kiser**, writer and former technology guru, is a truly interesting soul (those are his eyes!). He began selling lean, pastured pork to his friends from Meadow Green Farm in beautiful Rappahannock County ten years ago. Try his bacon—you will realize the connection between local and *taste* in a fundamental way.

**Just So You Know Dept:** We've just received a new shipment from your favorite local beef provider, John Whiteside, of Wolf Creek Farm. It's all part of our spring farm market, coming soon, which will be featuring locally grown produce, cheese, and meat from our region's **Buy Fresh, Buy Local** vendors.

Thank you for your orders this week! We look forward to serving you again.

It's a team effort...
RetailRelay.com
Free Pick-up • 3:00-7:00pm • Every Day
click for the schedule

## *What's New:*

- Babes in the Wood
- Meadow Green Farm
- Virginia Trout

---

### Babes in the Wood, Dillwyn, VA

From birth until the time they are taken to a USDA butcher, Babes pigs live happily unconfined in the woods. The sows even raise their young in the woods! They eat nuts and berries and root around like, well, pigs. No hormones or antibiotics. No nonsense. The result is the best quality pork available.

### Meadow Green Farm, Sperryville, VA

John Kiser's Yorkshire pigs live in a luxurious nineteenth-century barn when they're not grazing on fescue and clover-rich pasture outside. Pigs are nature's front-end loaders and theirs get their minerals directly from the iron-rich Rappahannock soil rather than antibiotic-laced corn feed. They roam, they dig, and they graze. John lets his pigs be pigs.

### Virginia Trout Company, Goshen, VA

Sometimes we find our vendors, sometimes they find us. Bryan Plemmons, of **Casta Line Trout Farms** in Goshen, gave us a call and said he had trout our customers might be interested in. We listened and checked it out. One of the oldest trout farms in Virginia, Casta Line got things going in 1965 and consistently garners Blue Ribbon honors from the Virginia State Fair.

The result is Virginia Trout, which gathers the best from five separate Highland County trout farms—each containing pristine mountain spring water. Trout are dressed or filleted immediately upon harvesting and frozen right away to preserve their freshness. Get your Omega-3s from this delicious fish!

---

**Exhibit 12-4** Sample promotional e-mail
Source: Retail Relay.

# Appendix 12-1

Customer lifetime value (CLV) can be calculated using a number of different methods. The most appropriate method is often governed by the features and restrictions of the data that is being analyzed. For a more complete discussion of methods for computing CLV, see "Customer Profitability."[1]

The data in the Excel file (UVA-M-0784X—located on the companion website, http://dmanalytics.org) has two important features that affect the way it should be analyzed. First, the data is organized by purchase occasion rather than by time period. Second, you can easily determine the probability that a customer who makes purchase number $t$ will go on to make purchase number $t+1$. Therefore, you can also determine the probability that any new customer making his or her first purchase will continue to purchase through occasion $t$. Stated another way, this data allows you to answer questions such as "What is the probability that a new customer will make purchases from Retail Relay on at least 10 occasions?" The data set contains information on 30 potential purchase observations.

Instead of the constant retention rate found in some models of CLV, we have purchase-occasion-specific rates. The CLV expected from a new customer can therefore be calculated by Equation 1:

$$CLV = \sum_{t=1}^{30} \frac{r_t M_t}{(1+i)^{(t-1)}}$$

(1)

where

$r_t$ is the probability that an individual will make purchases on at least $t$ occasions given that he or she has made one purchase. For the first purchase occasion, $r_t = 1$.

$M_t$ is the dollar contribution margin of a shopping basket at purchase occasion $t$, adjusted for distribution costs and coupon-redemption expenses.

$i$ is the relevant discount rate between any two purchase occasions. Because the average interpurchase time in this data is about three weeks, the relevant discount rate can be approximated by dividing the annual rate by about 17. More accurately, the annual rate ($a$) can be converted to the three-week rate using Equation 2:

$i = (1 + a)^{1/17.33} - 1$

(2)

It should be noted that the data provided in the Excel spreadsheet does not provide the retention rate ($r_t$), so some (minor) data manipulation is required. Finally, although the predicted CLV might increase if you had data beyond 30 purchase occasions, 30 is sufficient to provide a reasonably accurate estimate of CLV for the purposes of this case. The case provides data for what roughly a two-year CLV (30 weeks × average interpurchase time of three weeks = 90 weeks).

# Endnotes

1. Phillip E. Pfeifer, Paul W. Farris, and Neil Bendle, "Customer Profitability," UVA-M-0718 (Charlottesville, VA: Darden Business Publishing, 2005).

# Assignment Questions

1. What is the expected customer lifetime value of a newly acquired customer? Use an annual discount rate of 10%.

2. Do you think this value is likely to increase or decrease as Retail Relay grows into a larger company?

3. Is the Valpak promotion worth pursuing at a larger scale? What about door-hanger coupons?

4. Would you recommend any adjustments to the company's social media marketing campaign?

5. Should Retail Relay move forward with the Richmond expansion?

# 13

## Logistic Regression

## Introduction

Almost all of us are familiar with odds. What are the chances one thing will happen versus another? What are the chances you will succeed at work today? What are the chances your favorite game-show contestant will win today versus the chances he or she will lose?

What you might not be familiar with is how odds can be applied to marketing analytics. What are the chances a customer will buy your product versus the chances he or she won't? What are the chances you will retain a customer versus the chances you will lose him or her?

When you are using odds, you are examining two opposing outcomes. Any such unknown (one that can only be one thing or another) is known as a dummy variable. But if you know how to examine dummy variables properly, the results are anything but dumb.

## When Logistic Regression Trumps Linear Regression

A logistic regression is similar to any linear regression but with one important variation that has critical consequences.

Think about an important metric in marketing: customer retention. If Keepmoney Bank wants to use a regression analysis to examine whether it will retain a customer, it will set retention as its dependent variable. Rather than being normally distributed in a bell curve in the manner of continuous variables (Figure 13-1), however, a 1 will be assigned to represent customer retention and a 0 will represent customer loss. Only those two outcomes are possible. Again, this is a dummy variable, wherein what you are trying to predict is one of two options.

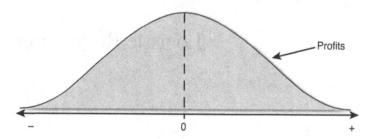

**Figure 13-1** A normal distribution

Source: All figures created by case writer unless otherwise specified.

Studies have shown that logistic regression is the best model for examining dummy variables such as customer retention.[1] But why can't Keepmoney use its trusty linear regression to determine the likelihood of customer retention given a set of independent variables? Again, linear regressions assume a bell-curve distribution of outcomes (what is known as a normal distribution) from negative infinity to infinity. Most things in life follow this sort of distribution. Think of human height or school grades—a few people typically earn Cs, a few more earn a B–, the majority will earn Bs, and a very few will earn an A+. But when examining a dummy variable such as customer retention, there is no curve across a range of outcomes. The outcome can only be 1 or 0.

If Keepmoney attempts to use a linear regression to examine customer retention, nonsensical predictions may result. The bank may find its chances of customer retention are greater than 1, meaning it has even better than a 100% chance of retaining a customer. Or the bank may find its chances are less than 0. You can round up for those predictions that are less than 0 or round down for those greater than 1, but the results of the regression will not be precise.

## Choice Behavior

The objective of logistic regression in this example is to represent consumers' choice behavior as accurately as possible. When individual consumers choose products, the value they place on the product does not typically increase linearly with increases in a preferred feature of the product. Instead, research indicates consumer valuation of a product typically follows an S-shaped curve with increases in the levels of a preferred attribute.

You can test whether the S-shaped curve represents consumers' choice behavior with a simple exercise. Imagine that on the x-axis you have the level of discount on a $300 plane ticket from Charlottesville, Virginia, to New York. Ask a group of your friends how many of them would purchase the flight. Then offer a discount of $20. How many additional people said they would buy the ticket? Probably not many. Increase the discount to $40. Maybe one person half-heartedly jumps in. At $60, you are likely to see a spike in purchasers. And from $60 to $100, the number of purchasers should increase at every level; however, at about $100, the number of additional purchasers will taper off, as you have reached the upper threshold.

In most real-life situations, this S-shaped curve represents how people make decisions. As a discount (or promotion) increases, the odds that people will make the choice to buy will increase. In this example, at a $60 discount, 2 in 10 people are likely to purchase the flight to New York; 8 in 10 are unlikely to purchase the flight.

## The Logistic Transformation

You now see that a linear regression would be insufficient to accurately represent individual consumers' choices. Figure 13-2 shows a distribution of probabilities from 0 to 1 representing the logistic function

$$p(customer\ retention = 1) = \frac{exp(u_p)}{1 + exp(u_p)}$$

where $u_p$ = utility consumer obtains from product $p = a + b_1X$.

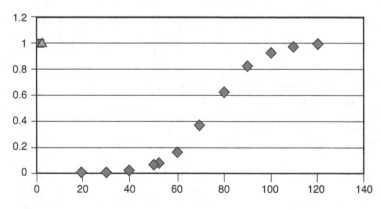

**Figure 13-2** Distribution of probabilities for a logistic distribution

4

The utility function ($u_p$), otherwise known as a value function, is used to describe the value a person places on a certain good or service. Take coffee, for example. To find the utility, or value, you might derive from a cup of coffee, you must consider all of the variables that might go into the decision to buy that particular cup: the taste, the price, the logo, the location of the store from which you buy it, your personal habits, and the jolt it gives you in the morning. For convenience purposes—and based on behavioral studies indicating how people process variables in an additive way—the value function is assumed to be linear.

The logistic function used to describe the ways in which consumers make choices takes the form of the exponent of the value function over 1 plus the exponent of the value function. The resulting distribution looks like an S-shaped curve, as shown in Figure 13-2. The predictions from this function are bound between 0 and 1 (meaning if one outcome is 0.1, the opposite outcome is 0.9).

5

Furthermore, the probability of success (retention) versus failure (churn) is $P \div (1 - P)$, where $P$ is the probability of retention. For example, if there are 10 outcomes with 1 success and 9 failures, the odds are 1/9. This ($P \div (1 - P)$) is what is known as the "odds function." Substituting for $P$ using the preceding logistic function, the odds function is equal to $e^{(a+b_1X)}$. If you are to make a transformation of this exponential function to a linear function via the natural log,[2] you will find the log odds function, which is $ln[P \div (1 - P)] = a + b_1X$ (Figure 13-3). This is equivalent to the value function.

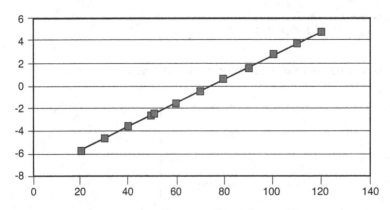

**Figure 13-3** Log odds function

Essentially, you have assumed a person has a linear value function or utility underlying his or her decision, then you have transformed that value into something useful about the chances he or she will make a decision. Therefore, the critical output of a logistic regression is the probability, or percent chance, a customer will stay with a company or leave the company, and that probability is defined in terms of the value the customer places on the company's product.

## Assessing Video Game Purchasers

How can a marketing manager use logistic regression techniques to find useful information about the ways people behave? Consider the data in Table 13-1, which tallies the number of sales of Xbox games through Best Buy's mobile app, as reported by Kaggle.[3]

**Table 13-1** Sales of Xbox Games Through Best Buy's Mobile App

| SKU | Game | Numsales | Abmedium | Browsetime | New | Regular Price | Customer Review Count | Customer Review Average |
|---|---|---|---|---|---|---|---|---|
| 1004622 | Sniper: Ghost Warrior—Xbox 360 | 53 | 1 | (0.00017) | 0 | 19.99 | 7 | 3.4 |
| 1010544 | Monopoly Streets—Xbox 360 | 12 | 1 | (0.00285) | 0 | 29.99 | 3 | 4 |
| 1011067 | MySims SkyHeroes—Xbox 360 | 3 | 1 | (0.00157) | 0 | 19.99 | 1 | 2 |
| 1011491 | FIFA Soccer 11—Xbox 360 | 85 | 1 | (479.80822) | 0 | 12.99 | 18 | 4.6 |
| 1011831 | Hasbro Family Game Night 3—Xbox 360 | 6 | 1 | 0.00094 | 0 | 9.99 | 2 | 3.5 |
| 1012721 | The Sims 3—Xbox 360 | 140 | 1 | (0.00031) | 0 | 19.99 | 13 | 3.8 |
| 1012876 | Two Worlds II—Xbox 360 | 5 | 1 | 0.00047 | 0 | 39.99 | 8 | 3.4 |
| 1013666 | Call of Duty: The War Collection—Xbox 360 | 41 | 1 | 0.00115 | 0 | 68.18 | 2 | 4.5 |
| 1014064 | Castlevania: Lords of Shadow—Xbox 360 | 15 | 1 | (0.00235) | 0 | 7.99 | 4 | 4.8 |
| 1032361 | Need for Speed: Hot Pursuit—Xbox 360 | 168 | 1 | (0.00039) | 0 | 19.99 | 45 | 4.2 |
| 1052221 | Marvel vs. Capcom 3: Fate of Two Worlds—Xbox 360 | 28 | 1 | (0.00092) | 0 | 19.99 | 11 | 4 |

Source: Kaggle, "Data Mining Hackathon on BIG DATA (7GB) Best Buy mobile web site," http://www.kaggle.com/c/acm-sf-chapter-hackathon-big (accessed November 5, 2013).

Each of the games shown in this data set boasts above-median sales compared with the other games available. In other words, a dummy variable has been set where "above-median sales" is represented by a 1, and "below-median sales" is represented by a 0. Now, which independent variables shown in the chart (time browsed, whether the game is new, price, number of reviews, and review average) are good predictors of being a 1—that is, above-median sales?

The output of a logistic regression of this data (Tables 13-2 and 13-3) looks similar to the output of a linear regression, and the most important data points, in addition to the coefficients, are r squared and P-value; other predictors of accuracy and significance go by a variety of names.

**Table 13-2** Output of Logistic Regression

**Summary Statistics**

| Variable | Categories | Frequencies | % |
|---|---|---|---|
| nrx_ind | 0 | 1128 | 44.183 |
| | 1 | 1425 | 55.817 |

| Variable | Observations | Obs. with Missing Data | Obs. Without Missing Data |
|---|---|---|---|
| Sales calls | 2553 | 0 | 2553 |
| Minimum | Maximum | Mean | Std. Deviation |
| 0.000 | 12.000 | 2.396 | 2.128 |

**Goodness of Fit Statistics (Variable nrx_ind)**

| Statistics | Independent | Full |
|---|---|---|
| Observations | 2553 | 2553 |
| Sum of weights | 2553.000 | 2553.000 |
| DF | 2552 | 2551 |
| –2 Log(Likelihood) | 3504.580 | 3216.666 |
| $R^2$(McFadden) | 0.000 | 0.082 |
| $R^2$(Cox and Snell) | 0.000 | 0.107 |
| $R^2$(Nagelkerke) | 0.000 | 0.000 |
| AIC | 3508.580 | 3220.666 |
| SBC | 3520.270 | 3232.356 |
| Iterations | 0 | 6 |

**Table 13-3** Model Estimates

| Source | Value | SE | Wald Chi-Square | Pr > Chi² |
|--------|-------|-----|-----------------|-----------|
| **Model Parameters (Variable abmedian)** | | | | |
| Intercept | (1.097) | 0.502 | 4.769 | 0.029 |
| New | (1.595) | 1.467 | 1.182 | 0.277 |
| Regular price | 0.006 | 0.011 | 0.279 | 0.597 |
| Customer review count | 0.066 | 0.030 | 4.943 | 0.026 |
| Customer review average | 0.399 | 0.116 | 11.878 | 0.001 |

The key difference in the logistic regression output is that the coefficients are not interpreted as such. For the coefficients to add value to your analysis, you must calculate the odds ratio. For example, if a logistic regression yields a coefficient $b$ of 2.303, the odds ratio says that for every one unit increase in the independent variable (such as the number of promotions), the odds that the dependent variable will be equal to 1 (the product is purchased) will increase by a factor determined by taking the exponent of the coefficient: $e^b = e^{2.303} = 10$. This is not the same as a direct linear transformation.

So, examining the P-values shown in the far-right column of Table 13-3, which variables can we say are predictive of whether a game will be a top seller? Customer review average, followed by the number of customer reviews, is the most significant variable. Price is relatively insignificant, in this case most likely because the price range of the games is small.

Using the coefficients determined in the regression analysis, the marketing manager can then determine how much the odds of a game being a top seller increase if review average increases by one point (Table 13-4). In other words, if a customer review average of 3 yields a certain probability of success, what happens if the average increases to 4? On average, the coefficient of customer review (coefficient $b$, the slope of the line) is 0.399, and the exponent of $b$ is 1.49, which means that a single-point increase in reviews increases the odds by a factor of about 1.5.[4]

**Table 13-4** Log Odds Ratio and Logistic Probabilities

| | | | |
|---|---|---|---|
| Coefficient of Customer Review Average ($b_{review}$) | 0.399 | | |
| $\exp(b_{review})$ | 1.490 | | |
| | | Customer Review Average = 3 | Customer Review Average = 4 |
| $U = bx$ | | 0.76 | 1.159 |
| $P(\text{sale}) = \exp(u) \div (1+\exp(u))$ | | 0.68 | 0.76 |
| Difference in probability | | 0.079 | |

# Conclusion

Marketing managers often want to predict customer behaviors that are not distributed across a range of outcomes. These are cases where only one of two behaviors is possible: buy or don't buy, customer retention versus customer loss, and so on. Here, if the manager attempts to use a traditional linear regression to examine the behaviors, nonsensical predictions can result.

But a logistic regression can be used to represent consumers' choice behavior. By transforming the value function into a logistic function, you can model how the value a consumer places on a product increases with a preferred feature of the product. The critical output of the logistic regression is therefore the increase (or decrease) in the percent chance a customer will perform a behavior based on a unit increase in a variable correlated with that behavior.

# Endnotes

1. Scott A. Neslin et al., "Defection Detection: Measuring and Understanding the Predictive Accuracy of Customer Churn Models," *Journal of Marketing Research* 43, no. 2 (2006): 204–211.

2. See Appendix 13-1 for more information on transforming an exponential function to a linear function via the natural log.

3. Kaggle is a user-generated business analytics community. For more information, visit http://www.kaggle.com.

4. For more information on how the odds ratio can be calculated, please see Appendix 13-2.

# Appendix 13-1: Logistic Regression—Understanding Exponential Functions

To understand logistic regressions, it is helpful to first examine exponential functions. Figure 13-A shows the classic example of an exponential distribution. When considering the cumulative sales of a product that has gained market acceptance over time (such as ultrasound machines), you see that sales are slow at first but begin to increase at a greater and greater rate once they have reached critical mass. In the graph, the red line is the actual data, or number of sales per year since introduction. What stands out is that the curve is not a straight line, whereas the ones used in linear regressions are. This is an exponential distribution.

The black line represents a function, created using a computer program,[1] which best accounts for the data shown in the graph. The regression analysis of the available data has produced a line defined by the form $y = 4.0858e^{0.3225x}$, where 4.0858 is the intercept of the line and the slope (0.3225) changes exponentially. The constant $e$ is an irrational number approximately equal to 2.71828, which is related to the rate of change in an exponential function and is the base of the natural logarithm. This function is found in a similar way as a straight-line function when performing a linear regression analysis.

One thing to note about this analysis is that the regression line fits almost perfectly. Because of the volume of data used, r squareds of up to 99% are possible, as compared with the r squareds of 20% to 30% you find when running linear analyses. This is because the data is aggregate and viewed retrospectively, whereas linear regressions attempt to describe the behavior of individuals. If the same analysis of cumulative ultrasound sales was conducted in year two, however, it would be difficult to predict what would happen in years three, four, or five, because r squared breaks down at that point.

What does this have to do with logistic regressions? Consider the green line in Figure 13-A, which represents the natural log of cumulative sales at each time period $x$. The line is nearly straight, meaning a linear regression analysis could produce an accurate function describing the data. In other words, a logistic transformation of exponentially distributed data allows you to view the outputs of the regression in the same way you would a linear regression.[2]

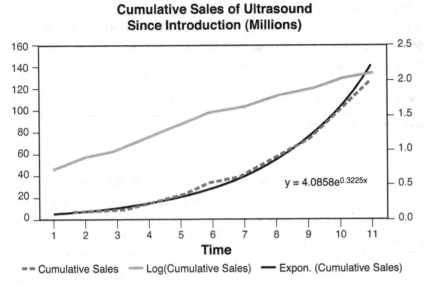

**Figure 13-A** An example of an exponential function

# Endnotes

1. For more information on how to perform a logistic regression using computer software, please visit http://dmanalytics.org/.

2. In algebraic terms, if $y = 4.0858e^{03225x}$, the natural log of $y$ will equal $4.0858 + 3.225x$, a linear function where the intercept is 4.0858 and the slope is 3.225.

# Appendix 13-2: Logistic Regression—Calculating Odds Ratio

Let's consider the log odds ratios presented in Table 13-A and the logistic regression output in Table 13-B. The log odds ratio is defined as the probability of observing an event $(p)$ versus the probability of not observing an event $(1 - p)$. In the context of the choice of games on the mobile app, you are considering the factor by which the log odds of purchasing a game increases when the review for the product increases from 3 to 4. A simple way to calculate this is to take the exponent of the coefficient of reviews from the logistic regression output. In this case, the coefficient of reviews equals 0.399. So the log odds will increase by a factor of 1.49 or 149% (exp(0.399)) when the reviews for a product increase by one unit.

**Table 13-A** Log Odds Ratio and Logistic Probabilities

| | | | |
|---|---|---|---|
| Coefficient of Customer Review Average ($b_{review}$) | 0.399 | | |
| exp ($b_{review}$) | 1.490 | | |
| | | Customer Review Average = 3 | Customer Review Average = 4 |
| $U = bx$ | | 0.76 | 1.159 |
| $P(\text{sale}) = \exp(u) \div (1+\exp(u))$ | | 0.68 | 0.76 |
| Difference in probability | | 0.079 | |

**Table 13-B** Model Estimates

**Model parameters (variable abmedian)**

| Source | Value | SE | Wald Chi-Square | Pr > Chi² |
|---|---|---|---|---|
| Intercept | (1.097) | 0.502 | 4.769 | 0.029 |
| New | (1.595) | 1.467 | 1.182 | 0.277 |
| Regular price | 0.006 | 0.011 | 0.279 | 0.597 |
| Customer review count | 0.066 | 0.030 | 4.943 | 0.026 |
| Customer review average | 0.399 | 0.116 | 11.878 | 0.001 |

# 14

## Retail Relay Revisited

## Introduction

Because Retail Relay (Relay) was operating like a start-up—all employees scrambling around to get everything done in the face of rapid growth—some important business processes had been left unattended. One of the processes that received little attention was how to use the customer-level purchase information in Relay's database to improve customer retention.

Relay understood that many of its existing customers were not only spending money with Relay, but were also purchasing some of their grocery products from other vendors as well. This kind of customer behavior was evident from even a casual examination of the customer-level purchase data. Some customers purchased from Relay infrequently and sporadically, so clearly, these customers must be shopping somewhere else during the interludes between their purchases from Relay. Because customers did not sign up for a subscription plan, Relay could never be certain if customers stopped purchasing from Relay (or "churned") or if they were merely dormant for a while. To overcome this challenge, Relay used a rule of thumb that classified customers as churned if their dormancy duration was more than two standard deviations above the customer's mean interpurchase time. For example, consider a customer with a mean interpurchase time of two months and the standard deviation in interpurchase time of three months. This customer is classified as churned if his or her dormancy duration is more than eight months.

Churned customers represented a loss of potential profit, and management believed that this loss was substantial. Yet Relay had not taken the time and energy to fully leverage its customer-level transaction data—an important customer-relationship asset—to improve customer retention. Because customers submitted their orders through Relay's website, Relay had a large and detailed database of customer orders. Among other information, when a customer placed an order, Relay knew which customer made the order, what items that customer ordered, the customer's entire order history, and the date and time of these orders. Relay decided to use the customer-level purchase data to better understand the factors that influenced customer retention. Were there any distinct characteristics of the retained customers that could instruct Relay about how to increase the retention of its not-so-regular customers?

Relay management knew that somewhere in this data lay the key to unlocking more of its current customers' grocery dollars. Now, it needed to dig until it found that key. Would a logistic regression analysis reveal the keys to improving customer retention? To begin this process, Relay decided to explore the customer summary file described in Exhibit 14-1.

# Exhibits

**Exhibit 14-1**  Retail Relay: Description of Customer Summary File

| Variable | Description |
| --- | --- |
| custid | Computer-generated ID to identify customers throughout the database |
| retained | 1 if customer is assumed to be retained; 0 otherwise |
| created | Date when the contact was created in the database—when the customer joined |
| firstorder | Date when the customer placed first order |
| lastorder | Date when the customer placed last order |
| esent | Number of e-mails sent |
| eopenrate | Number of e-mails opened divided by number of e-mails sent |
| eclickrate | Number of e-mails clicked divided by number of e-mails sent |
| avgorder | Average order size for the customer |
| ordfreq | Number of orders divided by customer tenure |
| paperless | 1 if customer subscribed for paperless communication (only online) |
| refill | 1 if customer subscribed for automatic refill |
| doorstep | 1 if customer subscribed for doorstep delivery |
| train | 1 if customer is in the training database |
| favday | Customer's favorite delivery day |
| city | City where the customer resides |

Source: Company documents.

# Section V

## Digital Analytics

This section explores the latest trends in marketing analytics powered by digital technology. Chapter 15, "Designing Marketing Experiments," provides the fundamental frameworks for design of effective experiments, which is one of the major drivers behind the explosion in digital analytics. Throughout this chapter, you are urged to provide time for design before running real-time digital experiments. The case series in Chapter 16, "Transformation of Marketing at the Ohio Art Company," allows you to contrast traditional television advertising experiments with a digital experiment on Amazon.com. The key insight surrounds the transformation of the treatment of marketing expenses, that is, from a fixed to variable cost, as the company shifts from offline to online advertising. The case also provides you the opportunity to critique experiment design and analyze results from an experiment.

Chapter 17, "Paid Search Advertising," provides the basics of search engine marketing and connects paid search advertising to customer lifetime value and customer management. The cases in Chapter 18, "Motorcowboy: Getting a Foot in the Door," and Chapter 19, "VinConnect, Inc.: Digital Marketing Strategy," expose you to paid search advertising and the metrics presented by Google analytics. Through these cases, you will be able to connect experiment design and optimal resource allocation.

In Chapter 20, "Cardagin: Local Mobile Rewards," the Cardagin case introduces mobile marketing, location, and time-sensitive data and coupons. The case allows you to apply spatial regression to understand characteristics of coupons that are successful in customer acquisition and the network effect benefits retailers obtain from participating in Cardagin. The mobile coupons presented in the case vary widely in face value, offer description, and time duration, which allows for a rich understanding of consumer preferences for mobile coupons.

# 15

## Designing Marketing Experiments

## Introduction

In his quarterly budget presentation, Larry Culp, brand manager for BigHoney cereal, requests funds for an advertising campaign highlighting new packaging that retains freshness better and longer. In response, Mark Weinberg, BigHoney CFO, asks Culp, "Can you convince me that sales of BigHoney will be hurt if you do not advertise?" As a follow-up, he asks, "You have requested $500,000 for a national campaign? Is that the right amount? Can you get the same result for $250,000?" How can Culp convince Weinberg?

Culp's challenge is typical for marketing managers who need to invest money in the marketing mix with the expectation that sales will increase in the future. Attributing an increase in sales to a specific marketing action is a major challenge because the effect on a brand of any single marketing activity is difficult to isolate; it consists of several levers being pulled at the same time, including price promotion, new product introductions, competitive actions, television advertising, PR events, and seasonality. Also, sales resulting from such inputs take time; a television advertisement is unlikely to compel a viewer to immediately jump off the couch, run to the store, and buy a soda. Isolating the influence of a specific event on consumer behavior can be a daunting task.

One way to isolate such influences is through experiments. In this example, Culp could, on a smaller scale, measure the effect of his proposed campaign on the brand's sales. Return on investment (ROI)—and a prospective budget—could then be estimated by projecting any identified lift to a national scale. But how do you design an experiment that will provide accurate results?

# Establishing Causality

Four key rules determine a causal relationship between two variables or factors. Consider Culp's challenge. The marketing campaign may be considered effective if:

- Launching the marketing campaign increases BigHoney sales.
- Not launching the marketing campaign causes no change to the sales figures.
- Launching the marketing campaign today affects sales in subsequent time periods.
- There were no other established external factors (such as competitive action) affecting the sales of BigHoney.

To clearly ascertain whether the targeted sales increase could be achieved without spending marketing dollars or whether any marketing spend is warranted, it becomes very important for Culp to establish causality.

# After-Only Experiment

An experiment provides a mechanism to manipulate one or more input factors while controlling all other factors and observe changes in an output of interest, such as sales or brand awareness.

A very basic experiment that can be designed by Culp is illustrated in Figure 15-1. Culp recruits 1,000 participating customers, half of whom—the test group—are exposed to the *new* advertisement highlighting the new packaging technology; the other half—the control group—are exposed to the *old* advertisements. If cereal purchases by all 1,000 customers are tracked, the difference in sales between the test and control groups will indicate the magnitude of the potential sales lift provided by the new advertising campaign. Such an experimental design is called *after-only* because you measure the sales of BigHoney among the participants of the experiment only after they are exposed to the advertisement.

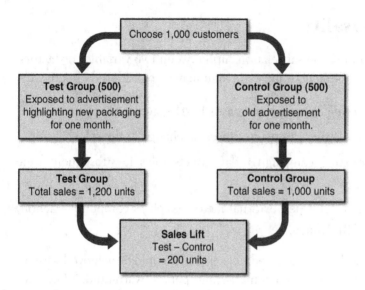

**Figure 15-1** After-only experiment design

Source: Created by author.

The after-only design satisfies two of the four conditions for causality: Sales increase in the short term and in subsequent periods. It cannot indicate whether the increase might have occurred without the new advertisement or whether preference differences existed prior to the experiment. The underlying issue here is the extent to which the participants in the test and control groups are similar *in terms of the factors relevant to the experiment.* The more similar the factors are and the more the two pools of subjects are exposed to the same external environment—store promotions, competitive reactions, even the same weather—then the more reliable the causal inferences are because the only difference would be the advertisement campaign to which each was exposed. So the experimenter could, with confidence, attribute a causal relationship between the marketing input and product sales.

## Test and Control Group Participants

For the experimenter, deciding how to distribute customers between the test group and the control group is critical. There are two primary ways to select control groups: randomization and attribute matching. *Randomization* involves allocating participants randomly between the treatment group and control group. With a big enough sample size, randomization will help improve the similarity between the test and control groups. Consider that Culp is using an e-mail advertisement campaign and has at his disposal a list of 1,000 BigHoney customers. In a random assignment, he would assign every other customer to the test group and the rest of the customers to the control group. Randomization creates fairly homogeneous test and control groups because it removes all sources of extraneous variation, which are not controllable by the experimenter. The chance that the test and control groups end up being different even with random assignment decreases as the sample size increases. For most practical marketing applications, a sample size needs to exceed at least 100 participants for a reliable random assignment process.

*Attribute matching* is used when the available sample size is not large enough to permit random assignment. Participants are assigned based on certain known attributes such as demography, geography, or annual income. If Culp were testing the effect of a TV advertisement campaign, he would be better off choosing cities that are similar in key demographic or psychographic attributes critical to BigHoney's sales.

# Before-After Experiment

A *before-after* design (Figure 15-2) requires an experimenter to measure the output of interest both before and after the participants have been exposed to the inputs.

In this before-after design for an e-mail advertising campaign, Culp would randomly divide the 1,000 participants into test and control groups, as with the after-only design. Both groups would be exposed to the old advertising campaign and sales in the respective campaigns recorded. Let $\Delta Sales_{before}$ be the difference in sales between the test and control groups when they are exposed to the old campaign. The test group is then exposed to the new advertising campaign, whereas the control group is still exposed to the old campaign. The difference in sales between the test and control groups now is termed $\Delta Sales_{after}$. The lift in sales due to the new advertising campaign is then calculated as $\Delta Sales = \Delta Sales_{after} - \Delta Sales_{before}$. Subtracting $\Delta Sales_{before}$ from $\Delta Sales_{after}$ allows the experimenter to control for preexisting differences between the test and control groups. This before-after design, along with random or matched assignment of participants, provides a belt-and-suspenders approach for controlling for all external differences between test and control groups.

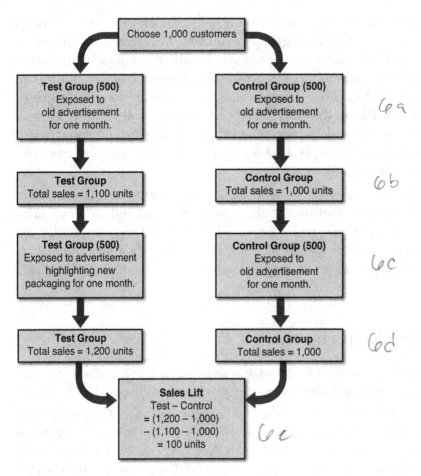

**Figure 15-2** Before-after experiment design

Source: Created by author.

If BigHoney cereal is sold to retailers for $1.59, and the cost of goods is 99 cents, the unit contribution equals $0.60. The lift of 100 units in the experiment translates to $60. If the cost of a single e-mail sent to a customer is $0.10, the cost of e-mails to 500 test-group customers is $50. The experiment suggests that the e-mail campaign provides an ROI of 20%. This ROI estimate can be used by Culp to plan national campaigns. Alternatively, if 500 e-mails provide $10 in contribution, the contribution from a single e-mail is $0.02. If the target lift from a national campaign is $100,000, the experiment suggests that Culp would require 5 million e-mails to attain the target lift.

# Field Experiments

When experiments are conducted within a natural setting, they are termed *field experiments*. In some industries, field experiments are a part of everyday business. Retail outfits regularly use catalogs or e-mails to conduct massive field experiments that assess consumer price sensitivity and optimal catalog design. One advantage of field experiments is that subjects are seldom aware that they are part of an experiment, so the collected data is more likely to represent the realities prevalent in the marketplace. The disadvantage is that it is very difficult to control extraneous variables or to manipulate inputs precisely.

Field experiments are also very transparent to the competition, and competitive reaction could cloud the results. If, during Culp's experiment, his competition, Big-Sugar, launches a promotion, the results could be overly pessimistic. But field experiments are still preferred because they allow the marketer to test a campaign with customers in a natural setting, increasing the accuracy of any prediction. In general, it is easier to experiment with pricing, product, or promotion decisions than with place or channel management decisions.

If Culp also wants to determine the best price for his new packaging, he can create different test conditions where advertising, promotions, and coupons are all the same, and the only difference is price. As part of the experiment, Culp could introduce Big-Honey with its new packaging in three cities (selected because they are similar in factors that affect BigHoney's sales). The only difference is that the products are priced differently in each city: $1.59, $1.89, and $2.15. The sales figures are then tracked in the three cities over time. The city where the product is priced at $1.59 could be expected to have higher sales volume—the question will be *how much* higher? The experiment results, based as before on the original cost of goods sold being 99 cents, are given in Table 15-1.

**Table 15-1** BigHoney Sales Data

|  | Product Price | Sales (In Thousands) | Profit (In Thousands) |
|---|---|---|---|
| City 1 | $1.59 | 1,000 | $600 |
| City 2 | $1.89 | 600 | $540 |
| City 3 | $2.15 | 500 | $580 |

Given this data, Culp is better off introducing the product at the $1.59 price point because it provides the highest profit.

# Web Experiments

Because they can be executed quickly and cheaply, web experiments have gained a significant edge over traditional offline field experiments. Consider the difference between TV and e-mail advertising campaigns for Culp. With TV advertising, Culp has to buy spots in different channels in the test markets with significant lead time. Once the video is shot, it is difficult, time-consuming, and very expensive to change it. Furthermore, the cost of the experiment increases rapidly with each new version that Culp would like to test. The e-mail advertisement, on the other hand, can be created much more quickly and at a much lower cost, making it easier and less expensive for Culp to test different versions.

The faster execution and lower cost of web experiments allows marketers to easily test the simultaneous influence of multiple inputs. When Culp wants to test three different campaigns, "Lasts Longer," "Tastes Better," and the current campaign, "Good for You," each at three different price points ($1.59, $1.89, and $2.15), he can create the full factorial design shown in Table 15-2.

**Table 15-2** Full Factorial Design

|  | Price | | |
| --- | --- | --- | --- |
| Advertisement copy | $1.59 | $1.89° | $2.15 |
| "Lasts Longer" | $1,315 | $1,112 | $1,206 |
| "Tastes Better" | $957 | $1,030 | $1,500 |
| "Good for You"° | $930 | $820 | $770 |

* Current conditions so can be considered controls.

Each cell in Table 15-2 represents a combination of advertisement copy and price point that is tested in the experiment. Because Culp is testing three types of copy and three price points, the total possibilities that need to be tested are 3 × 3 = 9. The profit from each combination is provided within each cell.

A TV advertisement campaign would have required Culp to recruit nine different cities for the experiment (one for each cell) as well as retailers in each city willing to manipulate the prices, a very expensive and time-consuming process. If BigHoney is sold direct to consumers through a website, then Culp can randomize the e-mails sent to consumers to match one of the nine cells in Table 15-2. The e-mail open rates, click-throughs to the website, and the subsequent purchases of consumers when they visit the website can be tracked for each consumer. This provides Culp with a much stronger sense of the effectiveness of the campaign because the same consumer is tracked from exposure to purchase.

The full factorial design also allows Culp to test combinations of the advertisement message and price point. In Table 15-2, you can see that the "Tastes Better" message with a price point of $2.15 provides the highest profit, followed by the "Lasts Longer" campaign at the $1.59 price point. You also can see that when the price is maintained at the current level of $1.89, the "Lasts Longer" campaign provides the highest profit. In this case, had Culp tested only the advertisement campaigns and not the different prices, he would have wrongly concluded that the "Lasts Longer" campaign provided the highest profits.

# Natural Experiments

In a *natural experiment,* a marketer observes the effect of certain naturally occurring incidents on customer behavior and other factors, such as sales volume. Recognizing such occurrences allows companies to learn about their customers at no or little additional expense. A classic example is Amazon collecting sales tax data from California residents. Analyzing the effect of a newly levied tax on sales volume will give Amazon an opportunity to discover how a sales tax affects online retailing. Amazon could compare sales before and after the sales tax introduction for customers who lived on either side of the state's border. The only change would be the newly introduced taxation of online purchases, which affects consumers only on one side of the border.

The most important part of identifying and analyzing natural experiments is to find test and control groups created by some external factor. Many marketers resort to geographic segmentation for natural experiments, but it will not always be a distinguishing characteristic. For example, when the Ford Motor Company introduced an employee pricing promotion, there was no natural geographic separation; all customers were offered the same deal. Instead, marketers compared sales in the weeks immediately before and after the program was introduced.

Ford Motor Company discovered that the jump in sales levels was accompanied by a sharp increase in prices. Customers presumed that they were getting a good deal, but the prices on many models were actually lower before the promotion than at the time of the employee discount prices. But customers responded to the promotion *despite* the prices, not *because* of the prices. The program led to many happy customers, even though they were paying higher prices.

# Conclusion

10

The accuracy of data obtained from a marketing experiment increases with the experiment's duration. For example, experiments that have shorter durations might not adequately account for the carryover effects of marketing interventions; however, marketing decisions are mostly sensitive to time, highlighting the tension between quick versus accurate decisions. The longer the gap between the field experiment and the full campaign, the less accurate the prediction from the field experiment. Yet the time required to obtain buy-in for the field experiment results could delay the timing of the full campaign and thereby the relevance of the field experiment. If an experiment involves salespeople, the mere knowledge of being in an experiment could change their behavior (the *demand effect*), leading to biased conclusions.

Experiments provide a bridge between new ideas and management decisions. Digital marketing has popularized experimentation in the marketing community. Organizations can succeed if they develop a system to learn from experiments and strive toward continuous improvement.

# 16

## Transformation of Marketing at the Ohio Art Company

## Transformation of Marketing at the Ohio Art Company (A)

The Ohio Art Company—among America's oldest toymakers—was headquartered in Bryan, Ohio, a small town in the northwest part of the state. Although Ohio Art made over 50 toy varieties including dolls and water toys, its flagship product was a drawing toy it had been selling for more than 52 years: the Etch A Sketch (EAS). In that time, over 100 million units had been sold to consumers in dozens of countries. Ohio Art's slogan, "Making Creativity Fun," demonstrated the company's commitment to arts and crafts products. Although most of its sales came from its toy business, Ohio Art also produced and sold custom metal lithography, which contributed one third of the company's revenues and a disproportionate share of profits.[1] In recent years, Ohio Art's toy business had experienced a bumpy ride, alternating between profits and losses throughout the 1990s and up through 2011. Product placement of EAS in the hit animated movie *Toy Story* was a shot in the arm for Ohio Art in 1995. In 1998, the company introduced a new doll called Betty Spaghetty, which was an initial hit with consumers, but its popularity and sales had waned over time. "Aimed at girls ages four and up, the small doll featured interchangeable limbs, spaghetti-like hair, and a variety of accessories, such as a cell phone, a laptop computer, and in-line skates."[2]

### Toy Supply Chain and Seasonality

Toy retailing had become more concentrated, with Walmart, Toys "R" Us, and Target accounting for the overwhelming majority of sales.[3] The need for lower costs (to compete effectively in the mass-merchant channel) forced Ohio Art to shift all production of its toys to China in 2001. Making an EAS in China and delivering it to the warehouse in Bryan, Ohio, cost the company 20% to 30% less than making it on-site.[4] The shift in production to Asia magnified the already high risks of introducing new products. Long shipping times and the seasonality of most toy sales meant that inventory management and tooling risks were significant. In 1998, a "'major retailer' abruptly canceled a $15.2 million toy order just before the holiday season. [Ohio Art] was left with a large amount of excess inventory and also was unable to cancel television advertising commitments that had been made in support of the holiday line."[5] Fortunately, in 1999, the company was again helped by the release of *Toy Story 2*, which featured a 30-second spot showing the Etch A Sketch. Management attributed the 20% increase in holiday EAS sales to that exposure.

The company's fiscal year ended January 31; November and December typically accounted for 45% of retail sales. Each of the other 10 months averaged close to 5.5% (see Figure 16-1). This same pattern was typical for almost all toys, including Ohio Art's.

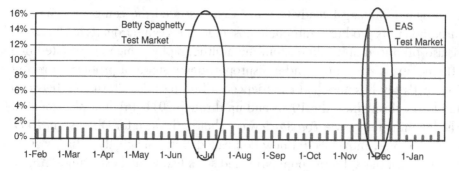

**Figure 16-1** Ohio Art toy seasonality

Source: Ohio Art. Used with permission.

### The Etch A Sketch Experiment

Although the EAS line had been promoted initially with heavy television advertising, by late 2006, advertising budgets for the EAS were below $1 million, most of which went toward reimbursing retailers for cooperative advertising. Too often, these funds did little more than fund temporary price reductions. No national television advertising had been done for several years. In late 2006, however, the company's advertising agency proposed a new campaign to enhance the toy's continued popularity. In part, this was due to a recent request by Target to include the EAS in its own television spot.

Although management was divided on whether an advertising campaign would be economical, it was decided to test the effectiveness of renewed television advertising through a field experiment that lasted from November 27 to December 16, 2006, a three-week period during which approximately 35% of retail toy sales normally occurred. Management intended to assess the results by comparing the test and control market sales of its largest retail customer (25% sales). This retailer had retail stores in all control markets and POS systems that allowed accurate monitoring of sales. The expectation was that observed sales increases would accrue to all retailers. Sales data from the previous year were not available because the merchant had removed EAS from its shelves for much of the year due to a pricing disagreement. The resolution of that disagreement had put EAS back on the shelves, and some of the management team thought that a sales boost through advertising would be a timely move to restore good relations between Ohio Arts and the retailer.

Television commercials for the EAS were aired during syndicated morning and evening talk shows, daytime soaps, and evening news programs only in Cincinnati, Ohio, during the three test weeks. There were internal concerns that Cincinnati might not be a good test market because it was in the same state as the company's headquarters. But research showed that not only was company location not a concern for buyers, but an overwhelming majority of consumers didn't even know that EAS was made and marketed by an Ohio company. Commercials were not aired in any other place in the United States during the test period. The breakdown of the total advertising spend in the three weeks is provided in Table 16-1. The cost of working with an outside agency to develop the test EAS commercials was $75,000. The media spend called for more than 100 spots, each with an average rating of 2.7 to be broadcast over the three weeks.[6] The $30,150 media spend in Cincinnati would be equivalent to a $5 million national budget.

**Table 16-1** Media Spend in Cincinnati

| Dates | Total Cost | Total Rating Points | Number of TV Spots |
| --- | --- | --- | --- |
| Nov. 27–Dec. 1 | $9,350 | 91.8 | 39 |
| Dec. 2–Dec. 8 | $10,200 | 106.3 | 44 |
| Dec. 11–Dec. 16 | $10,600 | 112.1 | 46 |
| **Total** | **$30,150** | **310.2** | **129** |

Source: Ohio Art. Used with permission.

Four other cities—Charleston, South Carolina; Cleveland, Ohio; Indianapolis, Indiana; and Pittsburgh, Pennsylvania—were chosen as controls to evaluate whether the EAS advertising led to increased sales (see Table 16-2 for city demographics). In choosing test market cities, several factors should generally be considered. First, the test city (or cities) must reflect market conditions in the product's market area, whether it was local, regional, national, or global. No city could represent all market conditions perfectly, and success in one city did not guarantee success elsewhere. Typical criteria for good test markets included similarity to planned distribution out-lets: representative population size, demographics, income, purchasing habits, and freedom from atypical competitive activity.[7]

**Table 16-2** Test and Control City Demographics

|  | Cincinnati | Charleston | Cleveland | Indianapolis | Pittsburgh |
|---|---|---|---|---|---|
| Median age | 36 | 33 | 33 | 34 | 36 |
| Median income (family) | $37,543 | $47,942 | $30,286 | $48,979 | $38,795 |
| Average family size | 3.05 | 2.39 | 3.19 | 3.03 | 2.95 |

Source: Ohio Art. Used with permission.

The greater Cincinnati area represented about 0.7% of the U.S. population. The average population of the control cities was around 2 million, which represented about 0.6% of the U.S. population. See Table 16-3 for sales data for EAS and another new Ohio Art product, Doodle Doug, in Cincinnati and the four control cities at selected stores of the major mass merchant.[8] Doodle Doug was not advertised, but sales were tracked in the cities as an additional control in interpreting the results.

**Table 16-3** EAS and Doodle Doug Weekly Unit Sales in Test and Control Cities (1/1/05–2/2/07)

| Dates | CINN EAS | Control Cities EAS | Total Chainwide EAS | Advertising Spending | CINN Doodle | Control Cities Doodle |
|---|---|---|---|---|---|---|
| Jan 1–Sep 1 Average | 11.2 | 79.1 | 1,396.6 | No | 101.3 | 440.4 |
| Jan 1–Sep 1 Std Dev | 5.4 | 27.3 | 319.4 | No | 29.8 | 120.8 |
| Sep 2–8 | 12 | 103 | 1,242 | No | 82 | 333 |
| Sep 9–15 | 12 | 71 | 1,130 | No | 71 | 317 |

| Dates | CINN EAS | Control Cities EAS | Total Chainwide EAS | Advertising Spending | CINN Doodle | Control Cities Doodle |
|---|---|---|---|---|---|---|
| Sep 16–22 | 10 | 87 | 1,184 | No | 52 | 280 |
| Sep 23–29 | 9 | 79 | 1,213 | No | 68 | 279 |
| Sep 30–Oct 6 | 10 | 96 | 1,178 | No | 58 | 248 |
| Oct 7–13 | 9 | 121 | 1,327 | No | 72 | 329 |
| Oct 14–20 | 14 | 101 | 1,349 | No | 95 | 331 |
| Oct 21–27 | 10 | 116 | 1,438 | No | 96 | 362 |
| Oct 28–Nov 3 | 11 | 118 | 1,582 | No | 201 | 651 |
| Nov 4–10 | 15 | 134 | 1,878 | No | 204 | 1,187 |
| Nov 11–17 | 24 | 214 | 2,597 | No | 277 | 1,325 |
| Nov 18–24 | 26 | 286 | 3,844 | No | 241 | 1,100 |
| **Subtotal for period** | **162** | **1,526** | **19,962** | **No** | **1,517** | **6,742** |
| Nov 25–Dec 1 | 61 | 370 | 4,604 | Yes | 217 | 926 |
| Dec 2–8 | 70 | 488 | 6,959 | Yes | 249 | 1,211 |
| Dec 9–15 | 109 | 740 | 9,867 | Yes | 347 | 1,643 |
| **Subtotal for period** | **240** | **1,598** | **21,430** | **Yes** | **813** | **3,780** |
| Dec 16–22 | 145 | 971 | 12,845 | No | 346 | 2,207 |
| Dec 23–29 | 39 | 312 | 4,298 | No | 157 | 1,009 |
| Dec 30–Jan 5 | 1 | 46 | 1,137 | No | 100 | 296 |
| Jan 6–12 | 12 | 62 | 1,137 | No | 80 | 310 |
| Jan 13–19 | 15 | 86 | 1,412 | No | 136 | 318 |
| Jan 20–26 | 23 | 65 | 1,424 | No | 83 | 297 |
| Jan 27–Feb 2 | 10 | 77 | 1,522 | No | 122 | 332 |
| **Subtotal for period** | **245** | **1,619** | **23,775** | **No** | **1,024** | **4,769** |

Source: Ohio Art. Used with permission.

One Ohio Art executive worried that the test would be difficult to read and suggested that a split-cable test[9] could be implemented in April of the following year for about $500,000. He believed the estimate of the projected sales lift from such a split-cable test would be much more accurate.

The suggested retail price for EAS was $12.99. The Travel, Pocket, and Mini Etch A Sketch were less expensive at $8.99, $4.99, and $2.99, respectively. Given unit sales for each product, the weighted average of all EAS products sold in the holiday time period was $10.00. It was this $10.00 price that was suggested for use in calculating the percentage increase required for a national campaign. The suggested retail price for Doodle Doug was $14.99. The company's average gross margin for the EAS products was 58%, and the average retail margin was 36%. (See Figure 16-2 for pictures of the EAS and Doodle Doug.)

**Figure 16-2** EAS and Doodle Doug toys

Source: Ohio Art. Used with permission.

## The Betty Spaghetty Experiment

In mid-2007, the company implemented another field experiment for a revamped Betty Spaghetty product line. The test had three objectives: (1) estimating consumer demand for the revised Betty Spaghetty line, (2) testing whether advertising could increase sales (and profits) obtained for the redesigned Betty Spaghetty, and (3) convincing the merchandise manager at a mass-merchant chain that those sales of Betty Spaghetty would justify the allocation of shelf space. For the Betty Spaghetty experiment, television and radio commercials were aired in Arizona for four weeks from June 17, 2007, to July 14, 2007. The company purchased 600 gross rating points (GRPs) for the television advertisements for a total cost of $31,500. The ads were aimed at girls between the ages of two and eleven and were aired on local cable channels, such as Nickelodeon and the Cartoon Network. Management also purchased 64 GRPs for radio commercials for a total cost of $8,022. The radio commercials were aired during morning and evening commutes. Each of the television and radio programs selected for the commercials reached about 1.8% of the population in Phoenix. The cost of developing the commercial through an outside agency was $150,000.

Management estimated that an equivalent ad budget for eight to ten weeks of pre-holiday advertising, factoring in certain economies as well as the higher seasonal cost of media, would be approximately $3 million. The average retail selling price of Betty Spaghetty during the test was about $15.00. Retailer and Ohio Art margins were about the same as for EAS, 36% and 58%, respectively. Given that some time would be required to read the test, obtain shelf space, and ship product to stores, management estimated that the four-week test market sales period represented about 10% of the total remaining sales potential for the year.

Table 16-4 reports weekly sales in 23 Arizona stores (test) and in 24 stores of the same mass merchant in California (control) for two versions of Betty Spaghetty. The stores represented 50% of the retailer's Arizona sales and 10% of California sales, respectively. Arizona and California represented 2% and 12%, respectively, of the retailer's national sales, and that same retailer was expected to account for 25% of total Betty Spaghetty sales. Management intended to use the test to help estimate Betty Spaghetty sales with and without advertising.

**Table 16-4** Weekly Unit Sales of Betty Spaghetty in Test and Control Cities

|  |  | Color Crazy Test (AZ) | Go-Go Glam Test (AZ) | Color Crazy Control (CA) | Go-Go Glam Control (CA) |
|---|---|---|---|---|---|
| | Week 1 | 30 | 56 | 1 | 12 |
|  | Week 2 | 28 | 59 | 5 | 18 |
|  | Week 3 | 51 | 51 | 7 | 36 |
|  | Week 4 | 54 | 40 | 17 | 46 |
|  | Total | 163 | 206 | 30 | 112 |
|  | Total/store/week | 1.8 | 2.2 | 0.3 | 1.2 |

Source: Ohio Art. Used with permission.

# Transformation of Marketing at the Ohio Art Company (B)

In March 2012, the Ohio Art Company, best known as the manufacturer and marketer of the classic toy, Etch A Sketch (EAS), had been distracted from its efforts to shift its marketing emphasis from traditional mass-marketing channels to more targeted digital marketing. Management believed such a shift would be necessary for the company to thrive in the next decade. The distraction came from the media attention surrounding recent comments made by a campaign manager of Republican presidential candidate Mitt Romney. Having been thrust into the middle of a political controversy, Ohio Art needed to decide how (and whether) to react to the growing media attention.

## Distraction or Opportunity?

When asked how a campaign might change tactics from primary to general elections, Romney's adviser Eric Fehrnstrom replied, "You hit a reset button for the fall campaign. Everything changes. It's almost like an Etch a Sketch. You can kind of shake it up and we start all over again."[10] The result was a media firestorm. Ohio Art received numerous calls from the media, and management knew it had to decide on a plan.

Management was concerned that investing time and financial resources to leverage the media attention might take resources away from the company's new star product: nanoblock construction toys. Because it appealed to a wide range of ages, it would be a great candidate for promotion through digital media. For both nanoblock and the traditional EAS line, digital, social media, and online retailers offered opportunities Ohio Art had yet to explore. Figure 16-3 suggests that there was significant room for further growth in both Internet and mobile advertising, due to the gap between the percentage of time consumers spent with Internet and mobile devices and the percentage of dollars advertisers devoted to these media.

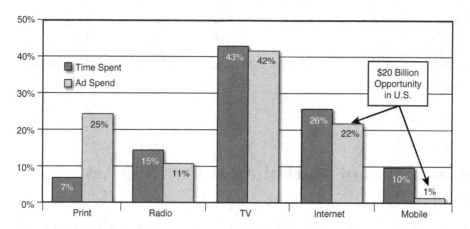

**Figure 16-3** Percentage of time spent using media versus percentage of advertising spend, 2011

Source: Adapted from Mary Meeker, "Internet Trends," Kleiner Perkins Caufield Byers presentation transcript, D10 Conference, May 30, 2012, 17, http://www.scribd.com/doc/95259089/KPCB-Internet-Trends-2012 (accessed July 26, 2012).

In addition to the Internet search and display ads, there were rapidly emerging opportunities to promote through Amazon.com and social media. Social media was particularly intriguing because management thought that outlet might offer new revenue models for the EAS brand. Up until this point, the EAS brand had been mainly leveraged through an increasing number of product variants (Figure 16-4), and the productivity of introducing more EAS product extensions seemed limited. Over 150 million EAS-related products had been sold by mid-2012.

**Figure 16-4** The EAS product and select variants

Source: Ohio Art. Used with permission.

Martin Killgallon, Ohio Art's VP of marketing, thought he could capitalize on the iconic nature of the brand by exploring partnership opportunities with other marketers. For example, the company had licensed iPhone and iPad covers that gave those devices the appearance of the EAS. iPad and iPhone mobile applications also mimicked the action of the EAS on the iPad and iPhone screens. These EAS apps, offered through Apple, Amazon, Google, and Barnes & Noble, had over 1.3 million downloads between mid-2010 and mid-2012. And interest in the timeless toy did not seem to be slowing down. In May 2012, a California start-up company created an accessory called "Etcher" as part of a project with Ohio Art: an iPad case styled after the EAS. It consisted of a bright-red plastic case with two familiar-looking knobs that were used for drawing horizontal and vertical lines. The system interfaced with an iOS app that replicated the toy's drawing experience. The iPad version allowed users to save and share their work with others on social networks or simply shake the screen to erase their creation and start over.

The company typically negotiated a royalty payment of 5% to 10% of gross revenue for licensed products such as this. The image of the EAS product was also often used in advertising as a prop, conveying fun and creativity in the context. Sometimes Ohio Art paid to be included (such as in the Target holiday commercials), and sometimes the company granted permission in return for expected favorable exposures (like the ESPN and BMW Mini commercials). Management thought there was more the company could do to capitalize on the high brand recognition and nostalgia associated with the EAS product, but it was unsure exactly what to do and how it might be monetized.

## A Shift in Strategy

Ohio Art made shifts in all aspects of its marketing mix in reaction to developments in the toy industry and the growth of online retailing. Management believed these shifts were investments that would make Ohio Art a stronger competitor in the upcoming years.

### Product

Instead of designing toys from the ground up and investing in its own tooling, Ohio Art began looking to license toys for exclusive distribution that were developed by other international toy companies or smaller entrepreneurial toy companies that were trying to gain access to stronger distribution and marketing capabilities. With this approach, focusing on new channels and monitoring marketing investments, the company believed it could reduce the risk of introducing new products. Early signs were that the strategy was working at least with its new nanoblock product, which seemed to have a lot of potential. Other licensed products included K's Kids (infant and toddler toys) and Clics (construction) for younger children and Air Picks (an "air guitar" toy that played famous guitar riffs) for preteens and older kids.[11]

### Channels

The traditional line of products (EAS and Doodlesketch) was stocked by the three largest toy retailers—Walmart, Target, and Toys "R" Us—as well as a number of other mass and discount retailers, including dollar stores and drug stores. For the new line of licensed products, including nanoblock, the company was shifting to specialty toy stores, plus Toys "R" Us and a few bookstores, such as Barnes & Noble and Amazon. com. Management believed that attempting to distribute the new products through mass merchandisers would reduce the enthusiasm of the specialty channels (including Toys "R" Us) to stock and promote these items. Also, broadening the distribution channels would make the company less vulnerable to sudden changes in stocking, merchandising, and promotion decisions by individual retail chains. By mid-2012, approximately 1,100 accounts stocked at least some of the nanoblock line. Of those, most were specialty toy retailers or accounts such as Urban Outfitters or Barnes &

Noble, which also sold hobbies and toys. Toys "R" Us and Amazon were expected to account for 65% of nanoblock units sold in 2012.

### Pricing, Discounts, and Margins

One of the reasons for moving to new channels was an attempt to escape the relentless price pressure, "unauthorized deductions," and promotional allowances required by large retailers. Specialty toy retailers tended to price products to earn 50% margins. These independent toy retailers were serviced by manufacturer representatives who typically earned commissions of 10% for sales to specialty stores. Mass retailer margins were lower. For a heavily promoted item, they were 35% or so, and for Ohio Art products, they were closer to 45%. Manufacturer representative commissions to this channel were lower: 4% to 5%. Ohio Art was determined that the new product line would not be subject to the same price pressure as the traditional line and intended to discontinue retailers that did not respect the suggested retail price levels.

### Marketing Communications

Historically, sales of the core EAS line had increased in response to such publicity as the featured role in the movie *Toy Story*, but the gains had been short-lived and might have been due to retailer reactions—more displays, better shelf space, fewer out-of-stocks, and the like—as much as consumer demand. Finding efficient ways to promote the line of Ohio Art toys was an ongoing challenge. Traditional marketing channels were not growing sales of EAS, and the nanoblock line was an impetus to try new strategies.

## Nanoblock History

Developed and manufactured by Kawada and first sold in Japan in October 2008, nanoblock allowed users to build detailed, intricate models because of their tiny size (Figure 16-5). The blocks, which were about one eighth the size of other popular building bricks, were made from high-quality ABS plastic and featured a double-ridged backing that enabled the tiny pieces to fit together almost seamlessly. They appealed to various age groups because of the variety of building sets offered.

Because of the blocks' instant popularity in Japan, large Japanese retail chains had dedicated much shelf display space to nanoblock. In addition to its regular lineup of products, Kawada also offered licensed products and special-edition products. The company also regularly added new items to its catalog, sometimes based on user-submitted ideas.

In late 2011, Ohio Art conducted an online survey to evaluate the demographics of its core customers. The survey revealed that almost 90% of its purchasers were between 25 and 54 years of age.[12]

**Figure 16-5** Sample nanoblock sets (suggested retail prices $9.99, $12.99, $19.99, and $164.99)

Source: Ohio Art. Used with permission.

With this valuable information about buyers, Ohio Art could now make informed decisions about marketing dollars for nanoblock. Specifically, Amazon aimed to use data, technology, and expertise to put the most appropriate products in front of the most qualified and receptive potential buyers. Amazon had built proprietary merchandising technology that allowed it to present a fully customized store to every consumer who visited its website. Companies selling on Amazon benefitted from Amazon's commitment to drive sales by putting the right products in front of the right customers.

A study of online shopping behavior reported that Amazon.com was the source used most frequently for product reviews and ratings. Amazon was used by 58% of respondents, compared with 45% for other retailers (such as Walmart and Best Buy), 41% for search engines (such as Google and Bing), 32% for manufacturers' websites (such as Nike and Lego), 25% for review sites (such as Epinions and CNet), 11% for Facebook, and 7% for Twitter.[13]

Amazon also offered a variety of targeted advertising options (see Table 16-5 for a description of the typical merchant services offered by Amazon.com) with rates that generally doubled for the toy category in the last quarter of 2011.

**Table 16-5** Merchant Services Offered by Amazon.com in 2011

| Name | Description | Rate° |
|---|---|---|
| Automated & Personalized Merchandising | Dynamically recommended products relevant to customers' current search and browsing behavior. | Free. |
| Community Gifting | Customers could create and share wish lists and gift registries. | Free. (Featured in a customer's wish list or gift registry) |
| Social Media | Featured in Amazon's toy blog, and Facebook and Twitter feeds. | Free. |
| Promotional Site Placement | Featured product on different parts of the main promotional site. | $7,500 to $2,000 per week for the main promotional site. Rates were highest for the center stage, followed by the right rotations, the logos at the bottom, and finally the banner at the top of the site. Advertisements were featured 20% to 50% of the time. |
| Product Detail Page Display | Better product details and descriptions on the product page. | $1,400 one-time fee. |
| Product Page Promotion | Placed promotions on the product page. | $5,000 per week. Promotions were featured 25% of the time. |
| Amazon Vine | Select group of customers posted opinions about new and prerelease items. | $2,500 one-time fee per product. |
| E-mail Outreach | Featured in Amazon's targeted promotional campaigns. | $12,000 per year for auto e-mail program. $0.15/mail for a single targeted campaign. |
| Search Results | Advertisement featured on top of customer's relevant search results. | $1,500 per month. |
| Brand Store | Customized, single, central destination for all the firm's brands and products. | $50,000 per year for cross-category store and $35,000 per year for a toy category store. |
| Gateway Placement | Placement on Amazon's landing page. | $65,000 to $32,000 per week, with higher rates for center placements, followed by right and then bottom. Ads were featured 10% of the time. |

* Rates are for Q1–Q3. Q4 rates are higher. Services can be customized for a specific merchant. The customized rates are not included here.

Source: Amazon.com.

According to Larry Culp, an Ohio Art sales rep, the company had always had a consistent presence on Amazon due to the EAS products. But the company had not done much to promote new products on Amazon until the debut of nanoblock. Amazon, like many technology-driven sites, used algorithms and collaborative filtering to determine search results' relevance. *Collaborative filtering* was a process used to generate product recommendations by matching the purchase histories of many different users. Without a minimum purchase volume, these recommendation algorithms did not have enough history to generate relevant recommendations for nanoblock.

One way the company was able to increase the potential for relevant recommendations was through Amazon's "Gold Box" promotion, where items were offered at reduced prices for an hour or two on a given day. Ohio Art decided to fund a promotion for its Eiffel Tower nanoblock set in the "Lightning Deals" section of Gold Box on March 4, 2012 (see Table 16-6 for sales data on select products). Companies paid Amazon to promote their products this way; fees were determined by the number of units companies made available for the deal multiplied by the discount (versus Amazon's normal price). In this way, companies were challenged to forecast properly; an overestimation would result in higher promotional costs while an underestimation would result in foregone sales. These "Lightning Deals" increased the number of user clicks on the nanoblock product, thereby increasing the relevance of Ohio Art and nanoblock. That, in turn, increased the number of appearances for Ohio Art's products even after the promotion ended. Ohio Art sold all 300 Eiffel Tower sets it offered at $12.99 in the "Lightning Deal." The rest of March volume was sold at the regular $19.99 price.

**Table 16-6** Sales Data on Selected Products

| Ohio Art Product | Sales Price | Jan–Feb 2012 | March 2012 | May 2012 |
|---|---|---|---|---|
| nanoblock Eiffel Tower | $19.99 | 274 | 686 | 219 |
| nanoblock Taj Mahal | $19.99 | 308 | 163 | 132 |
| nanoblock Castle Neuschwanstein | $19.99 | 244 | 184 | 146 |
| Classic EAS | $12.99 | 344 | 352 | 399 |

Finally, Amazon charged suppliers a 10% cooperative advertising fee. This fee was justified by Amazon providing search capabilities and using Google AdWords/Microsoft AdCenter to get top results in searches for merchants' products. For example, the top advertised spot in a Google search for "nanoblocks" was the Amazon.com link to Ohio Art's products. Ohio Art was trying to determine if Amazon was a great new channel or if the challenges associated with it would be just as tricky as those it faced in dealing with traditional retailers.

## *Opportunities*

EAS sales were stagnant, but nanoblock sales were growing. The targeted-audience data about nanoblock's customers coupled with a taste of Amazon's variable pricing motivated management to consider engaging in other new media. Ohio Art's ad agency recommended advertising that was playful and sophisticated for the adult audience. And the Amazon sales empowered management to recognize that it could push for positive return on investment rather than financing a large traditional ad campaign and then sitting around hoping for results. The new model of testing several tactics, discontinuing the ones that did not work, and honing the definitive successes was much more appealing—for all products, not just nanoblock.

Ohio Art utilized its Facebook.com/EAS page primarily for polls and factoids. Posts ranged from "Fun Fact: World's Largest #EtchASketch weighs 300lbs" to "Does this expertly sketched Mona Lisa make you smile or pout?" These efforts earned it over 7,000 fans by mid-2012. For the nanoblock Facebook page, Ohio Art produced a series of targeted poster ads (Figure 16-6), special offers, and announcements about fun things that were going on. With nanoblock in particular, the company attempted to create a forum for fans to communicate with each other, asking questions and sharing creations. The videos were quite popular on the nanoblock USA Facebook page, resulting in over 3,000 fans by mid-2012.

**Figure 16-6** Targeted nanoblock poster ads, spring 2012[14]

Source: Ohio Art. Used with permission.

There were several ways that companies could use blogs to promote their products. In 2010, Google Blogger introduced BlogSense accounts. Companies would pay for advertising on blogs that Google determined were related to their products. A percentage of the proceeds would go to the blogger. Of particular interest to Ohio Art was the fact that "Mommy Bloggers" had recently become very popular. Top Mommy Bloggers had thousands of daily visitors to their sites, many of whom were avid, loyal readers who deeply valued the writer's opinions. Companies could create incentives for these bloggers to promote or review their products on their blogs, which Ohio Art pursued in 2010 and 2011. The venture resulted in over 350 websites creating permanent links to the Ohio Art sites—http://www.world-of-toys.com/ (the retail website) and www.OhioArt.com. By mid-2012, the company was evaluating whether to attempt to convert certain Mommy Bloggers into affiliates. Affiliates would link to Ohio Art's website and receive commissions on sales that resulted from those click-throughs. Company-sponsored events, such as luncheons to demonstrate new products, functioned as forums to inform and entertain 20 or so bloggers at a time. The success of these small events was one argument for considering larger events (for example, inviting 350 bloggers to events sponsored by third parties or sponsoring booths at blogger conventions).

Ohio Art had also developed an interest in Pinterest, a content-sharing website where users could create, manage, and share theme-based "pinboards." Users could browse other users' pinboards, follow other pinners, and repin images to their own collections. Pinterest allowed users to share their pins on Twitter and Facebook, and with more than 12 million users (more than 80% female), it was the fastest social media site in history to break 10 million unique visitors.[15] Users typically pinned things such as recipes, décor, children's toys, and do-it-yourself crafts. But by the middle of 2012, Pinterest had not yet been explored by Ohio Art.

Overall website traffic was of interest to the company because direct-to-consumer sales represented the highest-margin sales and also because Ohio Art controlled that consumer experience completely, from product copy to price. As of mid-2012, search engines referred 22% of visits to the site. Thanks to the bloggers, there were 365 sites linking to OhioArt.com and 110 sites linking to World-of-Toys.com. Of the search-generated traffic, Ohio Art accounted for 25% of visits and some version of "Etch A Sketch" almost 40%.[16]

Ohio Art had e-mail addresses for approximately 18,000 customers, which were primarily collected from orders placed on the company's website. Many of those orders were for bulk quantities, intended for events where the number of products a customer needed exceeded what a local store might keep in stock. Ohio Art had used these e-mails to send new product announcements and promotional codes to encourage orders from its website.

# Conclusion

Management at Ohio Art was convinced that finding marketing investments that produced trackable, positive returns would be the key to its future success. It was no longer acceptable to take the risks associated with expensive national television ad campaigns and the associated inventory and receivables risk required to support broad retail distribution. The new philosophy was that as returns could be demonstrated, marketing investments could be rapidly scaled behind successful campaigns.

So, when Mitt Romney's campaign manager said the candidate's platform was "...almost like an Etch a Sketch," the Ohio Art team had a decision to make: either have its staff and ad agency jump into social media to capitalize on the opportunity or stay the course with other targeted efforts.

# Endnotes

1. "The Ohio Art Company," *International Directory of Company Histories*, vol. 59, (Farmington Hills, Michigan: St. James Press, 2004).

2. "The Ohio Art Company History," http://www.fundinguniverse.com/company-histories/the-ohio-art-company-history/ (accessed June 8, 2012).

3. Walmart had the highest market share at about 25%, followed by Toys "R" Us at 17%, and Target at 12%.

4. Joseph Kahn, "Ruse in Toyland: Chinese Workers' Hidden Woe," *New York Times*, December 7, 2003.

5. http://www.fundinguniverse.com/company-histories/the-ohio-art-company-history/.

6. One rating point was equal to 1% of the total population in a given area.

7. Charles W. Lamb, Joseph F. Hair, Carl D. McDaniel, and Daniel L. Wardlow, *Essentials of Marketing* (Cincinnati, OH: South-Western College Pub., 1999).

8. Unit sales figures are not provided in some weeks because EAS was not carried by the mass merchant in these weeks due to disagreements over price points.

9. Split-cable testing systems allow for delivery of separate advertising campaigns or a different level of advertising exposures to different groups of households within a given market and tracked purchases through consumer diaries or other panel data. This eliminated differences in retail environments, competitive activity, and other market characteristics among test and control groups.

10. Sam Stein, "Mitt Romney Platform 'Like an Etch A Sketch,' Top Spokesman Says," Huffington Post, March 21, 2012, http://www.huffingtonpost.com/2012/03/21/mitt-romney-etch-a-sketch_n_1369769.html (accessed July 23, 2012).

11. See the Ohio Art website for a complete listing of individual products: http://www.world-of-toys.com/category_s/58.htm (accessed July 30, 2012).

12. Christopher Tan is a self-proclaimed "nanoblock enthusiast" from Malaysia. He wrote a blog specifically dedicated to the product. See his post "Why nanoblock Is Cool!" September 21, 2011, http://www.inanoblock.com/2011/09/why-nanoblock-is-cool.html (accessed July 30, 2012) to understand more about the product and what types of consumers were interested in it.

13. "The 2011 Social Shopping Study," *Power Reviews*, June 2011, p. 14, http://www.powerreviews.com/assets/download/Social_Shopping_2011_Brief1.pdf (accessed July 24, 2012).

14. See the Facebook page for examples of video and poster ads created by the company advertising agency: https://www.facebook.com/nanoblockUSA.

15. Josh Constine, "Pinterest Hits 10 Million U.S. Monthly Uniques Faster Than Any Standalone Site Ever—comScore," February 7, 2012, http://techcrunch.com/2012/02/07/pinterest-monthly-uniques/ (accessed July 24, 2012).

16. "Statistics Summary for OhioArt.com," http://www.alexa.com/siteinfo/ohioart.com (accessed July 24, 2012).

# Assignment Questions

1. Why did the company think it *might* be a good idea to advertise the EAS products? What does the experiment tell you? How would you decide whether the more reliable and more expensive split-cable experiment would be worthwhile?

2. How does the EAS experiment compare with the Betty Spaghetty experiment? In your opinion, which experiment is more suitable for evaluating whether an advertising campaign is effective?

3. Use the test results to forecast sales for Betty Spaghetty, and prepare a production order for the factory in China.

4. Evaluate the Amazon.com promotion for nanoblock. Will such promotions lead the way or get in the way of distributing through independent toy stores?

5. Which products and what kind of social media campaigns do you believe have the most potential for Ohio Art? What actions would you propose in response to the media reactions to the comments by Romney's aide?

6. How might the company capitalize on the EAS's iconic brand status?

# 17

## Paid Search Advertising[1]

## Introduction

You're in the market for a baseball cap, an espresso maker, and a Ferrari F430 (lucky you). You decide you'd like to purchase each of the items in an online auction. You'd like to pay $10 for the hat, $1,000 for the coffee maker, and $150,000 for the Ferrari, so you set aside $151,010 to make sure you land your items.

Without understanding the nuances of the bidding structure, you decide to take an average of your total budget and allocate that as your bid amount on each item—$50,336.67 for the hat, $50,336.67 for the espresso maker, and $50,336.67 for the Ferrari.

Much to your dismay, you later learn you've won the auctions for the hat and espresso machine but missed out on the Ferrari. As ridiculous as the strategy sounds, this is what can happen when businesses run paid search advertising campaigns without trying to optimize or target their efforts to the business context and nuances of the system at hand.

Imagine that instead of different products such as hats and Ferraris, you are targeting customers with different levels of worth. Modern paid search advertising campaigns are based on the technology of online auctions—they allow businesses to bid on the opportunity to put their ads in front of certain types of customers. Fortunately, there is no need for companies to divide their budget equally and throw the same amount of money at every customer regardless of his or her expected value. Instead, the campaigns generate enough data about those customers to ensure that the companies know what the customers' values are before deciding whether it is worth it to place their ad in front of them.

Using linear and logistic regressions and cluster analyses, modern marketing managers can optimize their paid search advertising campaigns to ensure that they don't spend $50,000 on a customer who only wants to buy a hat. In this chapter, you will learn what paid search advertising is, the principal metrics used to track the success of the campaigns, the strategic objective of paid search, the relationship between customer lifetime value and search ads, how to overcome sparse data problems using keyword clouds, and the nature of Google AdWords's enhanced campaigns.

## What Is Paid Search?

Paid search advertising is one strategy companies can use to increase their digital visibility. It is part of a broader view of search engine optimization (SEO), the method of improving a company's performance in keyword searches on popular search engines (such as Google, Bing, and the like).

When a user types keywords into a search engine (for example, "car insurance"), two types of results are listed: websites the engine's algorithm has organically determined to be valuable and websites advertisers have paid to promote based on the keyword searched (Table 17-1). Because of the large amounts of data produced in paid search advertising campaigns, the returns from paid search advertising can be improved through marketing analytics, whereas organic search results are influenced more by website architecture.

The structure of paid search advertising has become increasingly complex as additional granularity has been introduced into the process, but the basis is still the maximum *cost-per-click* (CPC) bid, which is the highest amount an advertiser would be willing to pay for an individual click. The search engine will typically sell the link placement to the highest bidder at a rate just above the next-highest bid. This means the maximum cost per click a company would be willing to pay can be considerably higher than the average cost they actually pay. To control spending, search engines allow marketers to specify maximum daily spends. For more information on how search engines determine cost per click and an ad's rank among other search results, please see Appendix 17-1.

The search engine provider allows the advertiser to bid how much it would be willing to pay for the user to click on its link (a *pay-per-click* pricing structure). If the company's bid is high enough, its ad will be placed at the top of the page. Although payment is made only when someone clicks on the ad, the advertiser can be pushed farther down the page if competitors' ads are more effective at producing clicks. In Figure 17-1, Progressive is the first company listed in the organic search returns, and Progressive and Allstate are listed at the top of the two groups of paid search returns.

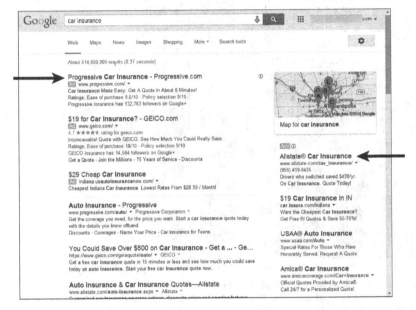

**Figure 17-1** Paid search results

Source: https://www.google.com/#q=car+insurance. Google and the Google logo are registered trademarks of Google Inc., used with permission.

Although search is only one of the platforms companies can use to increase their digital visibility, it is the dominant online marketing vehicle and is still growing (Figure 17-2). Display advertising has been growing faster than search in recent years, but digital media remains largely weighted toward search. Search advertising is distinctive from most other forms of marketing media in that it targets intent: It captures prospective customers right at the moment they are expressing an interest in a company's product. This makes for a powerful tool that can deliver a robust return on investment if the company can deliver an offer that resonates with the customer.

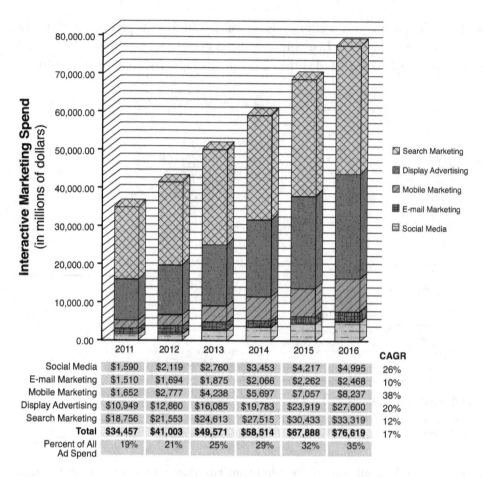

| | 2011 | 2012 | 2013 | 2014 | 2015 | 2016 | CAGR |
|---|---|---|---|---|---|---|---|
| Social Media | $1,590 | $2,119 | $2,760 | $3,453 | $4,217 | $4,995 | 26% |
| E-mail Marketing | $1,510 | $1,694 | $1,875 | $2,066 | $2,262 | $2,468 | 10% |
| Mobile Marketing | $1,652 | $2,777 | $4,238 | $5,697 | $7,057 | $8,237 | 38% |
| Display Advertising | $10,949 | $12,860 | $16,085 | $19,783 | $23,919 | $27,600 | 20% |
| Search Marketing | $18,756 | $21,553 | $24,613 | $27,515 | $30,433 | $33,319 | 12% |
| **Total** | **$34,457** | **$41,003** | **$49,571** | **$58,514** | **$67,888** | **$76,619** | 17% |
| Percent of All Ad Spend | 19% | 21% | 25% | 29% | 32% | 35% | |

**Figure 17-2** Interactive marketing spending in the United States from 2011 to 2016

Source: Forrester Research Interactive Marketing Forecasts, 2011–16.

Furthermore, modern paid search systems allow their advertisers to stipulate exactly what they are willing to pay for a given customer based on everything they know about him or her. This auction process can account for the specific search terms entered into a system ("car insurance" versus "cheap car insurance"), the type of device on which the search is being conducted, the time of day of the search, and the location of the person searching, allowing a company to bid different amounts based on how valuable they think the searcher might be. For example, data generated by companies using paid search advertising has shown that people are more likely to buy at certain times of the day than at others. Individuals searching at 1:00 a.m. might just be making a wish list, but those searching at 9:00 a.m. while at work typically are trying to be more efficient.

It is important to remember that paid search advertising is different from traditional advertising, which pushes a firm's message to consumers even when they are not looking for its products. Direct mail, store signage, and television advertisements (to name a few) are capable of creating demand by putting a company's message in front of people who have been identified as likely customers but who don't yet realize they want its products. This is a powerful form of advertising in that the advertiser has complete control of the campaign, but it isn't the way search works. Search is more akin to the yellow pages in that the advertisement for a plumbing service shows up when someone is looking for a plumber.

Again, paid search advertising can be an effective marketing channel, but it is most likely to capture only existing demand. If you have a new product or service that no one has ever heard of, search may not be as effective.

Google is the largest and most important player in the paid search advertising arena. The search engine has captured about 80% of the market for these types of ads and essentially makes the rules of the game. Bing is also a player, holding most of the remaining 20% of the market share. Comparison shopping engines such as Shopzilla and Amazon also deserve attention from companies whose products are sold in those arenas. Other pay-per-click advertising mediums such as the one offered by Facebook are focused on display ads pushed toward people who have expressed an interest in categories of products and lifestyles.

## Metrics of Search Advertising

Before examining the efficacy of a paid search advertising campaign, marketers should be familiar with several metrics used to understand web traffic in general. The *visits* metric measures the number of sessions on a website, whereas the *visitors* metric measures the number of people making those visits. (*Visitors* and *unique visitors* are the same metric.) When a user creates a shopping cart on a website that does not result in a purchase, this is known as abandonment, and the abandonment rate is the ratio of the number of abandoned shopping carts to the total number of carts created by users. Table 17-1 offers a list of terms useful for understanding paid search advertising metrics.

**Table 17-1** Paid Search Advertising Metrics

| | |
|---|---|
| Keyword | Term identified as one a customer might use to search for a given product. |
| CPC bid | The amount an advertiser is willing to spend to place its ad in front of a potential customer given the keywords entered, device used, geographic location, and other factors. |
| Quality score | An estimate of how relevant your ads, keywords, and landing page (website to which your ad points the customer) are to a person seeing your ad. |
| Realized CPC | The actual amount an advertiser spends to place its ad in front of a potential customer. This cost is determined as a function of bid amount, amount of the next-highest bid, and quality score. |

Source: Created by case writer. Definitions are adapted from Paul W. Farris, Neil T. Bendle, Phillip E. Pfeifer, and David J. Reibstein, *Marketing Metrics, The Definitive Guide to Measuring Marketing Performance* (Upper Saddle River, NJ: FT Press, 2010).

The success of a paid search advertising campaign is dependent on its ability to put the right message in front of the right consumer and influence him or her to perform an action. Impressions represent the number of opportunities consumers are given to see an advertisement. Many recorded impressions are not actually perceived by the intended viewer, however, so some marketers refer to this metric as "opportunities to see."

Less refined metrics for understanding how often an ad is viewed are page views and hits. *Page views* represent the number of times a website is accessed, and *hits* are a measure of file requests by a website. The notion of page views was intended to more accurately measure the number of times a site has been displayed to a user. But for marketing purposes, a further distinction must be made as to how many times an advertisement has been viewed by unique visitors. For example, the advertisement may be a banner ad that changes depending on the visitor. So, for a single advertisement served to all visitors on a site, impressions are equal to the number of page views. If a page carries multiple advertisements, the total number of all ad impressions will exceed the number of page views.

Cost per impression, cost per click, cost per order, and cost per customer acquired are the most critical marketing metrics for paid search advertisers. All three are calculated in the same way: by dividing advertising cost by, respectively, number of impressions, number of clicks, number of orders, and number of customers acquired.

Click-through rate is the percentage of impressions that lead a user to click on an ad. It describes the fraction of impressions that motivate users to visit the web location intended by the advertiser. Most Internet-based businesses use click-through metrics, and the growth of paid search advertising has made them more common. Advertisers should remember, however, that click-throughs are only a step on the road to a final sale, and other metrics must be observed to understand the true value of a paid search ad.[2]

# Strategic Objective

The goal of paid search advertising is in many ways to marry the ad a company is serving—and the price it is willing to pay for it—to the intent of the consumer at the moment he or she sees the ad (Figure 17-3).

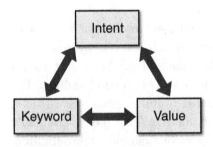

**Figure 17-3** Strategic objective
Source: Created by case writer.

The two most common types of ads are text ads, which contain roughly a dozen words (Figure 17-4), and product listings, which are more pictographic and are growing in importance for e-commerce (Figure 17-5). Both types of advertisement must have messages that are appropriate and attractive to a user based on what he or she is searching for.

**Figure 17-4** Google text ad
Source: Google search, https://www.google.com/search?q=achron+power+leds&oq=achron+power+leds&aqs= chrome..69i57.3188j0j8&sourceid=chrome&espv=210&es_sm=122&ie=UTF-8#es_sm=122&espv=210&q=power+leds (accessed November 14, 2013). Google and the Google logo are registered trademarks of Google Inc., used with permission.

**Figure 17-5** Google product ad

Source: Google search, https://www.google.com/search?q=led+lights&source=lnms&sa=X&ei=gOmEUuCeHpCg4AO 48IDwCQ&ved=0CAUQ_AUoAA&biw=1680&bih=943#q=led+lights&start=10 (accessed November 14, 2013). Google and the Google logo are registered trademarks of Google Inc., used with permission.

In paid search advertising, the goal of targeting ad copy to customers becomes even more difficult to achieve than it is when using traditional display ads. For a retailer such as Walmart that sells hundreds of thousands of products, that means creating appropriate ad copy for millions of possible search-term combinations. For example, the company might want to promote high-definition televisions with one group of advertisements and women's clothing with another. That means creating a campaign that hits the top search terms for televisions (for example, high-definition, hi-def, HD, flat screen, LCD, digital television) and a completely separate campaign for clothing (for example, blouse, skirt, dress, hosiery).

Management's challenge is not only understanding how to create copy that is relevant for those different potential search queries, but also performing controlled tests to ensure the copy resonates with the types of users who are encountering it. This improves the advertisement's click-through rate, and the search engine will come to believe that the ad is relevant and serve it to customers more often.

In addition to the ad copy, the landing page to which the customer is directed must be appropriate. Although it is simple to send every potential customer to a company's home page, most consumers expect to be taken directly to the product or service they are seeking.

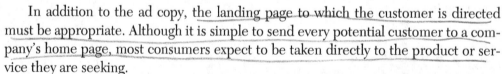

The most critical piece of the paid advertising system is bidding on ad space. Determining exactly how much a company is willing to pay for which customers and setting the system up to enter the appropriate bid are complex processes. This is also where marketing analytics enters into the process because field testing plays a critical role in optimizing bids. Because the value of all customers is not equal, the bid a company is willing to make on any piece of web traffic should be commensurate with the anticipated value of the traffic to the business. A good management system should measure the value extracted from each user and use that information to anticipate the value of similar customers in the future.

# CLV-Based Optimization

One way to get the most out of paid search advertising is to set customer lifetime value (CLV) as the objective function. In other words, the goal of the campaign should be to maximize CLV. In the earliest days of paid search advertising, firms typically focused on optimizing conversion rate. But all orders are not equally valuable, so measuring sales dollars rather than conversions (or number of orders) makes more sense. Consider the example of Sticks Kebob Shop in Table 17-2. Based on its analysis of the existing customer base, Sticks has realized that customers who first visited Sticks's website based on the keywords "kids healthy fast food" are more likely to belong to the Health Conscious segment of their customer base. Customers who first visit Sticks's website through the search keywords "convenient fast food," however, are more likely to belong to the Convenience segment. Sticks also knows from its customer database that customers in the Health Conscious segment have a CLV of $1,200 and customers in the convenience segment have a CLV of $700. This would imply that Sticks is willing to bid higher for the keywords "kids healthy fast food" than for "convenient fast food," even though the click-through and conversion rates for these keywords are similar.

**Table 17-2** Optimizing Paid Search Bids to Maximize CLV

| Keywords | Health Conscious | | Convenience | |
| | Click-Through Rate | Conversion Rate | Click-Through Rate | Conversion Rate |
| --- | --- | --- | --- | --- |
| "Kids healthy fast food" | 35% | 40% | 5% | 15% |
| "Convenient fast food" | 10% | 5% | 40% | 30% |
| CLV | | $1,200 | | $700 |

Source: Created by case writer.

But there is still more to the picture: Profit margin rates are also different depending on the product, and return rates can vary significantly. For example, people who buy paint rarely return it, but shoe buyers return their purchases regularly.

Different orders have different values to a business in the long term, so the goal of a company engaged in a paid search advertising campaign should be to use the data it has about its existing customers' behavior to optimize CLV. For companies looking to generate only sales leads through their online ads, the process is similar, as all leads are not equally valuable. Furthermore, what happens online isn't the whole story, as some consumers browse on a mobile device before making an in-store purchase.

Others shop on a laptop and then contact a call center. Companies must make an effort to capture some of this data in order to gain an accurate sense of CLV.

Although some of the elements of CLV might seem obvious to the marketing manager (a customer searching for "Lexus insurance" is more valuable than a customer searching for "cheap car insurance"), the ability to track the performance of a paid search ad granularly allows the manager to confirm intuition.

## Keyword Clouds

A challenge does arise for companies that use a large volume of keywords, such as big-box retailers. This leads to a number of keywords with relatively sparse performance (Figure 17-6), meaning not enough is known about the people who click on the ads after entering those words to make any significant claims about who they are relative to groups of people who click on other terms.

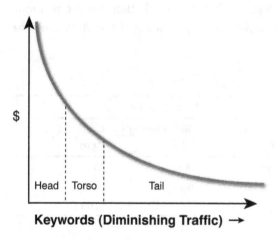

**Figure 17-6** The long tail of keywords

Source: Created by case writer.

To account for sparse data concerns, companies must attempt to aggregate data. For example, on the keyword level, the company might group certain words with their "cousins." The firm might have sparse data on "blue steel widgets," but it might recognize that the phrase "blue wood widgets" behaves in a similar fashion. By grouping these words into families of search terms, the business can build a statistically significant data set and make viable claims about the people who are attracted to the keywords (such as where they are from, how they surf the Internet, or whether they are likely to be repeat customers).

On the location level, although a firm might have little data on how a keyword performs in, for instance, Charlottesville, Virginia, it might be able to create a statistically significant amount of data on small cities in the southeast with above-average income levels. That data can then be used to make assumptions about what type of keyword will be effective in those types of geographic locations.

Because there is no downside to using a very large number of keywords (the cost only increases per click, not keyword), even smaller companies may discover some of their words do not produce a large number of clicks, meaning little is known about the customers who are drawn to those words. One technique that can be useful in creating keyword clouds to optimize paid search advertising campaigns is cluster analysis. Because keywords are tied to the intent of similar consumers or consumers who are part of the same market segment, marketers can group keywords just as they would customers in a given marketplace segment. For more about how to perform cluster analyses, see "Cluster Analysis for Segmentation" (UVA-M-0748).[3]

# Enhanced Campaigns

Google recognized early on that a keyword on a smartphone would be worth a different amount to a company than the same keyword on a home computer, and a keyword entered within a mile of a brick-and-mortar store would be worth more than the same keyword entered 100 miles away. So the company initially set up its system to allow users to create different campaigns for each modifier to a keyword. In other words, if a company had a base campaign of 10,000 keywords, it would create a separate 10,000-word campaign for those keywords searched on a smartphone and another 10,000-word campaign for those keywords searched on a tablet computer. If the company wanted to further modify the campaign for geography, it would have to create another three campaigns for searches within a mile of a brick-and-mortar store and another three campaigns for searches more than 100 miles from a brick-and-mortar store. This led to a replication model that was not scalable for large customers.

To correct this problem, Google rolled out enhanced campaigns in July 2013, a system that allows companies to modify their base campaigns. This meant firms had to condense back to a single version of every keyword and create a system where they could bid up for certain conditions or bid down for others. But one problem remains—the modifiers in the 2013 iteration are stacked on top of one another. For example, if a firm determined that smartphone traffic is worth 20% of desktop traffic because it is too hard to shop on the device, it might set its bid for keywords on smartphones to one fifth of its bid on desktops. But if the smartphone search is conducted

\10

within a mile of a brick-and-mortar store, the company might believe the traffic is worth the same as desktop traffic and want to increase the bid by a factor of five. In Google's current system, this also increases the cost of desktop traffic for that keyword by a factor of five if the desktop is located within a mile of a brick-and-mortar store. If the company wanted to further customize the campaign to double its bid for smartphone users within a mile of a brick-and-mortar store who also reside in a high-value geographic location, the desktop bid would again be doubled based on the larger bid, even if that were not the intention (Table 17-3).

**Table 17-3** Enhanced Campaigns

| Device | Bid Amount for "Television" | Bid Amount for "Television" within One Mile of Store | Bid Amount for "Television" within One Mile of Store in High-Value Geographic Location |
|---|---|---|---|
| Laptop | 5 (Base Bid) | 25 | 50 |
| Smartphone | 1 (20% of Base) | 5 | 10 |

Source: Created by case writer.

Search engines deliver reports that marry each click to the geography from which it came, and the goal of the manager is to synthesize that information to determine the value of each type of click. For smaller businesses, Google's optimize-conversion option delivers advertisements with some success. The rules are applied across the board, however, and don't take into account CLV or conditions unique to a company, such as promotions.

# Testing and Diagnostic Feedback Loops

As with any marketing measure, paid search advertising campaigns must be refined through numerous iterations. Marketing managers must gather the data available, revisit their campaigns, and make them more focused over time through testing and experiments.

So how does the ability to target customers based on the different factors analyzed by search engines actually work in reality? Imagine Suck-It-Up Vacuums determines that the average search for "vacuum cleaner" is worth $0.45 (Table 17-4). The company then determines that the value is reduced 5% by the location of the search and 2.5% by the day of the week, but increased 10% because the search is on a tablet, 3% because it is done on a wireless Internet connection, 7% because the search is done in the morning, and 13% because the person is a repeat buyer. All of these factors make the value of the search term at that moment $0.56.

**Table 17-4** Matching Bids to Value

| Modifier | Bid |
|---|---|
| Desktop—search engine | $0.45 |
| More than 10 miles from store | –5% |
| Smartphone or tablet | +20% |
| Free Wi-Fi hotspot | +3% |
| Early morning | +7% |
| Online retail checkout | +13% |
| Monday | –2.5% |

Source: Created by case writer.

As with any model, there is the danger of making assumptions based on incomplete data and omitted variables. Take a furniture retailer's campaign, shown in Figure 17-7. The company wanted to determine which regions were performing best nationally and found statistically significant differences in a variety of locations. Further inquiry, however, determined proximity to shipping locations was an omitted variable in the model. Shipping costs within 100 miles of the company's discrete distribution centers were reasonable, but outside those locations, the costs skyrocketed. Understanding that the conversion rate was higher within those regions, the company was able to correct its function to optimize CLV and target those zones more heavily than others.

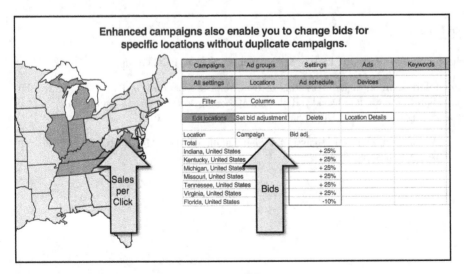

**Figure 17-7** Regional variance in value per click

Source: Created by case writer.

# Conclusion

Paid search advertising is a powerful tool for marketers looking to match their offers with consumers who are looking for their products. Because it is an auction-like system, wherein marketers bid an amount to put their ad in front of a customer, the data available from existing customers' behavior can ensure an optimal marriage between customer value and the price of the ad.

What's more, paid search advertising systems are only growing more powerful. For now, the consumer data is somewhat limited to location, device, and search time, but the future offers far-reaching possibilities. For example, consumers might be classified according to whether they have purchased anything from a company's website in the past or whether they have put something in their cart but never made a purchase. Search engines might also be able to feed marketers data about the speed of the Internet connection used by customers, whether they are at home or the office, whether they are traveling at five miles per hour or 60, whether they tend to buy online or offline, or whether they are existing customers of a competitor.

The basics of marketing analytics still hold true when analyzing the effectiveness of paid search advertising campaigns. The advertisements can be customized to the needs of the advertiser through varying bid amounts. Keywords represent customer intent, so they can be grouped in terms of their value just as customers can be grouped into segments. And, finally, the whole process can be improved over time through feedback loops, just like marketing measures in traditional channels.

# Endnotes

1. This chapter was cowritten with George Michie, Chief Scientist, RKG Group.

2. For more information on digital marketing metrics, refer to Chapter 9 of Paul W. Farris, Neil T. Bendle, Phillip E. Pfeifer, and David J. Reibstein, *Marketing Metrics, The Definitive Guide to Measuring Marketing Performance* (Upper Saddle River, NJ: FT Press, 2010).

3. Rajkumar Venkatesan, "Cluster Analysis for Segmentation," UVA-M-0748 (Charlottesville, VA: Darden Business Publishing, 2007).

# Appendix 17-1: Paid Search Advertising—Google Paid Search Bidding Engine[1]

Let us consider three firms, Geico, Progressive, and Allstate, bidding for the keywords "cheap car insurance." As shown in Table 17-A, Geico has stated that the maximum amount it is willing to pay for a single click is $0.40. Progressive and Allstate have stated their maximum bids as $0.65 and $0.25, respectively.

**Table 17-A** Cost-per-Click Calculations

| Advertising Firm | Cost-per-Click (CPC) Bid | Quality Score | Rank Number | Position | Actual CPC |
|---|---|---|---|---|---|
| Geico | $0.40 | 1.8 | 0.40 × 1.8 = 0.72 | 1 | $0.37 |
| Progressive | $0.65 | 1.0 | 0.65 × 1 = 0.65 | 2 | $0.39 |
| Allstate | $0.25 | 1.5 | 0.25 × 1.5 = 0.38 | 3 | $0.01 |

Source: Created by case writer.

Based on its proprietary algorithm, Google has assigned a quality score of 1.8 for Geico for the keywords "cheap car insurance." Progressive and Allstate have been assigned quality scores of 1.0 and 1.5, respectively. In general, a higher-quality score indicates that the firm's advertisement (and the firm's products) have a higher match with or relevance for the search keyword. This would imply that Google has determined that a consumer who searches for the keywords "cheap car insurance" is more likely to click on Geico's search advertisement than to click on Progressive's or Allstate's advertisements.

Google uses the product of the maximum CPC bid and the quality score to compute a company's rank number. A firm with the highest rank number is provided the top spot in the paid search advertising listing. The belief is that consumers are more likely to click on a paid search advertisement that is at the top of the list than on the ads lower down the list. In this example, Geico has the highest rank number (0.72) and is provided the top listing in the paid search advertisement section for the keywords "cheap car insurance," followed by Progressive, and then by Allstate. Although Allstate had a better-quality score than Progressive, it was given the third spot, because the maximum CPC bid provided by Allstate was much lower than Progressive's maximum CPC bid.

The final piece of information to consider is the actual CPC paid by the advertising firms. Although Geico was willing to pay \$0.40, Google charges them only \$0.37. The formula for calculating the actual CPC paid is

$$\$0.37 = 0.65 \div 1.8 + 0.01$$

\$0.37 is the minimum Geico would have to pay to obtain the number-one position because Progressive has a rank number of 0.65 and Geico has a quality score of 1.8. At the actual CPC of \$0.37, and a quality score of 1.8, Geico's rank number is 0.67—and for a CPC of \$0.36 and a quality score of 1.8, Geico's rank number would be 0.648. So, given Progressive's quality score and maximum CPC bid, Geico would need to bid only \$0.37 to have the highest rank number.

Similarly, even though Progressive's maximum CPC bid is \$0.65, its actual CPC is \$0.39. At a CPC bid of \$0.39, Progressive's rank number would be 0.39 (0.39 × 1). This would be sufficient for Progressive to have a higher rank number than Allstate.

This auction process is similar to the second-price sealed-bid system that is common in government contract jobs. In the second-price sealed-bid system, the winner of the contract is paid the price quoted by the second-lowest bidder, not the price the winning contractor itself quoted. In contrast, in a first-price sealed-bid system, the winner would be paid the amount they themselves quoted.

The variation in the paid search advertising world is the quality score. Academic research has shown that a second-price sealed-bid auction system increases the number of people willing to participate in the auction system and motivates people to bid at their true willingness to pay. The second-price sealed-bid system has been found to empirically have a higher average clearing price than a first-price sealed-bid system.

## Endnotes

1. The explanation in this Appendix is adapted from a Google tutorial, "Search Engine Optimization Starter Guide," 2010, http://static.googleusercontent.com/media/www.google.com/en/us/webmasters/docs/search-engine-optimization-starter-guide.pdf (accessed November 18, 2013).

# 18 ———————————

## Motorcowboy: Getting a Foot in the Door

## Introduction

Matt Weiss typed "sexy boots for men" into the Google search bar and sighed. He was part of a learning team at the Darden Graduate School of Business Administration participating in the Google Online Marketing Challenge, and the team's mission was to design a Google AdWords campaign for a company that had not used the service before. The team had chosen Motorcowboy.com (Motorcowboy), a web-based manufacturer of custom boots. To develop an effective keyword list, the team needed to understand how targeted consumers searched for boots online, and to do that, it would need to adopt those consumers' mind-sets. As Weiss peered out the window of his learning team room, he imagined how a cross-dresser might shop online for custom boots. He knew business school would change how he thought—but not like this!

Based in Richmond, Virginia, Motorcowboy sold custom, handmade leather boots and shoes direct to customers exclusively through its website. Owned and operated by Robert Maddux, Motorcowboy was effectively a solo enterprise—Maddux oversaw operations, finances, marketing, and website management.

Maddux maintained a relationship with a family-run supplier based in Thailand. The measurements required to make the custom footwear were provided by consumers using Maddux's proprietary self-measuring tutorial. By phone and e-mail, Maddux assisted customers with ordering and purchasing and then submitted each order directly to his supplier, who would mail the boots directly to the customer. Because Motorcowboy enabled its customers to design and request virtually any type of footwear, the business had amassed a broad portfolio of boot styles—cowboy, equestrian riding, movie replica, hiking and work, exotic material, and even superhero.

Motorcowboy's direct-to-consumer distribution strategy provided a number of benefits. With no salaried employees, Maddux spent roughly 10 to 15 hours each week responding directly to customer inquiries. Because customers paid shipping costs for the boots, and because fixed costs related to hosting and maintaining the website, 1-800 numbers, credit card expenses, and marketing were minimal, most operating margins trickled straight to his bottom line. Motorcowboy's streamlined operation enabled Maddux to capture roughly 45% to 50% gross margins on his products and still underprice competitors (Table 18-1).

**Table 18-1** Sample Sales Margins and Competitive Pricing at Motorcowboy

| Date | Buyer Location | Product | Price | Contribution |
|------|---------------|---------|-------|--------------|
| 4/19/2011 | Devon, UK | Classic RAF 1936 pattern Flying Pilot boots | $649 + $79 shipping | $324.50 |
| 6/15/2011 | Norway | Star Trek: Next Generation | $365 + $79 shipping | $180.00 |
| 4/13/2011 | Cloverdale, Western Australia | Captain Malcolm Reynolds boots | $449 + $79 shipping | $224.50 |
| | | Custom engineer/harness boots, $399 (comparable boots at competitor: $450) | | |

Source: Motorcowboy.

# Motorcowboy.com Decision Process

The decision-making process that ultimately led a customer to purchase customized footwear from Motorcowboy.com involved several steps, the timing of which varied significantly. For first-time purchasers, the initial step was a web search, probably using Google, for a style and/or size of boot unavailable in mainstream shoe stores. The second step, Maddux thought, was to visit the Motorcowboy.com site, often several times, and review the product line. Days or even weeks after the initial visit, prospective customers would call or e-mail Maddux with further questions. The purpose of these communications was generally to obtain reassurance that Motorcowboy could really produce customized footwear in such a wide variety and that the measurements would ensure a good fit. Maddux believed that, before most customers would be willing to pay for a product two months in advance of delivery, they had to develop enough confidence that it would fit properly and be of sufficient quality. After the call or e-mail exchange, a typical user might take another week to three weeks to submit the measurements and place an order.

Upon placing an order, customers were asked to review the "How to measure your foot" section of the website. Only at this stage, Maddux believed, did customers take the time and effort to complete the measurement process. Fulfillment of the order would then take seven to nine weeks. Customers received e-mailed pictures of the finished product prior to shipment to ensure that the finished product corresponded to expectations.

Maddux thought that, for every 100 visitors to the site, three to five would e-mail or call to express interest; of these, one or two would place an order. Seldom were orders placed without e-mail and phone interactions with the customer (less than 5% of orders); often, multiple e-mail exchanges with attached pictures, sketches, and revised price quotes were involved.

# Marketing at Motorcowboy

Before the Google Online Marketing Challenge, Motorcowboy's marketing strategy had relied on word-of-mouth advertising and strong organic search strength. Given the unique nature of Maddux's offerings, Motorcowboy often scored high for returns on "custom-made leather boots" and related searches. Maddux had acquired the business from its founder only 13 months previously and recently had begun attending police conventions to promote his products to highway patrolmen. The team saw opportunities for driving interest in selected niche segments.

To understand Motorcowboy's customer base, the Darden AdWords Challenge team met with Maddux, who identified the customer segments that supported the majority of Motorcowboy's sales and untapped segments that could benefit from Motorcowboy's value proposition.

Motorcowboy's product catered to customers who wanted boots with a custom fit but also customers who sought unique styles that catered to their unique needs and interests. Motorcycle police, required to wear boots all day long, appreciated the extreme comfort that came with custom boots. Cross-dressing men, who often had a difficult time finding stylish women's footwear to fit their larger feet, were willing to pay a premium for Motorcowboy's custom shoes. Role-play enthusiasts appreciated Motorcowboy's ability to design boots that perfectly matched those of such favorite characters as Batman or Hans Solo. In addition to these already healthy segments, Maddux wanted to grow the size of Motorcowboy's share in the equestrian and plus-size markets as well as the market for boots made of exotic materials, such as ostrich and stingray.

The Darden team compared its notes from the meeting with Maddux to Motorcowboy's 100 most recent sales and devised a formal segmentation (Table 18-2).

**Table 18-2** Darden Team's Segmentation of Motorcowboy Market

| Segment (Campaign) | Status | Prospects |
|---|---|---|
| Motorcycle | Maddux identifies patrolmen as whitespace area with big upside | Large segment, strong target |
| Music/move (costume) | Already accounts for significant portion of current sales | Niche market; Motorcowboy already appears high on organic search |
| Plus-size | New segment to target | Segment may be covered by custom-related searches |
| Cross-dresser | Believes segment is already purchasing product but hasn't yet targeted directly | Tiny segment but worth targeting with low spend |
| Equestrian | Related styles featured; segment may value custom-fit value proposition | Small segment but worth targeting with low spend |
| Custom | Accounts for majority of Motorcowboy's sales | Possibility of small lift |
| Exotic | Very small niche | Tiny segment but worth targeting with low spend |

# Search Engine Marketing (SEM)

*Paid search* was a form of Internet advertising offered by various search engines. Advertisements were tied to specific words/phrases so that, when these words were typed into the engine, the ads were displayed alongside the search results. Google, for example, sold "sponsored" listings, which appeared in a shaded box separate from natural search results. Organizations used paid search to increase their visibility in search engine results and drive traffic to their websites. Paid search was popular because it was contextual and targeted.

### How SEM Works

Businesses could choose to place ads on either the search engine results pages alone or both the search engine and its *network partners*—websites that partnered with the search engine to place advertisements on their web pages based on the content in the page in exchange for a share of revenue, as with a news website or a popular blog that attracted considerable traffic.

Advertisers were charged for paid search based on either the number of impressions or number of clicks on the advertisement. An *impression* was a single appearance of an advertisement on a search results page. Typically, the cost of advertisements was measured either in *cost per thousand impressions* (CPM) or *cost per click* (CPC). Most advertisers preferred to run a campaign based on a CPC basis, because clicks actually brought relevant traffic to the advertiser's website, whereas CPM was often better suited to a branding campaign with a goal of general visibility. One of the key metrics an advertiser used to determine the success of a search advertising campaign was the *click-through rate* (CTR)—the ratio of number of clicks to number of impressions.

There were two ways of determining CPC for an advertisement: *flat-rate* and *bid-based*. In a *flat-rate* model, the advertiser paid a fixed amount for each click on the advertisement. In a *bid-based* model (such as that employed by Google AdWords), each advertiser indicated a maximum bid on a given keyword; every time that keyword was used in a search, an automated auction determined the order in which text ads were displayed. Similar to a Vickrey auction, a winning bidder was usually charged the same, or only a penny more, than the next highest bidder to prevent advertisers from constantly tweaking bids to minimize costs.

## Dynamics of AdWords Campaign

Google AdWords gave businesses leverage over advertising expenditures. A campaign targeting a particular segment or highlighting a particular product would comprise ad groups—sets of headlines and short advertisement text blurbs—which corresponded to clusters of keywords and were optimized automatically by Google based on CTR performance (Figure 18-1).

The effectiveness of an AdWords account relied on both strategic keyword selection and astute bidding. Using highly targeted keywords (such as "top corporate-sponsored executive MBA program in Virginia") would result in low search volume but also low demand, so a user could bid low and still acquire top page positioning and high CTR. Conversely, getting top page positioning using more general terms (such as EMBA) would require setting a greater *maximum bid per click* (MPC). Bidding for expensive words ensured that the advertisement would get a high number of impressions but a low CTR due to competition from other sponsored links.

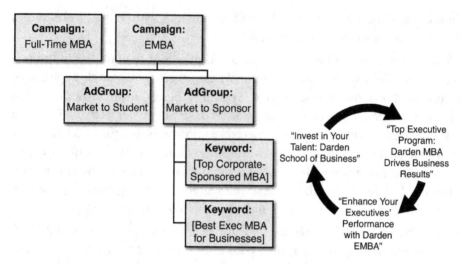

**Figure 18-1** Sample AdWords account structure

Source: Created by case writers.

# The 2011 Google Online Marketing Challenge

In 2008, Google opened the Online Marketing Challenge to college and graduate students anywhere in the world. By 2009, it had attracted more than 10,000 participants from more than 50 countries.

## Structure

Teams received a budget of $200—all of which had to be spent during the campaign—to advertise online using a Google AdWords account. The teams were required to work with a local business or nongovernmental organization (NGO) to create effective online marketing campaigns. Participants were advised to choose clients who had not yet tried AdWords.

The competition ran from January through June, during which a campaign was required to run for three consecutive weeks. Before the campaign started, a precampaign document describing the client's business and the team's proposed AdWords strategy was to be submitted to both the supervising professors and Google. After Google's receipt of the report, $200 was credited to the account. Campaigns were actively monitored, evaluated, and tweaked to maximize impact. At the conclusion of the three-week campaign, an eight-page postcampaign summary was submitted to Google.

The 2011 competition grouped participants into three regions: the Americas, EMEA (Europe, the Middle East, and Africa), and the Asia Pacific. A winner was picked from each region and, from among those three, an overall global winner was chosen. The regional winners were invited to a major Google office in their region; members of the global winning team were awarded a week's vacation in San Francisco, including a full-day visit to the Googleplex, the corporate headquarters in Mountain View, California, in the heart of Silicon Valley.

## Evaluation

Google used a proprietary algorithm to evaluate the marketing effectiveness of each AdWords account according to 30 factors. The algorithm selected the top 50 teams from each region, which were then narrowed down to five by Google AdWords experts. A group of academics assessed the pre- and postcampaign reports of those five and selected the regional and global winners.

The campaign statistics algorithm evaluated various campaigns based on the following five criteria:

- **Account structure**—How well did the campaign reflect the business?
- **Optimization techniques**—How well did the campaign implement best practices and suggested optimization techniques?
- **Account activity and reporting**—How well did the campaign leverage data from Google's reporting center in fine-tuning its approach?
- **Performance and budget**—How effectively was the budget used across keywords?
- **Relevance**—What was the CTR?

## Team's Strategy for the Competition

The team divided its campaign into the seven segments it had identified for Motorcowboy, each with multiple ad groups themed to specific aspects of that segment. The exotic materials campaign, for example, had an ad group for each type of material; someone searching for lizard boots would see an ad for lizard boots that would click through to a page of lizard boots on Motorcowboy's website.

Because the competition granted such a limited budget, and because Motorcowboy catered to such niche markets, the team decided to start with very specific keywords that would require lower bids than more general terms, believing that starting with a highly targeted approach would prevent exhausting funds prematurely in the search for high-value keywords. The team brainstormed lists of relevant keywords for each segment, then added qualifier terms related to Motorcowboy's unique value proposition, including *custom, handmade,* and *custom-made.* (See the data supplement on http://dmanalytics.org for the campaigns, ad groups, and keywords at launch.)

To generate the data needed to make decisions quickly, the team decided to allocate more money to the front end of the campaign. As the competition unfolded, it met regularly to determine how to tweak the campaign for maximum success. Each campaign, ad group, and keyword would be examined to determine whether it generated *quality* traffic, defined as searchers who spent time on the site and visited multiple pages. Such traffic was also described as having a low *bounce rate,* the rate at which visitors leave without moving beyond the landing page. The team also planned to monitor CTR, average ad position, and average CPC, and to change bidding as necessary.

### A Boot to the Backside: April 12–16

As the campaign got under way, the team closely monitored the results of its initial strategy. The team wanted to get enough data to start making decisions about which keywords were the most valuable and best targeted at the customer segment.

Four days after the launch, the team had only 28 clicks and $5.17 in ad spend (Figure 18-2). At this rate, it would spend less than a quarter of its total budget. Most of its terms were flagged by Google as "low search volume" and others as "below first page bid," meaning the bid price was too low for the ad to appear on the first page of search results.

From a long-term strategy perspective, the team saw the value of maintaining its long list of highly customized terms, but from a practical perspective, the team knew it had to spend $200 in the allotted 21 days. What should be the team's next steps? What were the trade-offs between this strategy and the original strategy? What metrics were most important when valuing the performance of keywords?

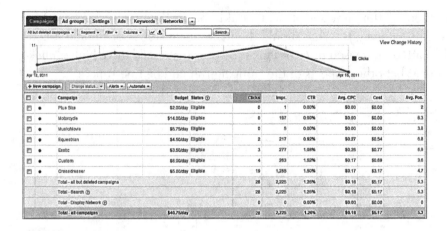

**Figure 18-2** Analytics of search terms

Source: Google Analytics.

# Reboot: April 17–20

Looking at its slow spend rate and the poor performance of many of its keywords, the Motorcowboy team decided to take a three-pronged approach: (1) bring in more general terms that didn't use the word *custom* or other qualifiers, (2) raise the bid price for the more popular terms to no higher than $0.60, and (3) pause terms that were driving impressions but not click-throughs.

With such low CTR, it was difficult to determine quantitatively which terms should get the price raise. The team sought to assess words on their qualitative merits, primarily with the question, "Is the person typing in this search going to be our customer?" With raised bid prices and new keywords, the team sat back to see what would happen. Over the following four days, the newly modified account generated 66 clicks and spent $23.75 (Figure 18-3).

Despite this uptick in spending and clicks, the team was still not going to reach the required spending level of $200. But the team did believe that the cumulative total of 94 clicks could provide data in Google Analytics on the quality of traffic (bounce rate, time on site, average pages visited) generated by different keywords.

The team thought this new set of data would enable them to make necessary modifications to its campaigns. What should the team's next steps be? Should it continue down the path of increased price or look for words that could drive higher click-through volume? What other aspects of the campaign should be fine-tuned?

| Campaign | Budget | Status | Clicks | Impr. | CTR | Avg. CPC | Cost | Avg. Pos. |
|---|---|---|---|---|---|---|---|---|
| Plus Size | $2.00/day | Eligible | 0 | 129 | 0.00% | $0.00 | $0.00 | 6.8 |
| Equestrian | $4.50/day | Eligible | 4 | 245 | 1.63% | $0.80 | $3.21 | 5.7 |
| Exotic | $3.50/day | Eligible | 4 | 632 | 0.63% | $0.31 | $1.24 | 5.7 |
| Music/Movie | $5.75/day | Eligible | 9 | 2,506 | 0.36% | $0.11 | $0.97 | 1.5 |
| Motorcycle | $14.00/day | Eligible | 10 | 278 | 3.60% | $0.48 | $4.84 | 5.7 |
| Custom | $6.00/day | Eligible | 14 | 402 | 3.48% | $0.37 | $5.20 | 3.1 |
| Crossdresser | $5.00/day | Eligible | 25 | 476 | 5.25% | $0.33 | $8.29 | 3 |
| Total – all but deleted campaigns | | | 66 | 4,668 | 1.41% | $0.36 | $23.75 | 3 |
| Total – Search | | | 66 | 4,668 | 1.41% | $0.36 | $23.75 | 3 |
| Total – Display Network | | | 0 | 0 | 0.00% | $0.00 | $0.00 | 0 |
| Total – all campaigns | $40.75/day | | 66 | 4,668 | 1.41% | $0.36 | $23.75 | 3 |

**Figure 18-3** Search data for April 17–20

Source: Google Analytics.

# Foot on the Pedal: April 21–April 28

Checking back periodically over the remainder of the competition, the Darden team continued with its approach of eliminating poor-performing terms (low CTR, poor analytics data) and adding the occasional new keyword. The team decided to increase bids to try for first or second ad position on ads that aligned well with Motor-cowboy's core offering that had shown good CTRs thus far. With time running out, the team was also willing to place bids in excess of $1.00 on expensive keywords that were appearing to generate strong results. Although it was hard to measure the value of each click-through given the long-lead nature of sales, the team believed that given the high profit margin on each purchase, driving the right type of traffic would create the value to justify a higher bid price.

With three days to spare, the team successfully exhausted its account and achieved a CTR of almost 5% during the final eight days (Figure 18-4).

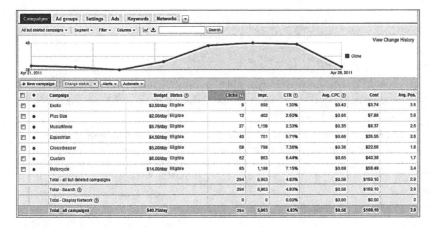

**Figure 18-4** Search data for April 21–28

Source: Google Analytics.

# Conclusion

After the competition, the Darden School team wrote the postcampaign report and debriefed with Robert Maddux, who reported a significant lift in inquiries during the competition period. Because Motorcowboy seldom processed orders through its site, however, Google Analytics would not be able to link those who connected to the site from the AdWords campaign with particular inquiries or purchases.

Parsing through the data from the competition, the team contemplated a series of conclusions and recommendations (Table 18-3). They wondered if customer lifetime value (CLV) would be a good concept for Motorcowboy and whether Maddux could use paid search advertising to increase CLV.

**Table 18-3** Darden Team Recommendations for Motorcowboy (By Campaign)

| | |
|---|---|
| Custom: | High CTR and increased time spent on site. A promising segment to continue targeting with AdWords. |
| Equestrian: | The Western ad group generated substantially more and higher-quality traffic than the general equestrian ad group. Future AdWords to emphasize Western (cowboy) boots. |
| Cross-dresser: | A highly searched campaign with low CPC. Some keywords had a high bounce rate, but several searchers spent a good deal of time on the website. Recommend continuing to invest in this segment. |
| Exotic material: | High bounce rate and low time on site; searchers did not seem to find what they were looking for. With low CPC, could potentially generate sales at low cost in the future. |

| | |
|---|---|
| Motorcycle: | Keywords were slightly more expensive, but it generated a high level of good traffic, particularly in the women's segment. |
| Music/movie (costume) | Some ad groups generated more and better traffic than others. Recommend focusing on those that did well, such as *Wonder Woman* and *Matrix*, and testing additional characters. |
| Plus-size: | Did not generate significant or quality traffic, perhaps due to demographics or the use of more generic search terms covered under the custom campaign. Recommend focusing on custom campaign to generate plus-size customers. |

# Assignment Questions

1. What elements of Motorcowboy's business model set it apart from its competitors? What does this mean for the brand's positioning?

2. Is AdWords a good marketing option for Motorcowboy? What other tactics could be used to generate new customers?

3. Discuss the team's initial plan and how the team adapted it as the campaign progressed. Why didn't the original plan generate enough traffic?

4. The equestrian campaign had an average cost per click (CPC) of $0.61. If the average price for a pair of cowboy boots is $550, with a 50% margin, what percentage of those clicking on an ad need to purchase a pair of boots in order to break even? What does this mean for the campaign?

5. One full-color, quarter-page ad in *POLICE* magazine costs $1,805 and reaches nearly 50,000 subscribers. What percentage of readership must visit Motorcowboy.com to generate the same cost per visitor as the motorcycle campaign, which had an average CPC of $0.69 in the last five days of the campaign? Should Maddux consider advertising in *POLICE*?

6. Is customer lifetime value (CLV) a relevant concept for Motorcowboy? What information would Maddux need to calculate CLV? What can he do to increase CLV?

# 19

## VinConnect, Inc.: Digital Marketing Strategy

## Introduction

Looking out the window of his office on a clear night in November 2012, Kevin Sidders contemplated his next steps. His company, VinConnect—an intermediary between European wineries and American consumers—had recently closed an offer for one of its partner wineries, and its numbers were slowly improving. But Sidders, the company's president, knew he needed to focus VinConnect's efforts on new marketing initiatives to more effectively reach its targeted audience and increase its customer conversion rate.

VinConnect's goal was to allow European wineries to sell their products "directly" (through VinConnect) to American consumers via offers delivered in e-mail. Since its launch, the company had signed up 19 partner wineries, and more than 900 people had subscribed to at least one of its winery mailing lists. It was a great start for a company that had been in business for just over a year, but Sidders knew he still had a tough road ahead.

When Sidders founded VinConnect in the fall of the previous year, the idea of European wineries selling directly to American consumers was completely novel. The initial challenge was introducing the concept to European wineries and convincing them of the benefits of the direct-to-consumer (DTC) model. Next, he had to build relationships with importers and distributors to ensure the model would work. Last, he needed to establish a reputation in the industry and put the VinConnect name and idea in front of wine buyers.

Given that there was tremendous market activity, marketing buzz, and technological innovation in the U.S. direct wine sales market, Sidders was concerned about differentiating his story and communicating his message to his target audience, and so decided to explore paid keyword search advertising. Would the powerful new tool be what he needed to get to the next level or would the data show that more traditional types of marketing were just as valuable?

By comparing the results of his Google AdWords campaigns and other outreach efforts and surveying his customers, Sidders found that the most effective ways to find qualified buyers were traditional marketing channels such as PR campaigns, strategic partnerships, and e-mail blasts. Sidders wondered if paid search advertising was even relevant for him and if it only attracted customers who would prove to harder to retain.

# Industry Description

The wine market in the United States had been growing consistently and was expected to have a market value of $33.5 billion by 2013.[1] As of 2012, Americans could buy one of more than 15,000 SKUs[2] from more than 5,000 brands. Table 19-1 illustrates the industry's growth, especially in DTC shipments:

**Table 19-1** Wine Industry Metrics

|                | 2013            | 2014            |
| -------------- | --------------- | --------------- |
| DTC shipments  | $1,468 million  | $1,584 million  |
| Total market   | $8,370 million  | $8,966 millon   |

Source: "Wine Industry Metrics," January 2014, Wines & Vines website, http://www.winesandvines.com/template.cfm?section=widc&widcDomain=home&widcYYYYMM=201401 (accessed February 18, 2014).

Alcohol sales and distribution in the United States was governed by laws that dated back to the repeal of Prohibition in 1933. The result was a mandatory three-tier system wherein the production, distribution, and sale of alcoholic products had to be done by a separate entity. Each state also had its own laws regarding all facets of the distribution, sale, and taxation of alcoholic products, which made the transportation of alcohol across state lines a complex process.

Despite all this, to drive growth, U.S. wineries developed new and more advanced marketing techniques. Many wineries were increasing spending on traditional advertisements, such as in-store campaigns and advertisements in print media, whereas others focused on using DTC marketing and social media efforts to build their brands.

# Direct-to-Consumer Sales

One area of particular focus for U.S. wineries was attracting private clients via direct sales models, including tasting rooms, online stores, mailing list offers, and/or wine clubs. DTC wine sales represented 3% of the overall market (or more than seven million cases sold) in the 12 months ending in April 2011.[3] Since then, there had been an increase in volume of over 8% to 11.5%[4] of the market. In October 2012, DTC shipments hit a new record with a total value of $222 million.[5] According to Wines & Vines, DTC sales through mailing lists, clubs, and tasting rooms were growing at twice the rate of the overall market and rapidly capturing share.

Although tasting rooms had been employed to do DTC marketing for decades, beginning in the twenty-first century, U.S. wineries began to innovate, using mailing list offers, wine clubs, and online stores. Over this period, wineries began developing methods by which they could (with enormous regulatory compliance overhead) sell and deliver their products direct to consumers across state lines. Once a winery put the requisite infrastructure in place, customers in remote (for example, out-of-state) areas were able to purchase wine direct from the winery and have it delivered to them. DTC wine sales provided benefits to both consumers and wineries (see Table 19-2).

**Table 19-2** Benefits of DTC Wine Sales

| Consumer | Winery |
|---|---|
| Convenience | Direct communication with private clients |
| Supporting the winery directly | Marketing messages delivered at point of sale |
| Access to hard-to-find wines | Encourages clients as brand ambassadors |
| Provenance | Price protection and control |
| | Opportunity to make special offers and sell older vintages |
| | Increase in three-tier demand as private clients buy more through traditional channels due to their affinity and relationship |

Source: Created by case writer.

VinConnect's model aimed to capitalize on the growth of the wine industry, specifically the increase within the DTC segment. The company enabled European wineries to market directly to private clients via mailing list offers, just like U.S. wineries were able to. In addition to helping create the mailing lists through customer acquisition, VinConnect developed marketing programs for private clients that provided a communications and commerce strategy, a legal and compliance infrastructure, logistics capabilities, and customer service.

European wineries faced a particular disadvantage in the U.S. wine market. Due to the legal and logistical challenges of the U.S. regulatory framework, European wineries had been unable to market to private clients in the United States, and therefore faced a competitive disadvantage and had a limited share of the U.S. luxury wine market. By finally allowing top European wineries to find and directly market to top U.S. customers, VinConnect enabled the wineries to take advantage of the benefits of DTC wine sales and to compete more effectively in the United States.

# VinConnect, Inc.

Prior to moving to Charlottesville, Virginia, Sidders lived in San Francisco, California, where he enjoyed discovering new wineries in the Napa Valley area. As he found emerging wines that were of high quality but limited production, he joined their mailing lists to have a direct relationship with them, support them financially, and ensure he would receive an annual allocation of highly sought-after wines.

Sidders' love of wine extended to French and Italian bottling, but he found the process of purchasing similarly high-quality, limited-production imported wines to be challenging. What might be available in one shop often wouldn't be in another, and the few bottles that might come to a local store often would sell out quickly. He turned to the Internet to continue to search for the wines, but that presented its own issues: He faced widely varying pricing and availability, he could never be assured of the provenance of the wine or how it had been stored or transported, and he had no direct relationship with the seller to ensure the wine's safe arrival (or recourse in the event it did not).

In response, Sidders founded VinConnect, Inc., in September 2011, to provide a way for the world's best wineries to sell their wines direct to private clients in the United States. VinConnect acted as the DTC channel in the United States for its luxury European winery partners by creating and administering mailing lists and club programs that enabled U.S. customers to buy wine directly. Each partner winery had its own mailing list and offered wines it selected at the frequency it chose (Exhibit 19-1). The wines were then transferred to the United States, forwarded along to VinConnect's warehouse in Sonoma, California, and shipped to customers.

When a consumer was interested in joining a winery mailing list, he or she could visit VinConnect.com (Figure 19-1) and click on one of the many "Join Now" options. From there, the potential customer entered his or her mailing address and selected which of the available winery mailing lists to join. Subscribers then began receiving periodic news and offers from those wineries. Each winery differed: Some made offers once a year and others allocated wine a few times throughout the year. For more information about VinConnect's subscribers, see Exhibit 19-2.

**Figure 19-1** VinConnect website
Source: VinConnect. Used with permission.

When a subscriber received an offer, he or she was asked to reply within a specific period of time, usually two weeks. At the close of the offer window, all orders were processed and customers received an order confirmation that included a general time frame for expected delivery. Delivery could take anywhere from two weeks to three months, depending on the type of allocation and where the wine was being sent. In 2012, VinConnect shipped to 38 states in the United States.

The customer response could come via e-mail or phone call, and if it was a first order, VinConnect would reach out to the customer directly in order to configure an account, including shipping and billing information. Once the order was confirmed, the customer did not hear from VinConnect again until the wine was received in inventory. At that point, the customer was charged and a receipt was sent. Tracking information was sent once the wine had been shipped.

# Recent Marketing Initiatives

When VinConnect first launched, it grew its list of subscribers through word-of-mouth advertising and by taking advantage of basic digital marketing, including

Twitter, Facebook, and organic Google searches. Having developed a profile of what he believed his target market to be, Sidders assumed that customers in the United States seeking wines produced by VinConnect's partner wineries would naturally be excited about this new avenue for purchasing direct. At an average of $80 per bottle, Sidders expected his company's gross profit margins to be around 30% to 40%. Unfortunately, the number of purchases had not been as high as he projected. Although people seemed to be excited about the VinConnect concept and the open rates for e-mails were high, those who received the wine offers often did not buy the wine. In an effort to attract the appropriate subscribers, Sidders invested in a number of different initiatives, including creating Google AdWords campaigns and strategic partnerships. The question was, which of the measures would be most effective at finding customers who would be more likely to buy wine than the existing base?

# Paid Search Advertising

Sidders created a variety of Google AdWords campaigns, each focusing on one of his partner wineries. Rather than using words about buying wine direct from wineries, he chose keywords that supported the idea that VinConnect was developed to create the connection between top European wineries and the American consumers who already appreciated its wines: Sidders used the proper names of the wineries that partnered with VinConnect. Exhibit 19-3 shows performance data for each of the keywords that attracted at least one visit to the VinConnect website. On average, VinConnect was spending $300 to $400 on Google paid search advertising per month. But the campaigns had not shown the return on investment that Sidders had hoped for, instead yielding only a small number of customer conversions (during the 14 months when paid search advertising was active) relative to other marketing channels (Table 19-3):

**Table 19-3** Keyword Conversions

| Keyword | Sign-ups |
| --- | --- |
| Borgogno | 11 |
| Castello dei Rampolla | 1 |
| Ciacci Piccolomini | 11 |
| La Spinetta | 9 |

Source: Company documents.

Sidders also launched a small pay-per-click Facebook campaign that showed few returns. The assumption was that the program did not attract the right consumers because Facebook's system allowed users to opt into certain categories rather than search for specific keywords.

## Public Relations and Strategic Partnerships

As soon as VinConnect was launched, participants in online forums on wine-centric websites, such as wineberserkers.com, began discussing the company. Then, in February 2012, the Terroirist wine blog contained an article profiling the company and Sidders, giving VinConnect exposure to the niche market it was created to benefit. Seeing the increase in subscribers due to this exposure, Sidders hired a public relations specialist to increase awareness of VinConnect and gain additional subscribers.

Throughout summer 2012, Sidders participated in a number of interviews, and VinConnect was featured in two notable articles. The first article, published June 14, 2012, was written by columnist Richard Jennings in his blog for the *Huffington Post*. In his commentary, Jennings wrote, "I'm very excited at this new option for U.S. wine lovers to buy direct from some of Europe's greatest. I also think Kevin and his team have done an admirable job in setting up a model that's as transparent and simply aimed at connecting producers with their U.S. fans as possible."[6] On August 28, 2012, Elin McCoy from *Bloomberg* wrote an article about VinConnect entitled "Former Credit Suisse Banker Sells Exclusive Wines."

To attract the attention of groups of individuals who would likely be ideal VinConnect customers, Sidders also began to pursue strategic partnerships with organizations that might have a particular interest in purchasing luxury wines. The first such partnership was with a national organization of business executives called the Business Leaders Association (BLA);[7] the organization had a wine-related special interest group that was focused on sharing and appreciating the world's top wines.

## Surveying the Customer Base

To measure the effectiveness of his marketing methods, Sidders contracted with an outside firm to design a 17-question survey and distribute it to three groups of VinConnect subscribers: customers, known as prospects, who opened VinConnect e-mails but did not buy wine (Group A); one-time purchasers (Group B); and frequent purchasers (Group C). Group A was 83% male, the majority (58%) of whom were between the ages of 31 and 50. Group B was 89% male and skewed slightly older: 51% were between the ages of 31 and 50, and 21% were between the ages of 51 and 60. Group C was 96% male and the oldest group of the three: 80% of the survey respondents were between 41 and 60 years of age. See Exhibit 19-4 for all relevant survey results.

Group C, the frequent purchasers, most often (41%) had heard about VinConnect through a news publication, such as the articles in the *Huffington Post* and *Bloomberg.* Group A survey respondents were most likely to have found VinConnect through a wine-related website (36%) or an online search (21%). Only 4% of the customers who purchased wine regularly had found VinConnect through a search engine such as Google.

In terms of the outlets from which the survey respondents most likely purchased wine, the frequent purchasers were less likely to buy from grocery stores or large retailers than the group that had never purchased a bottle from VinConnect. But both groups showed a willingness to purchase wine on the Internet. Purchasers in Groups A and B showed similar reasoning for making a decision to purchase a particular wine, but Group C reported two notable differences. Reviews and online scores rated most highly with the frequent-purchaser group, and quality/price ratio was less important for those buyers than for the other two groups.

Group C also showed marked differences in the aspects of the VinConnect model that attracted them to join. The frequent-purchaser group was more influenced by three factors in particular: (1) direct support (their purchases supported the winery directly), (2) priority offers (they had the first opportunity to purchase new releases before they were available in the United States), and (3) assured provenance (they had knowledge that the wine was authentic and traveled through winery-approved, temperature-controlled channels).

The survey was instrumental in proving to Sidders that the strategic partnership with BLA was successful at drawing new customers who were more likely to buy VinConnect wines than previous subscribers had been. Table 19-4 shows the performance of each of VinConnect's partner wineries, broken down by type of customer (Group B or C) and which marketing channels drew the customers to the company.

**Table 19-4** Winery Performance Data

| Winery | Sign-Ups | Group C | Group B | Revenue | Keyword | BLA | Facebook | Bloomberg/Huffington Post |
|---|---|---|---|---|---|---|---|---|
| Artadi | 0 | | | | | | | |
| Borgogno | 401 | | | | 29 | 31 | 7 | 7 |
| Castello dei Rampolla | 401 | 20 | 14 | 12,600 | 39 | 26 | 11 | 7 |
| Castello del Terriccio | 271 | 8 | 4 | 3,912 | 39 | 16 | 9 | 6 |
| Chateau Musar | 0 | | | | | | | |
| Ciacci Piccolomini | 283 | 10 | 1 | 2,031 | 31 | 16 | 8 | 9 |
| Clos de la Chapelle | 0 | | | | | | | |
| Clos de Tart | 595 | 8 | 9 | 26,641 | | | | |
| Dr. Loosen | 0 | | | | | | | |
| E. Pira—Chiara Boschis | 232 | 13 | 5 | 4,389 | 25 | 12 | 9 | 4 |
| Etienne Sauzet | 0 | | | | | | | |
| Fontodi | 274 | | | | 35 | 11 | 10 | 4 |
| Gourt de Mautens | 310 | 8 | 10 | 6,077 | 25 | 17 | 6 | 4 |
| Il Carnasciale | 1 | | | | | | | |
| La Massa—Giorgio Primo | 383 | 8 | 2 | 3,930 | 35 | 34 | 9 | 7 |
| La Spinetta | 411 | | | | 47 | 22 | 11 | 13 |
| Le Macchiole | 438 | | | | 34 | 34 | 12 | 8 |
| Louis Michel | 416 | 23 | 14 | 8,401 | 42 | 27 | 12 | 3 |
| M & S Ogier | 359 | | | | 28 | 23 | 7 | 3 |
| Massolino | 497 | 25 | 2 | 6,105 | 40 | 31 | 9 | 11 |

| Winery | Sign-Ups | Group C | Group B | Revenue | Keyword | BLA | Facebook | Bloomberg/Huffington Post |
|---|---|---|---|---|---|---|---|---|
| Monteverro | 0 | | | | | | | |
| Pegau | 420 | 18 | 8 | | 41 | 21 | 11 | 4 |
| Pelissero | 319 | 17 | 1 | 1,945 | 29 | 20 | 9 | 8 |
| Robert Weil | 0 | | | | | | | |
| Roberto Voerzio | 366 | 2 | 6 | 16,800 | 34 | 24 | 11 | 7 |
| Vall Llach | 0 | | | | | | | |
| Vielle Julienne | 444 | 2 | 2 | 133 | 39 | 31 | 10 | 4 |
| Vincent Girardin | 277 | 23 | 6 | 7,664 | 41 | 8 | 4 | 4 |

Source: Company documents.

# Conclusion

After the dust had settled on VinConnect's new marketing measures, the company had 20 partner wineries and more than 1,000 subscribers. Still, only a small percentage of those who had signed up and were receiving offers were actually purchasing wine. Sidders reviewed the analytics from his website from September 19, 2011, through November 19, 2012 (Exhibit 19-5). He knew he needed to determine what to do next to increase VinConnect's conversion rate and also to decide about how to allocate resources among marketing strategies to ensure the most profitability moving forward. He wondered which of the events of the previous months had had the largest effect on obtaining additional subscribers and which had helped VinConnect obtain actual customers. He asked himself: Was he even attracting the correct audience? Did he need to offer additional services?

# Endnotes

1. Research and Markets, "US Wine Market Forecast to 2012," March 13, 2012, http://www.researchandmarkets.com/reports/648785/us_wine_market_forecast_to_2012.pdf (accessed January 15, 2014).

2. Whole World Wines, "U.S. Wine Industry Info," http://www.wholeworldwines.com/challenge/us-wine-industry-info (accessed January 15, 2014).

3. *Direct-to-Consumer Shipping Report*, annual report from ShipCompliant and Wines & Vines, June 2011.

4. Direct-to-Consumer Shipping Report.

5. "Wine Industry Metrics," October 2012 data, Wines & Vines website, November 15, 2014, http://www.winesandvines.com/template.cfm?section=widc&widcDomain=home&widcYYYY MM=201210 (accessed February 18, 2014).

6. Richard Jennings, "New Direct-to-Consumer Channel for Top European Wines: VinConnect," *Huffington Post*, June 14, 2012, http://www.huffingtonpost.com/richard-jennings/new-directtoconsumer-chan_b_1592124.html (accessed January 15, 2014).

7. The organization has been disguised.

# Exhibits

### Exhibit 19-1  List of Wineries

| Winery | Top Wine(s) Varietals | Recent Top Scores | Price | Points of Distinction | Production |
|---|---|---|---|---|---|
| **Burgundy** | | | | | |
| Clos de la Chapelle | Pinot Noir | Low to Mid 90s | $$$ | Historic vineyard, old vines, organic/ biodynamic | Tiny |
| Clos de Tart | Pinot Noir | Mid 90s | $$$$$ | Legendary Grand Cru, low yields, built to age | Tiny |
| Etienne Sauzet | Chardonnay | Low to High 90s | $$–$$$$ | Refined, rich, floral | Small |
| Louis Michel | Chardonnay | Low 90s | $$–$$$ | Lean, mineral, pure Chablis—no oak used | Small |
| Vincent Girardin | Pinot Noir, Chardonnay | Mid 90s | $$–$$$$S | Pure, elegant, balanced | Medium |
| **Rhone Valley** | | | | | |
| Gourt de Mautens | Grenache blend | Mid 90s | $$$ | Hand-crafted, rich and intense | Tiny |
| Pegau | Grenache blend | Mid 90s to 100 | $$$– $$$$ | Traditonal—ripe, gamy, rustic, spicy | Small |
| M & S Ogier | Syrah | High 90s to 100 | $$– $$$$$ | Pure artisinal Syrah—deep, full, precise | Small |
| Vieille Julienne | Grenache blend | Mid 90s to 100 | $$– $$$$$ | Biodynamic, classic, elegant, very old vines | Tiny |
| **Piedmont (Barolo and Barbaresco)** | | | | | |
| Borgogno | Nebbiolo (Barolo) | Low to Mid 90s | $$–$$$$ | Traditional, classic, long aging | Small |
| E. Pira— Chiara Boschis | Nebbiolo (Barolo) | Low to High 90s | $$–$$$ | Feminine approach— structured, elegant, perfumed | Tiny |
| La Spinetta | Nebbiolo (both) | Mid 90s | $$–$$$$ | Rich, deep fruit, high quality across broad range | Large |
| Massolino | Nebbiolo (Barolo) | Low to Mid 90s | $$–$$$ | Structured, age-worthy, powerful | Small |

| Winery | Top Wine(s) Varietals | Recent Top Scores | Price | Points of Distinction | Production |
|---|---|---|---|---|---|
| Pelissero | Nebbiolo (Barbaresco) | Low to Mid 90s | $$–$$$ | Dynamic, consistent, refined | Small to Medium |
| Roberto Voerzio | Nebbiolo (Barolo) | Mid to High 90s | $$$$–$$$$$ | Iconic wines, very low yields, dense fruit | Tiny to Small |

**Tuscany (Chianti, Brunello, and Super Tuscan)**

| | | | | | |
|---|---|---|---|---|---|
| Castello dei Rampolla | Cab Sauv, Sangiovese, others | Mid 90s to 100 | $$–$$$$ | Biodynamic, pure, fruit-driven | Small |
| Castello del Terriccio | Cab Sauv, Sangiovese, others | Mid 90s | $$–$$$$ | Powerful, expressive, age-worthy | Small to Medium |
| Ciacci Piccolomini | Sangiovese (Brunello) | Low to Mid 90s | $$–$$$ | Classic, age-worthy | Small to Medium |
| Fontodi | Sangiovese (Chianti) | Mid 90s | $$–$$$$ | Powerful, rich, reference Chianti | Medium |
| Il Carnasciale | Caberlot | Mid to High 90s | $$$–$$$$ | Unique varietal, deep, complex, balanced | Tiny |
| La Massa— Giorgio Primo | Cab Sauv, Merlot | Low to High 90s | $$–$$$ | Rich fruit, great balance | Small |
| Le Macchiole | Cab Franc, Merlot, Syrah | Mid to High 90s | $$$–$$$$$ | Single varietals, powerful yet balanced | Small |
| Monteverro | Bordeaux blend, Rhone blend, Chardonnay | Mid 90s | $$$–$$$$$ | Ambitious, complex, rich, silky, polished | Small |

Source: "Winery Partners," VinConnect website, http://vinconnect.com/wineries/ (accessed January 31, 2014).

**Exhibit 19-2** Subscriber Information

| Customer | Referred By | Select Winery Mailing Lists | Date/Time of Signup | Date of Most Recent Change |
| --- | --- | --- | --- | --- |
| Customer 1 | | | 6/17/2011 13:02 | 7/5/2011 9:05 |
| Customer 2 | | | 6/15/2011 16:51 | 7/5/2011 9:05 |
| Customer 241 | Facebook ad | Clos de Tart (new sign-ups will be wait list), Louis Michel, Vieille Julienne, Borgogno, Massolino, La Massa, Le Macchiole | 1/5/2012 21:19 | 5/31/2012 8:22 |
| Customer 266 | Wineberserkers | Clos de Tart (new sign-ups will be Wait List), Louis Michel, M&S Ogier, La Spinetta, Pelissero | 1/24/2012 17:44 | 2/14/2012 9:51 |
| Customer 330 | La Spinetta | E. Pira—Chiara Boschis, La Spinetta, Massolino | 2/18/2012 7:22 | 7/17/2012 11:50 |
| Customer 390 | Google ad | Louis Michel, Borgogno, La Spinetta, Massolino, Roberto Voerzio, Le Macchiole | 3/14/2012 13:04 | 3/14/2012 13:04 |
| Customer 392 | Saw you on facebook | M&S Ogier, Borgogno, La Spinetta, Massolino, Roberto Voerzio, Castello dei Rampolla, La Massa, Le Macchiole | 3/14/2012 17:16 | 3/14/2012 17:16 |
| Customer 399 | YPO | Clos de Tart (new sign-ups will be wait list), Louis Michel | 3/16/2012 9:26 | 3/16/2012 9:26 |
| Customer 522 | Terroirist.com | Vieille Julienne, VinConnect Special Offers | 6/15/2012 23:55 | 10/16/2012 23:17 |
| Customer 592 | Richard Jennings Blog | Clos de Tart (new sign-ups will be wait list), Pegau | 7/12/2012 16:24 | 7/12/2012 16:24 |
| Customer 593 | | La Spinetta | 7/13/2012 9:48 | 7/13/2012 9:48 |
| Customer 924 | Post article 17 Oct 2012 | Louis Michel, Vincent Girardin, Pegau, Vieille Julienne, La Spinetta, Roberto Voerzio, Castello del Terriccio, Le Macchiole | 10/17/2012 16:40 | 10/17/2012 16:40 |

| Customer | Referred By | Select Winery Mailing Lists | Date/Time of Signup | Date of Most Recent Change |
|---|---|---|---|---|
| Customer 956 | | Clos de Tart (new sign-ups will be wait list), Louis Michel, Vincent Girardin, Gourt de Mautens, M&S Ogier, Pegau, Vieille Julienne, Borgogno, E. Pira—Chiara Boschis, La Spinetta, Massolino, Pelissero, Roberto Voerzio, Castello dei Rampolla, Castello del Terriccio, Ciacci Piccolomini, Fontodi, Il Carnasciale, La Massa, Le Macchiole, VinConnect Special Offers | 11/13/2012 7:26 | 11/13/2012 7:26 |

Source: Company documents.

**Exhibit 19-3** VinConnect, Inc., AdWords Campaigns and Keywords

| Campaign | Visits | Pages / Visit | Avg. Visit Duration | % New Visits |
|---|---|---|---|---|
| La Spinetta | 152 | 3.66 | 0:01:25 | 87.50% |
| Ciacci Piccolomini | 108 | 3.68 | 0:00:36 | 87.96% |
| Fontodi | 82 | 2.78 | 0:00:23 | 90.24% |
| Borgogno | 80 | 3.5 | 0:00:56 | 91.25% |
| Pegau | 78 | 3.58 | 0:02:00 | 78.21% |
| Massolino—Google Build | 68 | 3.82 | 0:01:01 | 83.82% |
| Clos de Tart | 49 | 3.49 | 0:01:26 | 85.71% |
| Pelissero | 49 | 2.71 | 0:09:29 | 81.63% |
| Castello dei Rampolla | 44 | 4.64 | 0:03:04 | 65.91% |
| La Massa | 40 | 3 | 0:00:36 | 87.50% |
| Le Macchiole | 39 | 3.54 | 0:00:33 | 92.31% |
| Louis Michel | 33 | 2.3 | 0:00:09 | 84.85% |
| Roberto Voerzio | 24 | 2.96 | 0:00:26 | 83.33% |
| Ogier | 21 | 3.81 | 0:01:45 | 80.95% |
| Chiara Boschis | 13 | 5.08 | 0:02:30 | 92.31% |
| Vieille Julienne | 11 | 2.18 | 0:00:03 | 81.82% |
| Castello del Terriccio | 10 | 2.4 | 0:00:04 | 90.00% |
| (Not Set) | 9 | 2.89 | 0:00:13 | 88.89% |
| Court de Mautens | 8 | 3.5 | 0:01:01 | 100.00% |

| Matched Search Query | Visits | Pages / Visit | Avg. Visit Duration | % New Visits |
|---|---|---|---|---|
| La Spinetta | 37 | 5.05 | 0:04:21 | 78.38% |
| (Not Set) | 30 | 2.33 | 0:00:15 | 93.33% |
| Ciacci Piccolomini | 24 | 3.25 | 0:00:28 | 75.00% |
| Clos de Tart | 24 | 3.79 | 0:02:21 | 87.50% |
| Castello dei Rampolla | 16 | 6 | 0:07:13 | 43.75% |
| Massolino | 14 | 4.29 | 0:01:32 | 78.57% |
| Borgogno Barolo | 13 | 2.77 | 0:00:15 | 92.31% |
| Ciacci Piccolomini d Aragona 2009 | 12 | 3 | 0:00:33 | 91.67% |
| Clos Pegau | 12 | 3 | 0:00:30 | 0.00% |
| Le Macchiole | 12 | 4.33 | 0:00:41 | 75.00% |
| Fontodi | 11 | 2.36 | 0:00:08 | 100.00% |
| Domaine du Pegau | 9 | 4 | 0:00:47 | 100.00% |
| La Massa Wine | 8 | 3.25 | 0:00:20 | 75.00% |
| Pelissero | 8 | 3.5 | 0:00:57 | 100.00% |
| Barolo Borgogno | 7 | 3.71 | 0:01:10 | 71.43% |
| Ciacci Piccolomini d Aragona 2006 | 7 | 2.29 | 0:00:13 | 71.43% |
| Ogier | 7 | 3.71 | 0:02:09 | 57.14% |
| Borgogno | 6 | 6 | 0:05:14 | 100.00% |
| Fontodi Chianti | 6 | 3 | 0:00:49 | 83.33% |

| Campaign | Visits | Pages / Visit | Avg. Visit Duration | % New Visits |
|---|---|---|---|---|
| La Spinetta | 109 | 3.8 | 0:01:49 | 84.40% |
| Ciacci Piccolomini | 92 | 3.82 | 0:00:37 | 86.96% |
| Pegau | 66 | 3.67 | 0:02:20 | 74.24% |
| Borgogno | 60 | 3.7 | 0:01:05 | 90.00% |
| Massolino | 55 | 3.42 | 0:00:55 | 83.64% |
| Clos de Tart | 49 | 3.49 | 0:01:26 | 85.71% |
| Castello dei Rampolla | 43 | 4.65 | 0:03:07 | 65.12% |
| La Spinetta Barbaresco | 42 | 3.33 | 0:00:25 | 95.24% |
| Le Macchiole | 39 | 3.54 | 0:00:33 | 92.31% |
| Pelissero | 37 | 2.84 | 0:12:32 | 83.78% |
| Fontodi | 32 | 2.56 | 0:00:21 | 93.75% |
| Louis Michel Chablis | 31 | 2.26 | 0:00:05 | 83.87% |
| La Massa Wine | 23 | 3.39 | 0:00:54 | 86.96% |
| (Content Targeting) | 21 | 2.1 | 0:00:17 | 95.24% |

| Matched Search Query | Visits | Pages / Visit | Avg. Visit Duration | % New Visits |
|---|---|---|---|---|
| Louis Michel Chablis | 6 | 2 | 0:00:00 | 100.00% |
| Fontodi Winery | 5 | 7.2 | 0:01:26 | 100.00% |
| Massolino Barolo | 5 | 10.8 | 0:02:51 | 60.00% |
| Pegau | 5 | 2.8 | 0:03:13 | 80.00% |
| Pelissero Wine | 5 | 2 | 0:00:00 | 80.00% |
| Borgogno Langhe Nebbiolo 2009 | 4 | 2.5 | 0:00:06 | 75.00% |
| Ciacci Piccolomini d Aragona Brunello di Montalcino 2007 | 4 | 2 | 0:00:00 | 100.00% |
| Gourt de Mautens | 4 | 5 | 0:02:02 | 100.00% |
| La Massa Winery Italy | 4 | 7.5 | 0:04:30 | 100.00% |
| La Spinetta Barbaresco | 4 | 2 | 0:00:00 | 75.00% |
| La Spinetta Moscato | 4 | 4.5 | 0:00:47 | 100.00% |
| La Spinetta Moscato d Asti Bricco Quaglia 2011 | 4 | 3.5 | 0:01:34 | 100.00% |
| Moscato d Asti la Spinetta | 4 | 5.5 | 0:00:51 | 75.00% |
| Pelissero Barbaresco | 4 | 3 | 0:00:11 | 50.00% |
| Roberto Voerzio Winery | 4 | 5 | 0:01:55 | 25.00% |
| Spinetta Winery | 4 | 3 | 0:00:25 | 100.00% |

| Campaign | Visits | Pages / Visit | Avg. Visit Duration | % New Visits | Matched Search Query | Visits | Pages / Visit | Avg. Visit Duration | % New Visits |
|---|---|---|---|---|---|---|---|---|---|
| Borgogno Barolo | 20 | 2.9 | 0:00:27 | 95.00% | 2007 Castello dei Rampolla Vigna d Alceo | 3 | 6.67 | 0:02:42 | 33.33% |
| Ogier | 18 | 4.11 | 0:02:02 | 77.78% | Castello dei Rampolla Sammarco | 3 | 2 | 0:00:00 | 100.00% |
| Fontodi Wine | 17 | 4 | 0:00:32 | 88.24% | Castello del Terriccio | 3 | 2 | 0:00:00 | 100.00% |
| Fontodi Chianti | 16 | 2.62 | 0:00:21 | 75.00% | Ciacci Piccolomini d Aragona 2007 | 3 | 4.67 | 0:00:31 | 100.00% |
| Ciacci Piccolomini Wine | 13 | 3.08 | 0:00:40 | 100.00% | Domaine Pegau | 3 | 2 | 0:00:00 | 66.67% |
| La Massa | 13 | 2.31 | 0:00:02 | 92.31% | Fontodi Chianti Classico | 3 | 2 | 0:00:00 | 66.67% |
| Massolino Barolo | 13 | 5.54 | 0:01:25 | 84.62% | Fontodi Wines | 3 | 2.67 | 0:00:07 | 100.00% |
| Domaine du Pegau | 12 | 3.08 | 0:00:13 | 100.00% | La Massa Winery | 3 | 2 | 0:00:00 | 66.67% |
| Pelissero Barbaresco | 11 | 2.36 | 0:00:04 | 72.73% | La Spinetta Moscato d Asti | 3 | 3.33 | 0:00:07 | 100.00% |
| Roberto Voerzio | 11 | 4 | 0:00:52 | 72.73% | La Spinetta Moscato d Asti 2011 | 3 | 2 | 0:00:00 | 100.00% |
| Castello Del Terriccio | 10 | 2.4 | 0:00:04 | 90.00% | La Spinetta Vermentino | 3 | 3.33 | 0:00:06 | 100.00% |
| Voerzio | 10 | 2 | 0:00:00 | 90.00% | La Spinetta Wine | 3 | 2.67 | 0:00:14 | 100.00% |
| (Not Set) | 9 | 2.89 | 0:00:13 | 88.89% | Le Macchiole Paleo | 3 | 3.33 | 0:01:07 | 100.00% |
| Chiara Boschis | 8 | 5.25 | 0:03:31 | 87.50% | Massolino Barolo 2007 | 3 | 2.67 | 0:01:23 | 100.00% |
| Vieille Julienne | 8 | 2.25 | 0:00:04 | 75.00% | Massolino Parafada Barolo | 3 | 5.33 | 0:04:21 | 0.00% |

| Campaign | Visits | Pages / Visit | Avg. Visit Duration | % New Visits | Matched Search Query | Visits | Pages / Visit | Avg. Visit Duration | % New Visits |
|---|---|---|---|---|---|---|---|---|---|
| Gourt de Mautens | 7 | 3.71 | 0:01:10 | 100.00% | Pelissero Barbera d Alba Piani | 3 | 3 | 2:30:26 | 33.33% |
| Chiara Boschis Barolo | 4 | 2.5 | 0:00:10 | 100.00% | Plan Pegau Lot 2009 | 3 | 2 | 0:00:00 | 100.00% |
| Fattoria la Massa | 4 | 3 | 0:00:43 | 75.00% | Roberto Voerzio | 3 | 4.67 | 0:00:35 | 100.00% |
| Domaine de la Vieille Julienne | 3 | 2 | 0:00:00 | 100.00% | 1990 Castello dei Rampolla Sammarco Toscana Rosso | 2 | 4 | 0:00:52 | 50.00% |
| Ogier Cote Rotie | 3 | 2 | 0:00:00 | 100.00% | 2 Btl Voerzio Barolo La Serra 2007 | 2 | 2 | 0:00:00 | 50.00% |
| Roberto Voerzio Barolo | 3 | 2.33 | 0:00:12 | 100.00% | 2006 Massolino Margheria Barolo | 2 | 3 | 0:00:23 | 100.00% |
| Domaine Louis Michel | 2 | 3 | 0:01:03 | 100.00% | Barolo Massolino | 2 | 4 | 0:00:41 | 100.00% |
| Castello dei Rampolla Chianti | 1 | 4 | 0:00:51 | 100.00% | Barolo Massolino 2000 | 2 | 2 | 0:00:00 | 50.00% |
| E. Pira Chiara Boschis | 1 | 14 | 0:03:42 | 100.00% | Barolo Massolino 2005 | 2 | 2 | 0:00:00 | 100.00% |
| Gourt de Mautens Rasteau | 1 | 2 | 0:00:00 | 100.00% | Borgogno Barbera d Alba 2008 | 2 | 2 | 0:00:00 | 100.00% |
| La Spinetta Barolo | 1 | 2 | 0:00:00 | 100.00% | Borgogno Barbera Superior | 2 | 2 | 0:00:00 | 50.00% |

Source: Company documents.

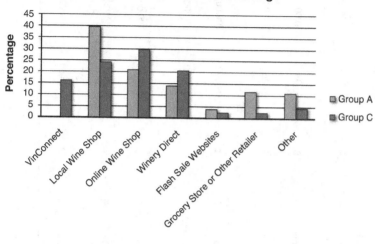

What percentage of your premium wine purchases occurred via the following?

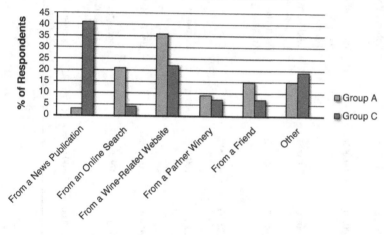

How did you hear about VinConnect?

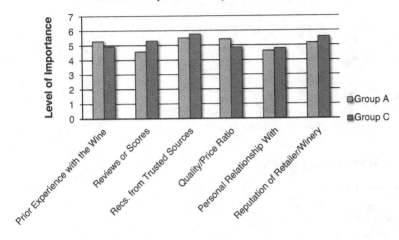

**How important are the following in your decision to purchase a particular wine?**

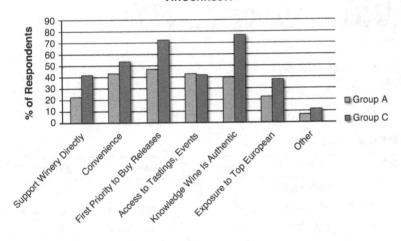

**Which of the following attracted you to join VinConnect?**

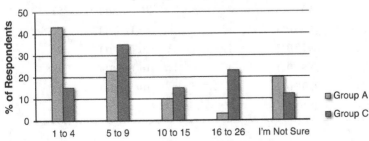

**How many VinConnect mailing lists have you signed up for?**

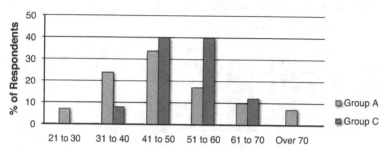

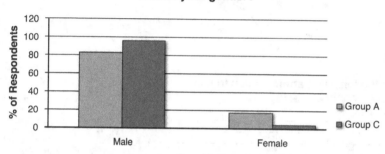

**Exhibit 19-4**  Relevant survey responses

Source: Company documents.

**Exhibit 19-5**  Total Website Visits by Date

| Day | Visits | Day | Visits | Day | Visits |
|-----|--------|-----|--------|-----|--------|
| 9/19/2011 | 11 | 9/30/2011 | 17 | 10/11/2011 | 15 |
| 9/20/2011 | 88 | 10/1/2011 | 5 | 10/12/2011 | 10 |
| 9/21/2011 | 61 | 10/2/2011 | 4 | 10/13/2011 | 11 |
| 9/22/2011 | 25 | 10/3/2011 | 18 | 10/14/2011 | 16 |
| 9/23/2011 | 9 | 10/4/2011 | 56 | 10/15/2011 | 24 |
| 9/24/2011 | 4 | 10/5/2011 | 37 | 10/16/2011 | 21 |
| 9/25/2011 | 7 | 10/6/2011 | 33 | 10/17/2011 | 30 |
| 9/26/2011 | 38 | 10/7/2011 | 17 | 10/18/2011 | 26 |
| 9/27/2011 | 29 | 10/8/2011 | 4 | 10/19/2011 | 14 |
| 9/28/2011 | 19 | 10/9/2011 | 5 | 10/20/2011 | 17 |
| 9/29/2011 | 16 | 10/10/2011 | 7 | | |

Source: Created by case writer.

# 20 —————————————————

## Cardagin: Local Mobile Rewards

*When you visit your favorite restaurant, the manager sometimes offers you a free dessert. The restaurant manager could provide such recognition for about 100 of their best customers, but what about the next 1,000 who are also regulars?*

—Rob Masri

## Introduction

On a still-nippy February afternoon, Rob Masri, CEO of Cardagin, a mobile marketing network based in Charlottesville, Virginia, scanned his iPhone app as he entered Eppie's, a local restaurant. Through the Cardagin app, Eppie's, an early member of the Cardagin network, could track a user's visits and offer personalized coupons on the spot. That day, Masri was able to redeem a 90% discount for lunch, over which he spoke passionately about Cardagin's fast progress, the decisions facing him, and the broader trends in mobile marketing.

Since its launch in September 2010, Cardagin had signed up more than 1,200 merchants in 30 cities over 20 states to offer loyalty programs through Cardagin's mobile app and raised over $5 million in venture funding. More than 25,000 customers have downloaded the Cardagin app, and the mayor of Charlottesville declared January 18, 2011, Cardagin Day. It was a great start for a business that provided a mobile-phone platform for merchants to access their loyal customers and for customers to obtain personalized rewards from all their favorite merchants in a single location. (Exhibits 20-1 and 20-2 provide an overview of Cardagin's initial launch growth and early user demographics.)

Masri recognized early on that using a smartphone as a marketing medium was an effective way to reach an increasingly mobile consumer base, and the initial challenge was convincing retailers of the value in reaching it. To do so, he would need to increase both the merchant and consumer networks, find new cities for the next expansion phase, and develop and price the next generation of services, helping merchants provide rewards for their customers that were personalized and effective. He had already identified a niche among smaller local businesses in college towns. A number of vendors were all simultaneously trying to capitalize on the mobile-coupon trends, so rapid expansion and effective couponing strategies were critical. (Exhibit 20-3 is a case study used by Cardagin to educate prospective clients.)

# Cardagin Network

By creating a mobile presence in Cardagin's mobile apps, local businesses had exclusive access to a modern customer-retention tool and could begin to identify, reward, and communicate with their best customers—the 20% who generated 80% of their revenue.

Cardagin created a network of local businesses (Figure 20-1). The larger the user base of consumers and merchants, the more valuable and beneficial the network. Using Cardagin's smartphone app, consumers could find their favorite local stores or explore new merchants, eliminating paper loyalty club cards and coupons, by tracking and managing points and rewards on a smartphone instead. By accessing the merchant portal on Cardagin.com, merchants could create a mobile presence and target advertisements and promotions to those local consumers most likely to buy their services or products. Through Cardagin's mobile loyalty technology, local businesses could monitor customer spending habits and make more intelligent and better-informed marketing decisions.

**Figure 20-1** Cardagin network
Source: Cardagin. Used with permission.

The Cardagin software enabled a merchant to target a specific subset of a customer base at specific times. Offers and rewards could be created "on the fly" for immediate effect, with GPS or location-based features making it possible to create and distribute advertisements and promotions much faster and more directly than a traditional television or newspaper advertising channel.

The Cardagin platform had two main components:

- The *mobile app* allowed consumers to use their smartphones to browse businesses, view offers, redeem coupons, join groups, receive notifications, earn loyalty points, and collect rewards. Cardagin offered a native app for the iPhone and for Android-enabled phones, eliminating dependence on Internet availability, as well as a mobile website for BlackBerry, Windows Phone 7, and browser-enabled feature phones. In addition to the consumer features, Cardagin's iPhone app allowed businesses to record transactions and award points at the point of purchase. For example, a business manager could log in to the Cardagin app, scan a customer's loyalty or redemption code, enter the purchase amount, and submit the transaction to be recorded on Cardagin's servers.

- The *Cardagin.com website* provided a self-service merchant portal for a business to easily manage its Cardagin account. Businesses could input location information (address, phone number, website, etc.); create advertisements, offers, and rewards; and track loyalty data and other metrics. Additionally, businesses could use the merchant portal to record purchases and award loyalty points (in lieu of a scan or point-of-sale integration). Although the main point of use for consumers was via the mobile app and website, Cardagin was in the process of developing a consumer web portal to allow users without smartphones to manage their loyalty points and rewards.

Cardagin gave local merchants an affordable alternative to traditional advertising. At a cost of $200 per month or about $6.67 per day, many local merchants could afford to enter mobile marketing space. Cost differences as compared with traditional sources are outlined in Table 20-1.

**Table 20-1** Traditional Advertising Costs by Source and Size[1]

| Yellow pages | Half-page ad | $6,000/year |
|---|---|---|
| Newspaper (25,000 circulation) | Quarter-page ad | $300/day |
| Radio spot | 30-second | $50/spot |
| TV spot | 30-second | $60/spot |
| Direct mail | Flyer | $1,000/month |

Source: Case writer estimates based on Charlottesville advertising market.

Once published, the advertisement or reward on the Cardagin app remained active until the merchant changed it, whereas most traditional channels charged for every rerun of the advertisement. Furthermore, these promotions could be more targeted than newspaper or television ads, and the retailer had no obligation to share any earned revenues from deals or points redeemed.

# The Pilot

To test the Cardagin concept in the marketplace, a two-part pilot program with a small sample (<10) of local businesses based in Charlottesville was conducted in the fall of 2010, during which participating merchants were provided Cardagin services free of charge. Merchant feedback suggested a need to tier the services by including a low-cost, entry-level product that allowed them to "dip their toes" into the mobile-advertising waters.

The firm responded with Cardagin Broadcast, which provided limited mobile advertising and tracking, and Cardagin Complete, which provided a full-service mobile loyalty component, consumer demographics, coupon redemption rates, and other data tracking. Differences between these products are highlighted in Table 20-2.

**Table 20-2** The Cardagin Product Line

|  | Cardagin Broadcast | Cardagin Complete |
| --- | --- | --- |
| Mobile ads | ✓ | ✓ |
| Access to Cardagin network | ✓ | ✓ |
| Track promotional views | ✓ | ✓ |
| Mobile loyalty program |  | ✓ |
| Track purchases and redemptions |  | ✓ |
| Targeted ads |  | ✓ |
| Access to reporting center |  | ✓ |

Source: Cardagin. Used with permission.

For retail clients to be willing to upgrade to full service, Masri would need to demonstrate the value of mobile marketing as a customer acquisition and retention tool. Mobile marketing garnered more data than traditional marketing activity, so a retailer could build a CRM (customer relationship management) database, enabling it to use customers' past behavior to devise tactical mobile-marketing campaigns to attract repeat purchases.[2]

A second pilot in the first half of 2011 expanded to areas outside of Charlottesville—to Northern Virginia and southern Pennsylvania, as well as Blacksburg, Virginia; Nashville, Tennessee; and Fort Worth, Texas. The second pilot tested three concepts: (1) proof of concept in non–college town markets, (2) consumer adoption of the Cardagin mobile app, and (3) market need and demand for a local mobile-advertising outlet (with and without the loyalty component). On the consumer front, the Cardagin website was launched, and the free iPhone and Android apps were released to the public. During this period, more than 400 businesses signed up and nearly 6,000 users created new accounts. Based on the first pilot, the case writers estimated the retention rate of merchants ranged from 75% to 89%. Usage data revealed that merchants who remained with the Cardagin network boasted higher penetration rates with Cardagin's user base (285 active users for retained merchants versus 21 active users for churned merchants) and more transactions per user (1,210 versus 58).

Each merchant on Cardagin provided at least one daily advertisement for consumers to view and redeem. Ads varied greatly among businesses. Many merchants provided a general-broadcast type of coupon, such as 10% off any product for two weeks or more, while others provided more personalized coupons for their best customers: buy one, get one 50% off, free state inspection with purchase of an oil change, or $2.00 off a lunch buffet. During this initial period, redemption information was not collected.

A new platform released in July 2011 could account for consumer redemptions based on consumer clicks, but it still could not verify if a click resulted in actual usage until businesses upgraded to the new loyalty component. At that level of service, data could be captured directly from a consumer's phone, either by scanning a quick response (QR) code or by the cashier manually entering a 10-digit alphanumeric code or the customer's mobile number.

## Merchant Portal

Key for retailers was the user-friendly merchant portal, a self-service mobile-marketing platform that allowed them to easily create, edit, and track offers and loyalty programs. After logging in to the portal, merchants could review business details and advertisements across multiple locations and easily manage their mobile advertising and loyalty programs (Exhibit 20-4a).

Following the execution of a promotion, merchants could use the portal to track coupon usage and customer loyalty metrics such as redemption rates and followers (Exhibit 20-4b). Self-sufficiency among retailers was the end goal, but as part of the firm's value proposition, customer service support would be required, initially in 100 markets across the United States.

## Consumer App

Once consumers downloaded the Cardagin app, they could search for participating merchants by name, ZIP Code, or locations nearest to them. Promotions provided by a merchant were then visible (Figure 20-2a). Clicking on a promotion brought up a bar code (Figure 20-2b) that could be scanned by the merchant's data capture device, which could be an iPhone or iPod Touch, to redeem the reward.

### Merchant Network

An important aspect of Cardagin's value proposition was the possibility of a merchant network. By aggregating within a specific geographic area under the Cardagin banner, merchants could not only reward and retain existing customers, but also acquire new customers via network partners.

Masri focused his efforts on college towns, using a grassroots campaign fostered by a brokered sales force. The college-town locale provided access to a younger consumer base and single-location merchants underserved by national providers. Masri also approached university alumni and athletics associations with the Cardagin solution and offered those groups the option of providing exclusive offers for their members from merchants in the Cardagin network. For the merchants, Cardagin provided a way to access members of a lucrative but elusive group. (Exhibit 20-5 provides an overview of Cardagin services.)

2a. Sample Reward

2b. Redemption Screen

**Figure 20-2** The Cardagin app consumer's view

Source: Cardagin. Used with permission.

## Competition

Cardagin faced competition from a well-entrenched industry. Coupons were distributed through various mediums (such as print, e-mail, and mobile phones). The digital-coupon industry included daily discounts geared toward customer acquisition as well as other mobile loyalty program providers.

## *Printed Coupons*

During the economic recession of 2008–2009, U.S. annual coupon usage increased for the first time since the early 1990s, and 2010 marked the largest single-year distribution quantity of consumer packaged goods (CPG) coupons ever recorded in the United States: 332 billion. Redemption peaked in 1999 at 4.6 billion, then averaged 2.6 billion between 2006 and 2008, rising again in 2009 and 2010 to 3.3 billion, representing consumer savings of an estimated $3.7 billion (Figure 20-3).

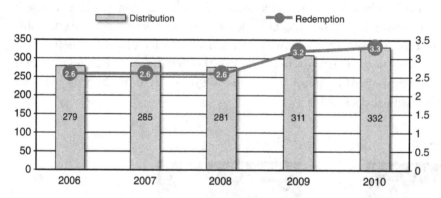

**Figure 20-3**  U.S. CPG coupon distribution and redemption volume (in billions)

Sources: NCH Marketing Services, Inc., *Annual Topline U.S. CPG Coupon Facts Report for Year-end 2010;* Todd Hale, *The Coupon Comeback,* April 13, 2010, http://blog.nielsen.com/nielsenwire/consumer/the-coupon-comeback/ (accessed November 9, 2011).

Despite growth within all other classes of trade, conventional grocery stores or supermarkets still accounted for the highest coupon redemption rates (Table 20-3).

**Table 20-3**  Total Coupon Redemption Volume by Retail Channel (In Percent)

|  | 2008 | 2009 | 2010 |
|---|---|---|---|
| Grocery stores | 59.9 | 60.6 | 59.7 |
| Mass merchandisers | 25.0 | 24.4 | 23.9 |
| Drug stores | 6.5 | 6.2 | 6.6 |
| Military commissaries | 4.9 | 4.2 | 4.1 |
| Other[3] | 3.9 | 4.6 | 5.7 |

Source: NCH Marketing Services, Inc., *Coupon Facts Report 2011.*

Newspaper inserts remained the primary method for the distribution (89%) and redemption (53%) of coupons, but with more and more consumers making digital coupons part of their shopping routine and more than $1.2 billion in savings issued in

2010, the digital coupon market dramatically outpaced the growth of newspaper coupons by approximately 6 to 1.[4] While online coupons represented only 1% of overall coupon distribution, they had grown to nearly 10% of redemptions in 2009 and had been the industry growth engine in recent years.[5] Other paperless coupon distribution methods, such as electronic checkout (39%), digital promotions (31%), and shelf pad (30%), also helped drive 2009's significant growth in coupon redemptions (Table 20-4).[6]

**Table 20-4** Total Coupon Distribution Volume by Media Type (In Percent)

|  | 2009 | 2010 |
|---|---|---|
| Freestanding insert (FSI) | 85.9 | 87.7 |
| All other media | 14.1 | 12.3 |
| In-store handout | 5.6 | 5.2 |
| Direct mail | 2.6 | 2.4 |
| Magazine | 2.4 | 2.2 |
| In/on pack and cross-ruff[7] | 1.4 | 1.1 |
| Other[8] | 2.1 | < 2.0 |

Four sustainable trends were likely driving the rapid shift in coupon redemption: (1) dramatic global penetration of mobile devices and media (for example, smartphones, tablets, QR codes, and location-based services), (2) social media fueling changes in consumption patterns, (3) retailer recognition and active participation in mobile couponing (such as linking consumer to loyalty card data and personalization of coupons and rewards), and (4) the promising future of mobile wallets, which allowed consumers to carry the contents of a wallet (such as a credit/debit card, coupons, and shopping lists) on a phone.

## Daily Deals

Groupon was the largest and fastest-growing firm in the group buying space, and its daily deal service provided more than 50% of its sales revenue. Like Cardagin, Groupon's value proposition also centered on giving local firms access to local markets, although Groupon sought to leverage the vast network of consumers registered to its service and to drive customer acquisition to local businesses. Cardagin's focus was on customer retention and building customer loyalty. Groupon's payment model was also different. Groupon collected a prepayment from the consumer and then paid the merchant a percentage of that payment; Cardagin did not sell coupons to consumers and received no shared revenue. Instead, Cardagin relied on monthly subscription fees paid by the businesses.

With a surplus supply of deals and low barriers to entry, it was expected that competition within the industry would grow quickly. Through its acquisition of Punchd, a customer loyalty program based on the "buy-10-get-1-free" punch-card system, Google fueled speculation that it was adding a loyalty component to its checkout product, Google Wallet. AT&T was planning to enter the market through Yellowpages.com.[9] Amazon.com had invested in LivingSocial. Yelp.com, the restaurant review site, considered creating its own version of daily deals.

### Mobile Coupons

Companies such as Coupon Rover, Coupons.com, Yowza!!, and Coupon Sherpa provided coupons on mobile apps, but the majority were focused on national brand stores and not local merchants. Mobile applications provided by Foursquare, SCVNGR, and Gowalla capitalized on the trend in social games, allowing people to check in at certain locations and earn rewards or go on scavenger hunts and play games with customers. Location services such as Placepop allowed consumers to check in when they visited a merchant and redeem offers based on frequency. Placepop in particular also allowed users to suggest rewards and create unique loyalty programs with the merchants directly.

Mobile loyalty companies such as Sundrop, Punchd, and PlumReward were the most similar to Cardagin. They provided loyalty solutions to help retain customers but no customer acquisition package. Cardstar, KeyRing, and CardKing provided consumers with a way to store the plastic cards and key fobs of local and national businesses on their mobile phones, but they did not create the loyalty programs for those businesses nor did they store information on a customer's transaction. Industry analysts believed that the ability to provide relevant consumer information to merchants would determine which services survived long-term.[10]

# Conclusion

Cardagin received positive reviews from local television, social media, industry blogs, and entrepreneurship magazines, including *TechCrunch, Inc.* magazine, *CNET*, and *VentureBeat*. What remained for Masri was to develop a simple yet convincing comparison of costs and returns between Cardagin and traditional local channels. What kinds of promotions were more effective for which consumers and when?

Masri had to prioritize his marketing spending. Should he focus on acquiring new merchants or retaining existing ones? How much could Masri spend on acquiring a new merchant? What was the value of a single merchant to Cardagin's network? He wondered if the size of the existing merchant network helped him attract new merchants and consumers to the Cardagin platform. He also wondered how he could quantify this positive network effect. How can the data from Cardagin's network inform his decisions?

# Endnotes

1. Advertisements in many of these channels had to be run multiple times in order to be effective.

2. Ariya Priyasantha, "How to Harness the Power of Mobile Couponing," Mobile Marketer, July 20, 2010, http://www.mobilemarketer.com/cms/opinion/columns/6809.html (accessed October 12, 2011).

3. Includes convenience stores, warehouses/clubs, and variety/discount stores (such as the Dollar Store).

4. Kantar Media press release, January 5, 2011.

5. Jack Neff, "Coupon Clipping Stages a Comeback," *Advertising Age*, November 1, 2010, http://adage.com/article/news/newspaper-print-coupon-clipping-stages-a-comeback/146816.

6. Todd Hale, "The Coupon Comeback," Nielsen, April 13, 2010, http://www.nielsen.com/us/en/newswire/2010/the-coupon-comeback.html.

7. A *cross-ruff* coupon is distributed as part of a product's packaging but is only redeemable for future purchases.

8. Includes newspapers, digital/online, and handouts away from store.

9. Kris Ashton, "AT&T to Offer Deals on Its YP.com Site," Daily Deal Media website, May 2, 2011, http://www.dailydealmedia.com/369att-to-offer-deals-on-its-yp-com-site/ (accessed October 13, 2011).

10. Issie Lapowsky, "Horse Race: No Hole Punch Required," *Inc.*, November 2010.

# Exhibits

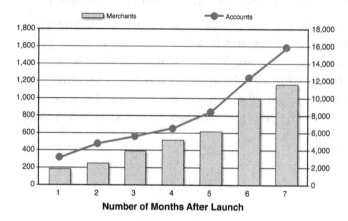

**Exhibit 20-1** Cardagin growth in numbers of merchants (left axis) and accounts (right axis)
Source: Cardagin. Used with permission.

**Exhibit 20-2** Key Metrics for Cardagin Users

| Age | |
|---|---|
| < 18 | 0.9% |
| 18–24 | 17.5% |
| 25–34 | 30.8% |
| 35–44 | 25.2% |
| > 45 | 25.5% |
| **Education** | |
| High School | 10.0% |
| Associate's Degree | 6.7% |
| Bachelor's Degree | 50.0% |
| Graduate Degree | 21.7% |
| Postgraduate Degree | 11.6% |
| **Marital Status** | |
| Married | 50.2% |
| Single | 45.1% |
| Divorced | 4.8% |
| **Gender** | |
| Male | 46.4% |
| Female | 53.6% |

Source: Cardagin, based on demographic information obtained during customer registration of version 1.0; such information was no longer required in subsequent versions.

# Cardagin
## Case Study

www.cardagin.com

## The Local Merchant

A local coffee and donut franchise in Charlottesville, VA struggled with coupons and paper punch cards for years. Andy, the local franchise owner, spent on average $12,000 per year to attract customers to his store with limited success.

Andy wanted to learn more about his customers - who used coupons, who picked up punch cards and who spent what? He chose Cardagin for his marketing and customer retention needs.

*"Using Cardagin, we acquired a group of customers who want to hear from us, who care about us and who respond to our offers."*

*Andy, local franchise owner*

## The Setup

Andy worked with Cardagin to devise a multi-part mobile marketing campaign targeting University of Virginia students. As the students returned from summer break, Andy offered an exclusive promotion that could only be redeemed through Cardagin: "**any** drink, **any** size for **free**!" This exclusive offer ran for one week and was designed to attract customers to Andy's store and join his loyalty program, powered by Cardagin.

The following two weeks, Andy ran another exclusive offer on Cardagin: "**any** drink, **any** size for **$0.99**!" This offer, while still aggressive, helped Andy engage his new customers on his new platform. During the final two weeks of his mobile campaign, Andy ran a final offer: "**any** drink, **any** size for **$1.19**!" As customers redeemed the offer, Andy encouraged his staff to remind every customer to join his mobile loyalty program and earn points for every dollar they spend.

*Marketing Tip*

*Having staff encourage all customers to join your new loyalty program, powered by Cardagin, gives you insight into the value of a customer.*

## The Results

So, what happened? As a result of creative marketing and using Cardagin's unique mobile technology, Andy was able to generate substantial revenue for his business. More importantly, Andy's new loyalty program, powered by Cardagin, generated repeat customers instead of one-time deal hunters, and gave Andy insight into a group of customers that he can engage and reach at anytime. Here's a look at the numbers:

Redemptions: **How many drink offers were redeemed?**
- Free drink offer: 531 in one week
- $0.99 drink offer: 329 in first week, 268 in second week
- $1.19 drink offer: 231 in first week, 184 in second week

Short-Term Gain: **What was the immediate impact of the campaign?**
- Campaign revenue: $1,084.88 (excluding additional purchases)
- Hundreds of new customers within a specific demographic
- Upsell opportunities of higher margin items

Long-Term Gain: **What were the long-term benefits of the campaign?**
- Repeat customers who are rewarded for their loyalty
- Direct line of communication with engaged customers
- Transaction log of who spent what, when and where
- Viral marketing from loyal customers who share savings and rewards via social media outlets and who recommend Andy's business to their friends and family

## The Bottom Line

Cardagin helps Andy identify his best customers. He now knows that Karen R., Richard G. and Matt S. come in everyday for their morning coffee. The lifetime value of these customers, and others like them, is priceless to a local business. Using Cardagin, Andy has a modern, meaningful and cost-effective way to reach, engage, reward and retain those customers who mean the most to his business.

**Exhibit 20-3** Overview of Cardagin services for prospective clients

Source: Cardagin. Used with permission.

## Exhibit 20-4 The Cardagin merchant portal

4a. Merchant Portal

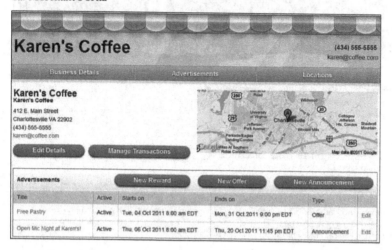

4b. Information Reporting

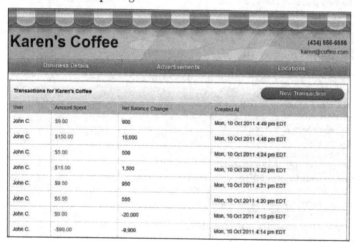

Source: Cardagin. Used with permission.

**Exhibit 20-5** Overview of Cardagin services for Eppie's restaurant

## Network Effect of Being Listed with Other Local Businesses

5a. List View

5b. Map View

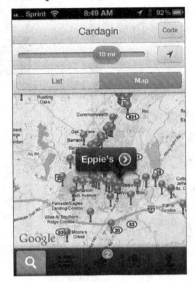

5c. Business Storefront

## Mobile Presence in Cardagin

### 5d. Business Information

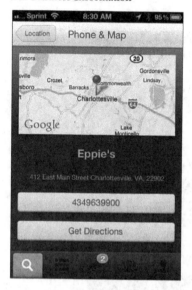

### 5e. Points Screen

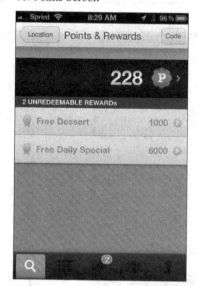

### 5f. Redemption Screen

Source: Cardagin. Used with permission.

# Assignment Questions

1. When is a mobile coupon considered successful for the retailer, the consumer, and the mobile-coupon-service provider?

2. What aspects of Cardagin determine retailer adoption and consumer adoption?

3. How do you compare the returns from mobile coupons and local newspaper advertising or coupons?

4. Run a regression of the logarithm of number of redemptions (1numredeem) on industry category dummies, free shipping, all-free, discount percentage, and coupons offered by competition weight by spatial distance.

5. What recommendations can you give retailers regarding coupon design from the regression output?

# Section VI

## Resource Allocation Revisited

We revisit resource allocation in this section with Chapter 21, "Dunia Finance LLC Revisited." This case implements analytics to optimize the cross-sell operations of Dunia. Chapter 22, "Implementing Marketing Analytics," concludes the book by presenting practical advice to ensure widespread adoption of marketing analytics within an organization.

# 21

## Dunia Finance LLC Revisited

## Introduction

Ali Hurbas, head of the Strategic Analytics Unit (SAU) at Dunia Finance LLC (Dunia), was in the middle of an effort to use data extracted from the Dunia data warehouse to establish potential customers' customer lifetime value (CLV). This would then be used in a spreadsheet model intended to evaluate particular cross-selling activities in terms of the resulting aggregate CLV.

The link between alternative forms of contacting customers and CLV was really the confluence of many linked relationships between variables, each one relatively straightforward on its own account. When all these relationships were put together, however, the model had a somewhat complex appearance. Hurbas was sorting out how to express his model to his colleagues at Dunia, including senior management.

For a product to succeed, the deciding factor was profitability, which was driven by profits and average loans outstanding. The focus on profitability was one of the leading-edge practices adopted by the Dunia SAU team, ensuring that a holistic assessment was done on the overall value of the relationship and not on one-dimensional metrics. The profit and loss (P&L) statement incorporated all relevant revenue and expense items associated with the product. Dunia measured return on assets on an annualized basis.

Customers fell into particular categories based on two characteristics: risk score and propensity to respond. The risk score was between 500 and 1,000, and company practice was to divide that range into 10 bins that increased by 50 points. Propensity to respond had five possibilities: very low, low, medium, high, and very high. Customers were placed into one of 50 categories based on these two variables (10 risk-score bins × 5 levels of propensity to respond).

Each category had a specific number of customers at any time, a number referred to as the category size. The approval rate for Dunia granting a personal loan to a customer would depend on the category the customer fell into. Such a customer, if granted a personal loan, would provide to Dunia a given Risk-Adjusted Yield from Interest Margin and Annual-Fee Revenue less Credit Losses.

Profitability depended on two important variables:

Receivables per Customer = Average Credit Limit × Expected Average Credit Limit Utilization

Annual Funding Cost = Receivables per Customer × Funding Cost

These variables feed into the calculation of various components of CLV. Documentation of the spreadsheet model is shown in the indented list in Exhibit 21-1. Each line in the indented list represents a variable that appears as a column in the spreadsheet. Exhibit 21-2 shows all relationships of model variables to other variables or to data fields in databases from the data warehouse. Where variables on the right side of an equation come from an equation involving other variables or fields, the next level of indentation shows the equations for those variables.

This spreadsheet model can serve as the basis of a what-if analysis of alternative cross-selling activities involving e-mails and calls. When a 1 is put in a cell in one (and only one) of the columns D, E, F, or G for a particular category in a row, the CLV will change. Hurbas and his colleagues could then experiment with various activities for the categories. As combinations of activities are considered, the number of calls is shown in column I; the total is at the bottom of that column. It is possible to use the spreadsheet to explore the set of activities having a given total call level that produces the greatest CLV.

# Optimizing the Cross-Sell Operations

Ali Hurbas, head of the Strategic Analytics Unit at Dunia Finance LLC (Dunia), believed he might be able to set up the customer lifetime value model to find the optimal combination of cross-selling activities involving calls and e-mails. He planned to use the Excel Solver add-in feature. He needed to identify the objective, choose the decision variables within the model, and define constraints.

Dunia had set the budget for the current period to (United Arab Emirates dirhams) AED 100,000. Due to limitations for people, space, and equipment, management had also set a maximum of 50,000 calls allowed.

In which categories should Hurbas select which activities to provide the best plan for cross-selling credit cards to personal loan customers? Carefully explain and justify your recommendations. How would you achieve buy-in for implementing your plan?

# Exhibits

**Exhibit 21-1** Indented List of the Relationships Among Variables in the Spreadsheet Model

CLV Gain = Category Size × Approval Rate × CLV × Sumproduct(Activities:Response Rates) – AcquisCost per Booking × Bookings – Telesales Cost

   CLV = Net Contribution × [(1+Discount Rate) ÷ (1 + Discount Rate – Retention Rate)]

   Telesales Cost = Category Size × Cost for Category

Source: Created by case writer.

**Exhibit 21-2** Indented List of Data Relationships Used to Calculate Variables in the Spreadsheet Model

Bookings = Sumproduct(Activities:Response Rates) × Category Size × Approval Rate

  Net Contribution = Risk-Adjusted Yield – Marginal Cost

    Risk-Adjusted Yield = Interest Margin + Annual Fee Revenue – Credit Losses

      Interest Margin = Annual Interest – Annual Funding Cost

        Annual Interest = Interest Earning Receivables × APR

          Interest Receivables = Receivables per Customer × Revolving Ratio

            Receivables per Customer = Average Credit Limit × Expected Average Credit Limit Utilization

          Annual Funding Cost = Receivables per Customer × Funding Cost

        Credit Losses = Expected Annual Credit Losses × Receivables per Customer

          Receivables per Customer = Average Credit Limit × Expected Average Credit Limit Utilization

Source: Created by case writer.

# 22

## Implementing Marketing Analytics

## Introduction

Marketing analytics powered by "big data" holds the promise to shift marketing strategy from an intuitive discipline to a fact-based, decision-making process. Despite its potential, widespread adoption of marketing analytics within organizations remains a challenge. The following road map for improving implementation of marketing analytics is based on our interactions with more than 100 executives in conferences, executive education seminars, case study development, and consulting projects.

The starting point for implementation of marketing analytics is top management support and the integration of the marketing analytics function in business processes. Given this launching pad, firms must address issues related to organizational structures, analytics processes, and organizational change to foster implementation of analytics (Figure 22-1). Within this framework, managers should ask seven key questions to start the journey toward a marketing analytics–driven culture.

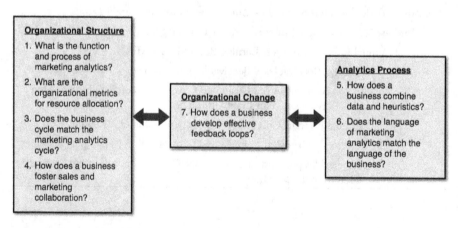

**Figure 22-1** Road map for implementing marketing analytics

# Organizational Structure

## 1. What Is the Function and Process of Marketing Analytics?

The objective of marketing analytics is to shift from intuition-based to fact-based decision making. It is important to understand that effective marketing analytics entails a combination of attribution of sales to different marketing mediums, optimization, and allocation of marketing resources; accounting for consumer response (including search, online chatter, store visits, and purchasing behavior); and business outcomes (including unit sales, revenues, market share, and customer lifetime value). Without taking such a holistic approach and considering market conditions and competitive activities, organizations cannot see the full effect of marketing and this leads to a gap in the credibility of marketing analytics.

Field experiments are the first step in taking action on the recommendations of marketing analytics. A test-and-learn environment is essential for this adoption. However, in reality, ongoing tests of media budgets are possible only in the presence of fluid marketing and media management. Often, budgets are allocated to specific media types, but a holistic perspective allows for flexibility across media vehicles. Marketing analytics professionals, on the other hand, need to understand the organizational culture and capabilities of data and IT systems.

Even if an organization develops a holistic analytics function and provides fluid budgets to media vehicles and the analytics professionals are embedded within the organization's systems and culture, management's need for control may lead it to reject models. A way around this is to customize models for managers and train them on how to use and understand them.[1] Simulation software and scenario planning are, therefore, essential for implementation of analytics. Analytics professionals need to recognize the limits of the models underlying their predictions and recommendations. Simulation software that lets managers change the business parameters or assumptions and evaluate consequences would go a long way toward developing comfort with analytics among managers.

## 2. What Are the Organizational Metrics for Resource Allocation?

Successful implementation of the budgeting process necessitates focusing on better allocation rather than on total budget optimization. Profit functions typically have a flat maximum (Figure 22-2). In other words, it is typical to find that net profit does not increase after a certain level of marketing spending, even if unit sales continue to increase with marketing spend.

Managers are, therefore, better off not optimizing the total budget but rather focusing on reallocating resources across media channels for a fixed budget.

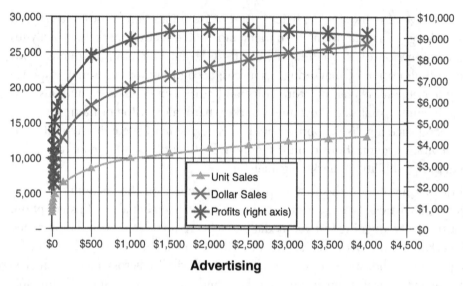

**Figure 22-2** The flat maximum principle of profits

It is important that organizations decide the metrics for evaluating the effectiveness of marketing spending up front and share those metrics widely. It is best to use a wide range of metrics to evaluate marketing investments. Return on investment (ROI) is, however, the most common metric in assessing the value of marketing tools because it is easiest to use in analytical marketing-mix models. Optimization recommendations that use ROI to a large extent recommend reduction of marketing budgets because the returns from marketing investments are not linear, as is typical in many capital projects. Market response functions typically follow an S-shaped curve (Figure 22-3), where small investments in marketing do not lead to sales response. Beyond a certain threshold, incremental marketing investments start providing returns. Beyond an upper limit, however, additional investments do not lead to a corresponding increase in sales. Such an S-shaped function takes into account typical marketing phenomena such as diminishing returns and long-term carry-over.

As shown in Figure 22-3, ROI calculations that are based on total returns and total marketing investments ignore where a brand is on the market response curve. The key is, therefore, to look at the return on marketing investment (ROMI), or the return on marginal investment.

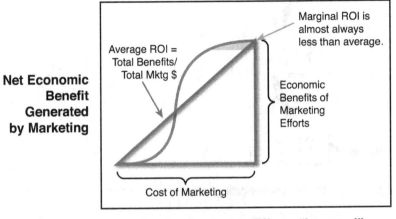

**Cost of Marketing Efforts "Invested"**

**Figure 22-3** Marketing ROI is not linear

ROMI is calculated as a "contribution attributable to marketing (net of marketing spending), divided by the marketing 'invested' or risked."[2] The challenge with ROMI is identifying sales that are attributable to marketing. Marketing analytics and smart experimental designs can be very useful in identifying the lift in sales attributable to marketing investments. As shown in Figure 22-3, ROI is typically higher than ROMI. Optimization of marketing based on ROI would, therefore, normally recommend a lower investment in marketing than ROMI because ROI attributes all of a firm's sales to marketing investments. A ROMI-based strategy takes a more measured approach and accommodates nuances in consumer response to marketing.

## 3. Does the Business Cycle Match the Marketing Analytics Cycle?

The cadence of business and analytics decisions must be synchronized. For example, purchasing television spots in advance can provide greater discounts (sometimes as high as 50%) and provide structure for media planners and the sales force. But this forward buying also establishes lock-in and comes at the expense of flexibility, which is often necessary for testing the effects of reallocations recommended by marketing analytics. It is, therefore, necessary to take into account media purchase cycles and synchronize the marketing analytics and sales force activities with this cycle. A proposed analytics and decision cycle is provided in Figure 22-4.

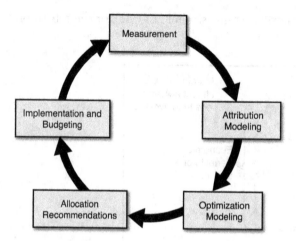

**Figure 22-4** Synchronization of management budgeting and allocation cycles

### 4. How Does a Business Foster Sales and Marketing Collaboration?

Technology developments (especially the Internet) have provided customers access to more information on products than ever before. In this environment, consumers are increasingly conducting their own research online before meeting the salespeople, which changes the dynamics of a sales call. Salespeople, on the other hand, also have access to information on consumer behavior and can use technology to address customer queries in real time during a sales call. Marketing can develop insights on customer behavior, which can help the sales force by providing better quality and more leads.

Organizations, therefore, need a unified view across all sales and marketing channels to drive predictability and improve revenue. But this is challenging because salespeople and marketers generally have different metrics. Further, marketers tend to speak a language that sales teams seldom understand. Common obstacles for sales and marketing collaboration include different languages between sales and marketing and the lack of credibility among salespeople for someone without sales experience. Marketing can improve the transparency of the sales process by tracking customer progress through different stages of the sales funnel. This increased transparency can form the basis for collaboration between marketing and sales. But it is important for marketing to map customer insights to the sales funnel and explain how the insights can improve the sales process.

# Analytics Processes

## 5. How Does a Business Combine Data and Heuristics?

Marketing decisions should depend on the information gathered, but it is never possible to gather all the information. It is, therefore, important to blend analytics with heuristics to create a better marketing-mix model by integrating nonmix lessons learned over time. For example, consider a situation wherein the goal is to use analytics across marketing elements to maximize the return. The reality, though, is that according to analytics, short-term trade ROI is going to be higher than short-term advertising ROI. This is because trade marketing has an immediate effect on sales, whereas advertising normally has a smaller short-term effect. The total value from advertising is realized over time, whereas most of the value for advertising is realized within the short term.

Although it is easier to lift sales with short-term levers such as price discounts rather than with long-term levers such as new customer acquisition, it is not the best decision to reallocate all advertising money to trade. So a business would need to consider including metrics beyond sales, such as brand and advertisement awareness or word of mouth, to evaluate the value of marketing-mix elements.

The biggest challenge to accomplishing this is incorporating heuristics into the analytics process in the long run. The solution is to learn over time. By following a measurement cycle—"plan, execute, measure, evaluate, learn"[3]—companies can apply knowledge learned from previous projects to compare and contrast insights into new projects.

## 6. Does the Language of Marketing Analytics Match the Language of the Business?

Consultants typically view the messaging of the results as the key reason for lack of implementation of the findings. Three factors help develop a persuasive story using marketing analytics. The first step to telling a good story is to clearly define, explain, and widely share the primary metric for evaluating resource allocation. By increasing transparency and clarity, analytics teams can improve their influence on the process. Second, analytics managers need to ensure that the model is in sync with brand strategy and other data to which executives are exposed. This helps the message of the model fit the larger story. Finally, simple and readable models have a much stronger impact on decision-making. Data visualization and simulation software help open the black box and help managers play with the marketing analytics system to understand its process and benefits.

# Organizational Change

## 7. How Does a Business Develop Effective Feedback Loops?

Feedback loops can be developed by setting performance or ROMI thresholds, making recurring improvements, and celebrating accomplishments of both the marketing analytics and brand teams.

It is useful to start with an idea of the end goal of the analytics-driven organizational change in mind. This determines the expected long-term payoff and allows management to establish key criteria for accepting initiatives proposed by analytics. Communicating the end goal and the criteria early in the journey improves the relevance of analytics activities.

An organizational change journey must be mapped to reach the end goal. The journey begins with customer insight. Focusing on only profit will lead to little relevance for the brand and to increased issues with customer churn and dissatisfaction. It is, therefore, important to focus analytics on understanding actual shopping behavior, rather than the sophistication of the models. The key is to drive customer behavior by understanding customers' attitudes and the determinants of their attitudes. Customer transactions and profits would result from developing a system that delivers on customer needs.

The journey, therefore, begins with understanding the customer data available within an organization and developing systems for capturing data that is unavailable but necessary. Analytics then drives customer insights, which can be combined with management heuristics to develop customer management decisions. The success of this process depends on managers' willingness to separate fact from fiction and look to data to test their business and customer hypotheses. During this process, it is important to keep a focus on customer feedback as the basis for evaluating the strategy. A customer-focused incentive structure would also enable long-term management focus on continuous customer feedback–based improvement.

# Looking Ahead

More than 40 years later, John D. C. Little's observations are still relevant:[4]

"People tend to reject what they do not understand. The manager carries responsibilities for outcomes. We should not be surprised if he prefers a simple analysis that he can grasp, even though it may have a qualitative structure, broad assumptions, and only a little relevant data, to a complex model whose assumptions may be partially hidden or couched in jargon and whose parameters could be the result of obscure statistical manipulation."

Firms have the ability to do extensive analysis and develop sophisticated marketing analytics tools. But there is still a gap between analytics and action, communication and buy-in, and testing and learning. It is likely that firms and their analytics functions need more marketing, and less science. Organizations have learned how to measure customer value and infer insights from customer data, but connecting these insights to the decision maker is still a missing piece.

# Endnotes

1. G. L. Lilien, A. Rangaswamy, G. H. Van Bruggen, and K. Starke, "DSS Effectiveness in Marketing Resource Allocation Decisions: Reality vs. Perception," *Information Systems Research* 15, no. 3 (2004): 216–235.

2. Paul Farris, Neil Bendle, Phillip Pfeifer, and David Reibstein, *Marketing Metrics: The Definitive Guide to Measuring Marketing Performance*, 2nd ed. (Upper Saddle River, NJ: Pearson Business Publishing, 2010).

3. Paul Flugel and Dafna Gabel, "Marketing Mix Analysis: Heuristics to Empower Action," conference presentation, Marketing Science Institute, http://www.msi.org/conferences/presentations/marketing-mix-analysis-heuristics-to-empower-action/ (accessed April 23, 2014).

4. John D. C. Little, "Models and Managers: The Concept of a Decision Calculus," *Management Science* 50, no.12, supplement (2004): 1841–1853.

# Index